D1789224

Before and Beyond
the 'Big Society'

Before and Beyond
the 'Big Society'

John Milbank and the Church of
England's Approach to Welfare

Joseph Forde

James Clarke & Co.

James Clarke & Co

P.O. Box 60
Cambridge
CB1 2NT
United Kingdom

www.jamesclarke.co
publishing@jamesclarke.co

Hardback ISBN: 978 0 227 17780 8
Paperback ISBN: 978 0 227 17777 8
PDF ISBN: 978 0 227 17778 5
ePUB ISBN: 978 0 227 17779 2

British Library Cataloguing in Publication Data
A record is available from the British Library

First published by James Clarke and Co., 2022

*This book is dedicated to the memory of my parents,
Peter and Kathleen, both of whom died when I was young,
and to all that they gave to me.*

Contents

Acknowledgements

Writing a book on a topic as broad as welfare and the Church of England, and, specifically, placing its handling of the 'Big Society' project in historical and theoretical context, means one is – at least to some degree – reliant on the work of others. I am indebted to all of the authors cited in the references and particularly the following, whose work has often provided the inspiration for this study: Nick Crowson, Nicholas Deakin, Eliza Filby, Geoffrey Finlayson, Derek Fraser, Matthew Grimley, Chris Harman, Matthew Hilton, James McKay, Jean-François Mouhot, Justin Davis Smith and Nick Spencer.

It was in the 1980s, while I was an undergraduate in history at Lancaster University and later a postgraduate in history at the University of Sheffield, that I developed my passion for historical research and writing, and much of what follows is indebted to the teaching I received at that time, particularly from Dr Harro Hopfl, Dr John Hedley Brooke, Dr Ralph Gibson, Dr Alan Wood and Dr Martin Blinkhorn at Lancaster University and Dr Michael Bentley at the University of Sheffield. More recently, whilst undertaking the research for the PhD on which this book is based, I benefited from the excellent support and encouragement I received from the teaching teams and my fellow postgraduate students at the Urban Theology Union (UTU) in Sheffield and at Luther King House Educational Trust in Manchester. At UTU the Revd Dr Alan Billings, the Revd Dr Keith Hebden and the Revd Dr Christine Dutton were helpful and encouraging at every stage, and a special word of thanks must go to the Revd Dr Ian K. Duffield, my senior research supervisor, for his flexibility of approach and theological and editorial guidance. At Luther King House, the Revd Dr Jonathan Tallon's tutoring was invaluable, as was the assistance I received from the Academic Registrar, Clare Richardson. A word of thanks must also go to the library staff at Luther King House and the University of Manchester for their resourcefulness.

The Revd Dr Malcom Brown, Director of Mission and Public Affairs for the Church of England, was generous in agreeing to be interviewed for the PhD, and a special thanks is therefore offered to him for giving his time and attention to that project.

My two PhD examiners, Canon Professor Mark D. Chapman (University of Oxford) and Revd Dr Graham Adams (Luther King House), provided pertinent criticisms of my thesis and valuable suggestions for turning it into a book, for which I am also grateful.

Thanks must also go to historian and friend David Price CBE, for sharing his thoughts with me on the historical aspects of the research over dinner in Oxford in 2017.

I am also indebted to Adrian Brink (Director) and Samuel Fitzgerald (Assistant Editor) at James Clarke & Co. for their professionalism in seeing this book through the press, to Dorothy Luckhurst for her diligent copy-editing, and to Wendy Baskett for her skilful indexing.

I should also like to pay a debt of gratitude to the NHS, and to my former colleagues and the many other fascinating people I encountered working for it, who have no doubt helped shape my views on the British Welfare State, particularly Dr Elizabeth Carlin and Ms Roz Norman.

The responsibility for all of the interpretations, judgements and deficiencies contained in the book is, of course, my own.

Finally, I would like to thank my wife, Carole, for more than she can ever know, and my two daughters, Eleanor and Amy, for their love and inspiration.

Introduction

Background

The provision of welfare is germane to much of Christ's teaching, not least His depiction of how one can inherit the kingdom:

> Then the King will say to those on His right hand, 'Come, you blessed of My Father, inherit the kingdom prepared for you from the foundation of the world: for I was hungry and you gave Me food; I was thirsty and you gave Me drink; I was a stranger and you took Me in; I was naked and you clothed Me; I was sick and you visited Me; I was in prison and you came to Me.'[1]

It is on that basis, writing as a Christian, that the idea for this book emerged out of a sense of bewilderment I had about a change in direction the Church of England had taken to welfare following the financial crash of 2008, when, in 2010, it offered qualified support to the Coalition government's 'Big Society' project. This was an initiative that sought to rebalance welfare provision in the United Kingdom – by making it less statist and more localist and voluntarist in its delivery. As such, the thinking underpinning that project challenged some of the assumptions on which the post-war British Welfare State had been founded. Prior to 2010 the Church of England had been a staunch defender of the Welfare State. The favourable response it gave to the 'Big Society' project during its first two years, suggested a paradigm shift may have occurred in its thinking on welfare, and I wanted to identify and scrutinise the reasons

---

[1] Matthew 25: 34–36. *New King James Version Reference Bible* (Nashville, TN: Thomas Nelson Publishers, 2019).

for that change of direction, as well as the implications stemming from it for those in need of welfare provision, then and since.

The Church of England has played an important role as a provider of welfare throughout its history and particularly since the early nineteenth century; it has also contributed substantially to shaping the way welfare has been provided by others – including governments of the day. Yet, the Church of England's level of influence on shaping the political landscape is not what it once was. This partly reflects the steep decline in affiliation and observance that it has witnessed since the early 1960s, which forms part of the context for this study. Despite that trend, however, the extent to which, in 2010, the Cameron-led Coalition government called upon the Church of England to deliver on key aspects of its 'Big Society' project suggests that its influence on shaping, and, in part, delivering on a government's welfare agenda, is far from negligible. It also remains one of the largest providers of welfare in the UK. These are reasons why the approach it takes to welfare matters: to its affiliates; to affiliates of other Christian denominations; to members of faith-based organisations that are not Christian but which see the provision of welfare as a vital component of a civil society; to those of no faith who take the same view; and to all those who find themselves in need of welfare support. It therefore merits academic and wider, societal scrutiny, as the consequences – not least for the poorest in society – can be considerable, and it is for that reason that I felt drawn to undertake this study.

The influence that, since 2008, John Milbank has had on reshaping the welfare agenda in the Church of England and, since 2010 – via his input into the Blue Labour project – the welfare agenda in the Labour Party has been considerable, as have the consequences for the Church of England. Milbank is a theologian with an international reputation who has made a substantial contribution to Anglo-Catholic theology, particularly since the publication of his major work, *Theology and Social Theory*, in 1990.[2] His founding, in the late 1990s, of Radical Orthodoxy, the theological school that has since gained a reputation for being one of the most influential on post-modern and post-liberal approaches to Catholic orthodoxy, has further cemented his reputation as an important thinker for his times. Moreover, since 2008, in a flurry of journalistic and other, more academic, writings, Milbank has made a concerted effort to apply some of his theological insights to the contemporary British

---

[2.] J. Milbank, *Theology and Social Theory: Beyond Secular Reason*, 2nd edn (Oxford: Blackwell, 2006).

political context, not least with regard to the provision of welfare. These works are the sources of much of the analysis that follows and have been written in a more accessible style than has been his trademark.

As Milbank's thinking on welfare can be located in one strand of Anglican Socialist thought, it is examined by looking at it through the lens of the Anglican Socialist tradition. His writings – on the rise of capitalism and the modern, Western state, Christian Socialism, Blue Socialism, Blue Labour, post-liberalism, the British Welfare State, voluntarism, the 'Big Society' project, and the Church of England's post-war role in the provision of welfare – feature prominently in what is the first analysis and evaluation of Milbank's Blue Socialist thinking on welfare *vis-à-vis* its influence within the Church of England. The Anglican Socialist tradition has also played an important part in shaping the Church of England's positioning on welfare since the middle of the nineteenth century,[3] and this book explores that aspect of its history and the part it played in influencing its handling of the 'Big Society' project.

Blue Labour advocates, such as Milbank, see the Welfare State as an overly centrist, bureaucratic, often remote and inefficient welfare delivery vehicle, favouring a more voluntarist and localist approach to aspects of welfare provision currently being provided by the state. As such, since 2009, they have offered the Labour Party a more radical, alternative approach to welfare than anything it has seen since the founding of the Welfare State in the 1940s: one that challenges the Fabian-inspired, social democratic thinking on welfare that it had embraced since the early 1920s, and which, in the immediate post-war years, had underpinned much of the Attlee administration's drive to establish a welfare state, and which was so influential on shaping aspects of Labour's post-war defence of it. It is because of its radical departure from Labour's post-war positioning on welfare that the Blue Labour political phenomenon merits critical assessment, not least for those who see it as a threat to the Welfare State and the social democratic ideology that underpins it.

[3.] For more on this see, for example, M. Brown (ed.), *Anglican Social Theology* (Croydon: Church House Publishing, 2014); M. Chapman, *Bishops, Saints and Politics* (London: T&T Clark, 2007); M. Grimley, *Citizenship, Community and the Church of England* (Oxford: Oxford University Press, 2004); D. Nicholls, *Deity and Domination: Images of God and the State in the Nineteenth and Twentieth Centuries* (London: Routledge, 1989); S. Spencer (ed.), *Theology Reforming Society: Revisiting Anglican Social Theology* (London: SCM Press, 2017).

Milbank was also influential in shaping Red Tory thinking on welfare that emerged in 2009–10 – principally in the writings of Phillip Blond,[4] one of his former PhD students. This was also highly critical of the post-war, welfare state settlement and for similar reasons to how Blue Labour thinkers had come to see it. Red Tory thinking was also influential in shaping aspects of Prime Minister Cameron's political outlook, and his support for the 'Big Society' project reflected that. Yet, it is the influence Milbank has had on reshaping the Church of England's strategic thinking and policy formulation on welfare since 2008 that this book is primarily concerned with examining.

My Approach

Writing as a Christian, does not, I would argue, preclude one from examining this subject from a standpoint that places a need for historical evidence to be at the centre of one's interpretation of past events, and fully respects the need for academic detachment in the way one examines it, whilst acknowledging that the study of history can never be a totally objective science.[5] It is on that basis that, on one level, this book can be seen as a study in the history of ideas as well as one in contemporary political theology, as the approach throughout has been to examine these events by setting them in their wider political, historical and theoretical context. A wide range of historical sources has been examined, including a number of official Church documents. Yet, there will always be a question about how far documents, however 'official', actually speak for, or describe accurately, the Church's attitudes/views at a given point in time. Like all forms of historical evidence, they have their limitations in what they can reveal about the past, not least when one is writing about an organisation as complex as the Church of England. What may have been the views of members of the House of Bishops at a synod, for example, as recorded in the minutes, or the views of a church committee as recorded in an official report, cannot be assumed to have been those held by the congregants on the pews, for which there may be no historical record. Accepting the limitations

---

4. P. Blond, *Red Tory: How Left and Right Have Broken Britain and How We Can Fix It* (London: Faber & Faber, 2010).

5. A useful introduction to this topic can be found in M.D. Chapman, 'The History of Theology and Historical Theology', in Chapman, *Bishops, Saints and Politics*, pp. 1–6.

inherent in the use of historical documents as sources of evidence on which to base one's interpretation of past events does not invalidate that approach, however. What it does do is make writing about history an imperfect quest, but an important one, nevertheless, if we are to learn anything from the past.

The Book's Structure

The book is split into three parts. Part One sets the scene by analysing three strands of the Anglican Socialist tradition with specific reference to their perspectives on welfare and the Church. It also provides a summary analysis of the history of welfare provision in Britain since the early twentieth century. This enables Milbank's thinking on welfare and the Church to be examined in historical and theoretical context, as a contribution to the Anglican Socialist tradition out of which it has emerged (Part Two), before examining it in the context of the Church of England's relation to the political field of welfare since 2008 and, specifically, its response to the 'Big Society' project (Part Three). It also enables the Church of England's handling of the 'Big Society' project to be examined in historical and theoretical context (Part Three).

Part One

Part One provides a historical and theoretical backdrop on the origins of the British Welfare State and the post-war welfare state consensus and its collapse, as seen through the lens of the Anglican Socialist tradition. In chapter one, I describe three distinct strands of Anglican Socialist thinking on the modern state. These have shaped their advocates' views on the role the state should perform in the transition to a Christian socialist society, and the role the Church might play in that process, not least with respect to its interface with the state's welfare arm. I examine how two of these strands remain highly relevant for locating and understanding the role the Church of England might perform in the provision of welfare in the future.

John Milbank's thinking on welfare and the Church is also considered. In chapter two his Blue Socialist outlook is contrasted with R.H. Tawney's perspective on the state and welfare. David Nicholls' thinking – including its influence in bringing about a revival of interest in English political pluralism since the early 1970s and on shaping aspects of Milbank's later thinking – is also examined. Milbank's thinking in relation to the two dominant strands of economic perspective that have characterised the post-war history of the welfare state consensus and its collapse – Keynesianism for the period 1945–76 and neoliberalism for the period since – is also analysed.

Part Two

Part Two examines the Blue Socialist thinking of John Milbank with reference to its key theoretical underpinnings and to some alternative perspectives and criticisms of them. In chapter three I analyse his perspectives on the Middle Ages, the Reformation, Protestantism and the rise of capitalism, the Church and the modern, liberal-capitalist state, and Christian Socialism. I also provide arguments that challenge Milbank's historical perspective on religion and the rise of capitalism, as well as his thinking on Blue Socialism. Chapter four provides an evaluation of Milbank's Blue Socialist perspective on the Welfare State *vis-à-vis* the voluntary sector, and the Church of England's post-war role in the provision of welfare, and his proposed Blue Socialist, post-liberal alternative vision of the role he argues the Church of England should perform in the provision of welfare.

Part Three

Chapter five explores whether the thinking on welfare in the Church of England in the period since 2008, particularly its handling of the 'Big Society' project, can be located in the themes and perspectives on the Church, state and welfare that have been developed by writers from within two strands of the Anglican Socialist tradition. It examines John Milbank's Blue Socialist thinking on the 'Big Society' project, and the influence it had on shaping the Church of England's response to it, in the context of other perspectives from within Anglican Socialism, and from within the Radical Orthodoxy grouping as regards Phillip Blond's *Red Tory* analysis. The chapter also examines whether the Church of England's positioning on welfare underwent a paradigm shift in 2010.

In chapter six I offer some reflections on the research and its findings and, based on them, reach conclusions to the lines of argument that are relevant for shaping the Church of England's approach to welfare henceforth.

An epilogue briefly considers the events that have taken place since I completed my research for this book in early 2020; specifically, the implications the Covid-19 pandemic and its impact on the public purse may have for the conclusions that I have reached on the shaping of the Church of England's approach to welfare in the years to come.

Consistent with the decision to examine these matters through the lens of a historical tradition – Anglican Socialism, Part One focuses on providing a historical and theoretical backdrop to much of what follows.

Part One

Locating John Milbank's Thinking on Welfare and the Church within the Anglican Socialist Tradition

Chapter One

Three Anglican Socialist Strands: Welfare Statist, Christendom, Revolutionist

Introduction

A central argument of this book is that two strands within the Anglican Socialist tradition are particularly relevant to understanding the Church of England's handling of the 'Big Society' project. This is because the debate that took place on welfare in the Church of England in the aftermath of the financial crash of 2008 and the squeeze on public expenditure that followed, closely paralleled these two strands of thinking. First, the Welfare Statist strand, since the 1940s, has seen the Welfare State as a key provider of welfare support to those in need of it and thus contributed to the goal of achieving a Christian Socialist vision of society gradually via parliamentary democracy, a more progressive taxation model and publicly funded, state-managed, government welfare departments as part of the overall mix. Second, the Christendom strand, since the early-twentieth century, has seen the state as a hindrance to the goal of achieving a Christian Socialist society. Instead, it has emphasised a need to empower groups and individuals in civil society, including the Church, rather than state-managed government departments, with more responsibility for the delivery of welfare, and thus to restore something of the pre-Reformation, Christendom vision of the role of the Church in society.

The debate has often been between those who – essentially, but not uncritically – have been defenders of the Welfare State and those who have taken a more unequivocally critical view of it. These more critical writers have argued instead for a more communitarian, localist and voluntarist approach to aspects of welfare provision, with an enhanced role for the Church of England in the delivery of welfare, whilst still retaining aspects of state welfare provision that the Church of England and voluntary sector are insufficiently resourced and/or equipped to provide.[1]

A third, revolutionist strand, primarily held by some Anglican Socialists in the interwar period and a smaller number in the 1970s and 1980s (and even fewer since), has seen state provision of welfare as a 'sticking plaster', only partly covering up the wounds of a corrupt capitalist order – one that needs to be overthrown by force via a popular revolution waged by the oppressed classes and replaced by a new socialist political, economic and social order. That strand has been included in the analysis in chapter one for the purpose of historical completeness and as a contrast to the other two strands, though few Anglican Socialist writers now advocate it.

The central aim of this chapter is to analyse these three strands of Anglican Socialism with reference to their historical and theoretical lineage, so that, with respect to two of them, their relevance to the contemporary debates around the provision of welfare and the approach to be taken on welfare by the Church of England can be analysed. John Milbank's thinking on welfare and the Church can also be located within the Anglican Socialist tradition. After briefly summarising five key terms, the chapter will include a section on socialism and the state, followed by sections on the three Anglican Socialist strands.

Key Terms

Socialism

For this book, socialism refers to a strand of political philosophy that emerged in the nineteenth century in opposition to perceived economic and social injustices caused by capitalism. In significant part, it attributes these to the private ownership of the means of production, distribution

---

[1] We shall see that John Milbank is one of these writers, though he argues that his post-liberal vision of a politics of virtue is not simply a 'rehash of communitarian thinking' but builds 'on the communitarian critique of liberalism'. See J. Milbank and A. Pabst, *The Politics of Virtue: Post-liberalism and the Human Future* (London: Rowman & Littlefield International, 2016), p. 7.

and exchange by a relatively small number of capitalists, who are then able to wield considerable power over the working classes, who only have their labour power, skills and intelligence to sell for a living. From this perspective, capitalism has resulted in high levels of exploitation, inequality and other injustices that a socialist transformation of society, based *inter alia* on securing a much wider level of social ownership over the productive forces, and greater levels of working-class representation in the political, economic, social, cultural and intellectual features of society, is intended to remedy.[2]

Anglican Socialism
By this is meant the tradition within Anglicanism that emerged in the 1840s and 1850s, principally around the thinking of F.D. Maurice, later developed by many others,[3] that has sought to fuse secular strands of socialist philosophy with Christian theology and practice. Common to both has been an emphasis on advancing social justice by improving the lot of the industrial and post-industrial working-classes, the poor and dispossessed, with an emphasis on expanding their political, economic, social, educational and cultural levels of access and reward – the intention being to reduce inequalities and class-defined barriers to human flourishing.[4] Although Maurice was not an Anglo-Catholic, the Anglican Socialist tradition has primarily been Anglo-Catholic in its origins and development, though it has been and remains a strand of Anglicanism with wider influence within the Church of England.[5]

[2.] For a useful introduction to British Socialism, see M. Beer, *A History of British Socialism* (Nottingham: Spokesman Books, 1984). See also K. Laybourn, *The Rise of British Socialism* (Stroud: Sutton Publishing, 1997).

[3.] On Maurice, see J. Morris, *To Build Christ's Kingdom: An F.D. Maurice Reader* (Norwich: Canterbury Press, 2007). John Ludlow, Charles Kingsley and T.H. Hughes are examples of other prominent writers in the early period of the Anglican Socialist tradition. Their contributions are skilfully covered in C. Raven, *Christian Socialism 1848–1854* (London: Frank Cass & Co., 1968).

[4.] See K. Leech, 'What Happened to the Anglo-Catholic Socialists?', 2011. This article is held on a private web site (WordPress.com) for which access can be obtained on request at the following link: https://robbbeck.wordpress.com/2011/10/28/what-happened-to-the-anglo-catholic-socialists/.

[5.] For example, the Victorian Anglican Socialist, Charles Kingsley, was a broad-church Anglican. See Brenda Colloms, *Charles Kingsley* (London: Constable, 1975). F.D. Maurice, though not an Anglo-Catholic, refused to

Christendom Theology

For this study, Christendom theology refers loosely to a strand of Catholic theology that is highly critical of the Protestant Reformation, which brought about the collapse of medieval Christendom. Christendomists see the Reformation as a time when the Christian Church was depoliticised and fractured, a time when the Christian faith increasingly retreated from the public to the private sphere, a time when Catholic thinking on the common good was reinterpreted in favour of a theo-political and liberal 'secular' political outlook, that placed more emphasis on the private goods and the interests of individuals as a path to human and spiritual flourishing, and contributed to the rise of capitalism. Christendomists locate these events as the outworking of a modernist/rationalist turn in philosophical thinking that occurred in the late medieval period, which *inter alia* challenged the Catholic pre-modern theological perspective on nature and grace, leading to a separation of the two, which they reject. Contemporary Christendom theologians such as John Milbank, see the emergence in the twentieth century of post-modern philosophical perspective as a welcome challenge to modernist/rationalist thinking and, in some respects, a return to pre-modern philosophical strands that have more in common with pre-Reformation, Catholic understandings: both ontological and epistemological.

Unsurprisingly, Anglican Socialists in the Christendom strand such as Milbank, have tended to be wary of the rise of the political state and its 'separation' from the Church that occurred in the early modern period, seeing the political state as a threat to the Church's theo-political sovereignty and overall standing in society. Some Christendomists aspire to a vision of a restored Christendom, with a re-politicised Church and a post-liberal political and economic epoch in which a Catholic world view could, once again, regain its pre-eminence.[6]

---

be labelled a broad-church Anglican. See T. Brown, 'Anglican Way or Ways', in M.D. Chapman, S. Clarke and M. Percy (eds), *The Oxford Handbook of Anglican Studies* (Oxford: Oxford University Press, 2018), p. 626.

[6.] For more on the theological and philosophical aspects of Christendom thinking, see, for example, S. Murray, *Post-Christendom: Church and Mission in a Strange New World* (Milton Keynes: Paternoster, 2005). For more on the historical circumstances that led to the decline of Christendom,

English Political Pluralism

By this is meant the thinking of English pluralist writers such as John Neville Figgis, who, as David Nicholls has accurately summarised, envisaged 'a situation in which members of the state pursue their chosen ends in life, as individuals and associated in voluntary groups, with as little interference from coercive governmental authorities as is possible in the context of order and peace',[7] and, 'when the state does not itself pursue some national policy which purports to realise a common good'.[8] Hence, for English pluralists, the primary role of the state should be to 'maintain order by settling disputes between individuals and groups'.[9] This is not to be confused with an alternative, and very different, use of the term pluralist within American political theory, which 'defines democracy as a form of stable and institutionalised political competition in which organised interests strive to control government through taking part in electoral contests and/or strive to influence the policies a government adopts'.[10]

Nor is it to be confused with the use of the word to mean that one religion cannot be the sole or exclusive source of all religious truth. Not all English pluralist writers have been Anglicans (e.g. Harold Laski and G.D.H. Cole) but several have, and it is these that this study will focus on.

Welfare State

By this is meant what the historian Asa Briggs has described as follows:

> A 'welfare state' is a state in which organized power is deliberately used (through politics and administration) in an effort to modify the play of market forces in at least three directions – first, by guaranteeing individuals and families a minimum income irrespective of the market value of their work or their property; second, by narrowing the extent of insecurity by enabling individuals and families to meet certain 'social contingencies' (for example, sickness, old age

---

see M. Greengrass, *Christendom Destroyed: Europe 1517–1648* (London: Penguin, 2015).

[7] D. Nicholls, *The Pluralist State* (London: Macmillan, 1975), p. 8.

[8] Ibid., p. 10.

[9] Ibid.

[10] P. Hirst, *The Pluralist Theory of the State* (London: Routledge, 1989), p. 3.

and unemployment) which lead otherwise to individual and family crises; and third, by ensuring that all citizens without distinction of status or class are offered the best standards available in relation to a certain agreed range of social services.[11]

It can be argued that the British Welfare State embodies these three principles in its aims.

Socialism and the State

Since the publication in 1821 of G.W.F. Hegel's *Outlines of the Philosophy of Right*, a work that explores the complex interface between family, civil society, the administration of justice and the modern state, and argues that freedom is enhanced rather than diminished via the application of state enforced laws, a debate has raged about the extent to which the modern state diminishes or augments freedom.[12] Moreover, though by no means confined to socialist writers, the debate has often been conducted by them. For example, Karl Marx, in his *Critique of Hegel's Philosophy of Right*, reached different conclusions to those of Hegel about the extent to which the modern state augments individuals' freedom.[13] For Marx, the modern state was the bureaucratic preserver of a status quo, that owing to the existence of private property – something he advocated should be abolished – resulted in the subjugation of an entire class, the proletariat, and hence a negation of their freedom. By contrast, Ferdinand Lassalle, a socialist who had been influenced by Marx's works and, in 1863, had founded the General German Workers' Association, nevertheless saw the state very differently from Marx.[14] For Lassalle, the modern state was not a class-based power superstructure there to preserve the

---

[11.] A. Briggs, 'The Welfare State in Historical Perspective', *Archives Européennes de Sociologie*, Vol. 2, no. 2 (1961), p. 228. Cited in R. Lowe, *The Welfare State in Britain Since 1945*, Third Edition (London: Palgrave Macmillan, 2005), p.17.

[12.] G.W.F. Hegel, *Outlines of the Philosophy of Right* (1821) (Oxford: Oxford University Press, 2008).

[13.] K. Marx, *Critique of Hegel's 'Philosophy of Right'* (1843) (Cambridge: Cambridge University Press, 2009).

[14.] A.J. Berlau, *The German Social Democratic Party 1914–1921* (New York: Columbia University Press, 1949), p. 21.

interests of the dominant bourgeois class and thus the subjugation of the proletariat class – something Marx had argued would 'wither away' once private property and the resultant exploitation had been abolished and a classless society had been achieved. Rather, for Lassalle, the state was a necessary arm in the administering of justice to individuals, essential for a socialist transformation of society – a position that Marx later criticised in his essay, *Critique of the Gotha Programme*.[15]

This difference of perspective on the modern state between Marx and Lassalle resembles others that have since occurred in the history of the Marxist tradition: between those who have advocated the need for a revolutionary overthrow of the capitalist state apparatus and its replacement as a precondition for establishing a socialist society, such as Vladimir Lenin and Leon Trotsky;[16] and those who have seen the modern state as a necessary instrument of administrative and political justice, capable of being reformed to play an essential part in the delivery of a socialist transformation of society via parliamentary democracy, such as Antonio Gramsci and Palmiro Togliatti.[17]

Within the history of Anglican Socialism, the role the modern state can play in advancing a Christian Socialist agenda has also been a major theme. One strand of thought, which can loosely be called 'Welfare Statist' and which can be traced back to Hegel,[18] sees a positive role for the modern, liberal-capitalist state and the potential it affords, via parliamentary democracy, for advancing a Christian socialist transformation of society. Two influential Anglican Socialist thinkers who held this view were William Temple and, in his later writings,

---

15. K. Marx, *Critique of the Gotha Programme* (1875) (London: Lawrence & Wishart, 1905).

16. V.I. Lenin, *The State and Revolution* (1917) (Washington DC: Regnery Publishing, 2009) and L. Trotsky, *The Permanent Revolution and Results and Prospects* (1929) (Seattle: Red Letter Press, 2010 edition).

17. A. Gramsci, *Selections from the Prison Notebooks* (London: Lawrence & Wishart, 1971) and P. Togliatti, *On Gramsci and Other Writings* (London: Lawrence & Wishart, 1979). For more on the differences between Gramsci's and Trotsky's thinking on socialist strategy and the state, see J. Forde, 'Popular Front Strategy in France and Spain in the 1930s: Betrayal or Reaffirmation of the Socialist Cause?' (Unpublished MA dissertation, University of Sheffield, 1987).

18. For more on this, see Nicholls, *Deity and Domination*, pp. 180–88.

R.H. Tawney.[19] Their thinking, in their lifetime and since, has played a significant part in influencing the politics of the British Labour Party and was important for establishing the Welfare State in the 1940s, although, as we shall see in chapter two, the liberal thinking of William Beveridge and John Maynard Keynes was also important. The lineage of Temple's and Tawney's thinking on the modern state can, in part, be located in the Hegel-inspired British Idealist movement of the mid-nineteenth to early-twentieth centuries: writers such as T.H. Green, F.H. Bradley and B. Bosanquet.[20]

Another strand of Anglican Socialism which I have called the Christendom strand, became more prominent at the beginning of the twentieth century, though it had some earlier antecedents.[21] The Christendom strand was in direct opposition to British Idealist thinking, and contributed to the English political pluralist movement of the early twentieth century, and to a revival of interest in that perspective since the early 1970s. Writers such as John Neville Figgis, V.A. Demant and Maurice B. Reckitt[22] (the latter two having been considerably influenced by a revival in Christendom thinking following the publication in 1922

[19.] W. Temple, *Christianity and the State* (London: Macmillan and Co, 1928) and *Christianity and Social Order* (1942) (London: Shepheard-Walwyn, 1976). See also R.H. Tawney, *Equality* (1931) (London: Unwin Books, 1964).

[20.] For more on this, see Grimley, *Citizenship*. Grimley sees William Temple more as a 'liberal' than as a Christian Socialist. This is not a view shared by other writers such as Alan Wilkinson, who, in *Christian Socialism: Scott Holland to Tony Blair* (London: SCM Press, 1998), locates Temple more within the CSU tradition and hence as a Christian Socialist. The same view is taken by J. Fletcher, *William Temple: Twentieth Century Christian* (New York: Seabury, 1963), and by P.D. Jones, *The Christian Socialist Revival 1877–1914* (Princeton: Princeton University Press, 1968). It is this latter view that the present writer shares.

[21.] The Oxford Movement, in some respects, reflects this strand of thinking. See, for example, S. Brown, P. Nockles and J. Pereiro (eds), *The Oxford Handbook of the Oxford Movement* (Oxford: Oxford University Press, 2017).

[22.] J.N. Figgis, *Churches in the Modern State* (London: Longmans, Green & Co., 1913), V.A. Demant, *Religion and the Decline of Capitalism* (London: Faber & Faber, 1952) and *Theology of Society: More Essays in Christian Polity* (London: Faber & Faber, 1947). See also M.B. Reckitt, *The Meaning of National Guilds* (New York: Macmillan, 1918), and M.B. Reckitt (ed.), *Prospect for Christendom* (London: Faber & Faber, 1945).

of a pivotal work called *The Return of Christendom*)[23] were critical of the thinking underpinning the British Idealist perspective on the modern state. Their views were to influence two Anglican Socialists of a later generation: David Nicholls and John Milbank, both of whose writings have been sympathetic to them.[24] The English political pluralist perspective also had antecedents in the English Romantic Movement of the early to mid-nineteenth century. For example, William Cobbett, in his book, *Rural Rides* (1830), was wary of what he perceived as an increasingly over-encroaching, industrialising (and dehumanising) capitalist economy and state polity on the English countryside and its rural way of life,[25] with insufficient heed being paid to the voices at the grassroots.

A third strand of Anglican Socialism can loosely be called revolutionist, having been influenced by the writings of Marx and by some of his later followers. This strand has tended to be more revolutionary in its aspirations, seeing the modern state as an instrument of capitalist exploitation, and hence something to be overthrown by force in the interests of advancing the socialist cause. It can be located in thinkers such as Conrad Noel and Jack Putterill from within the Catholic Crusade, an organisation established in 1918 by Noel around the parish church of Thaxted in Essex (Noel disbanded the Catholic Crusade in 1936). The Catholic Crusade was partly influenced by the Bolshevik Revolution that had taken place in Russia in October 1917, as well as by its aftermath, including the state collectivisation of farms which, according to one analyst, Noel had favourably likened to the Catholic medieval estates.[26] Like Marx, Noel was fully committed to common ownership of land and industrial resources:

> Many members of the Church of England are socialists and would establish a commonwealth whose people should own the land and the industrial capital and administer them

---

[23.] A Group of Churchmen, *The Return of Christendom* (New York: The Macmillan Company, 1922). C. Gore wrote the introduction but did not identify himself with the essayists' views.

[24.] See Nicholls, *The Pluralist State*, and J. Milbank, *The Future of Love: Essays in Political Theology* (London: SCM Press, 2009).

[25.] See W. Cobbett, *Rural Rides* (1830) (London: Penguin Classics, 2001).

[26.] See J.R. Orens, 'Conrad Noel: Vision and Paradox', in K. Leech (ed.), *Conrad Noel and the Catholic Crusade: A Critical Evaluation* (London: The Jubilee Group, 1993), p. 33.

cooperatively for the good of all. Such public ownership
they regard as urgent and as a necessary deduction from the
teachings of the church.[27]

Noel was also influenced by the writings of Trotsky, who, like Marx,
throughout his lifetime advocated a revolutionary overthrow of capitalist
states by the use of force as the only way of achieving a transition to
socialism. Consistent with this revolutionary thinking, Noel stated that
the Catholic Crusade's aim was 'to smash the British Empire and all
empires to bits' and that it stood for a 'revolutionary attitude in politics,
and the establishment, if necessary by force, of a classless cooperative
society on communist lines'.[28]

    This strand of thinking also later influenced Anglican Socialists such
as Kenneth Leech, who, in 1974, founded the Jubilee Group – a loose
network of radical Anglo-Catholic Socialists that met until around 2003
and had some thinkers in its ranks who were influenced by Marxist ideas.
Leech stated in 1989: 'While Christianity and Marxism are the most
distorted traditions in the modern world, an alliance between prophetic
Christianity and progressive Marxism, offers the last humane hope for
mankind.'[29] However, unlike Figgis and Temple, Noel and Leech did not
develop a theory of the state in their works, and as their revolutionist
perspective is also not one that features much in contemporary debates
within Anglican Socialism, it is a strand of the tradition which, for the
purposes of this study, we can leave behind at the conclusion of chapter
one. For now, though, we turn our attention to the Welfare Statist strand.

---

[27] C. Noel, *Socialism in Church History* (London: Frank Palmer, 1910) p. 7.
     Cited by K. Leech, 'Turbulent Priests', *Marxism Today* (February 1986),
     pp. 11–13.
[28] Cited by Leech, 'Turbulent Priests', p. 11.
[29] K. Leech, *The Radical Anglo-Catholic Social Vision*, a lecture given at
     the Centre for Theology and Public Issues, University of Edinburgh,
     on 13 March 1989 (Edinburgh: CTPI, 1989). Available at: https://books
     .google.co.uk/books/about/The_Radical_Anglo_Catholic_Social_Vision
     .html?id=NwR0Zk5WME8C (accessed on 23 April 2016), p. 7.

The Welfare Statist Strand

The term 'welfare state' was popularised by William Temple in 1928 when, as Bishop of Manchester, he undertook the Henry Scott Holland Memorial Lectures, subsequently published as *Christianity and the State*, where he characterised the First World War as:

> a struggle between the idea of the State as essentially Power – Power over its own community and against other communities – and of the State as the organ of community, maintaining its solidarity by law designed to safeguard the interests of the community. The Power-State might have yielded to sheer pressure of circumstances in course of time; but it is contrary to the psychology of the Power-State to suffer conversion; it was likely to fight before it let a Welfare-State take its place.[30]

Thus, for Temple, it was necessary for the Allied powers to have fought Germany and to have diminished its 'Power-State'. However, this perspective, as the above quote suggests, was far from being non-statist, a theme that his later work of 1942, *Christianity and Social Order*,[31] was to develop. Rather, Temple had a different vision of what the state could potentially achieve as an 'organ of community'. He saw the need for it to be more than the British 'minimalist' state that he perceived as having been deficient in its ability to address some of the social problems that many of those who had fought in the First World War had since endured, not least the consequences of prolonged unemployment, poor educational opportunity for their children and, for some, poor housing. However, as we have seen, he was also critical of what he described as the German 'Power-State' that, in some respects, he saw as being a cause of the First World War.[32]

Temple's thinking in *Christianity and the State*, was, in part, derived from a theology of the state that he was developing at that time and that his later work of 1941, *Citizen and Churchman*, was to articulate more fully.[33] He had been influenced by the Christian Socialist writings of

---

[30.] Temple, *Christianity and the State*, pp. 169–70.

[31.] This is the work that most fully reflects Temple's thinking on welfare.

[32.] That is, the 'Bismarckian', authoritarian style state that pre-dated the democratic reforms brought about under the Weimar Republic.

[33.] W. Temple, *Citizen and Churchman* (London: Eyre & Spottiswoode, 1941).

F.D. Maurice and those in the Christian Social Union of 1889 to 1919, such as Henry Scott Holland and Charles Gore, who had argued for the need for a moral state, dovetailed with a national church as part of an organic nation.[34] Temple joined the CSU whilst he was at Oxford and remained in it for several years.[35] In 1908 he stated: 'Socialism … is the economic realization of the Christian Gospel. There is no middle path between the acceptance of Socialism and the declaration that the Gospel cannot be applied to economics, and this is Manicheism. The alternative stands before us – Socialism or Heresy; we are involved in one or the other.'[36]

Charles Gore, a leading member of the CSU, had stated in his preface to *Lux Mundi* (1889) that the principal role of the Church was to 'throw herself into the sanctification of each new social order'[37] – and that included secular states. W.J.H. Campion, in the same volume, declaring that, despite its limitations, 'the State is sacred: it is "of God"',[38] argued that a Christian view of government via the state necessitated that it must realise 'the common good'.[39] Similarly, Temple, in *Citizen and Churchman*, described the state as:

> the source and upholder of Law, and its sphere is all that is appropriately regulated by Law. It is not its own end. It is an organ of the community, indispensable to the continued existence of the community but entirely subordinate to it. Its end is the welfare of the community. And the community consists of persons. It is not an entity existing somehow in detachment from its members; it is essentially those persons united in social unity.[40]

---

34. S. Spencer, 'William Temple and the "Temple Tradition"', in Spencer (ed.), *Theology Reforming Society*, pp. 85–107.
35. J. Kent, *William Temple: Church, State and Society in Britain, 1880–1950* (Cambridge: Cambridge University Press, 1992), p. 12.
36. W. Temple, 'The Church and the Labour Party: A Consideration of Their Ideals', *The Economic Review* 18, no. 2 (1908), pp. 190–202. Cited in Spencer (ed.), *Theology Reforming Society*, p. 86.
37. C. Gore (ed.), *Lux Mundi* (1889) (London: John Murray Press, 4th edn, 1890), p. ix.
38. W.J.H. Campion, 'Christianity and Politics', in Gore (ed.), *Lux Mundi*, p. 444.
39. Ibid., p. 449.
40. Temple, *Citizen and Churchman*, p. 26.

Thus, for Temple, 'the State exists for the citizens, not the citizens for the State'.[41] Crucially, for Temple, however, the state was also 'a servant and instrument of God for the preservation of Justice and the promotion of human welfare'; as such 'the State has a moral *and spiritual* function [my italics]. It is not possible to divide human interests into two categories – the material and the spiritual – and to assign the former to the State, the latter to the Church.'[42] Therefore, for Temple, Christians, although embodying a higher loyalty to God than to any state, could nevertheless give to a state conditional approval if its purpose was to enhance the welfare of its citizens. We shall see in what follows that the 'spiritual function'[43] Temple ascribed to the state, as well as his view that it was a 'servant and instrument of God', are antithetical to the broad thrust of Christendom theology, which sees the Church, not the state, as the kingdom of God in embryo and thus the place where spiritual functionality resides. The state, by contrast, is seen by exponents of Christendom theology such as David Nicholls and John Milbank as essentially secular and a product of the modernist challenge to Christendom that the Protestant Reformation represented.[44] A key theme of this book is that this contrasting theology of the state held by Welfare Statist Anglican Socialists and Christendom Anglican Socialists explains some of the differences in their perspectives on the provision of welfare.

Temple's vision of a welfare state, though rooted in the Anglican Socialist tradition, built on work that had already been undertaken to improve the lot of the disadvantaged by Asquith's Liberal administrations from 1908 to 1916. Lloyd George, Asquith's Chancellor of the Exchequer between 1908 and 1915, had established a more progressive income tax regime to fund old age pensions and provide some redistributive assistance to the unemployed and the wider pool of disadvantaged.[45] Temple's vision was more ambitious in scope and resourcing, however, and contributed to the thinking of William Beveridge and his report of 1942 that modelled the Welfare State project, which will be considered in chapter two. Temple was a member of the Labour Party in the years

---

41. Ibid., p. 28.

42. Ibid., p. 36.

43. Ibid.

44. Nicholls even claimed that any 'attempt to sanctify the secular order, breaking down any distinction between sacred and secular, has totalitarian implications'. D. Nicholls, *God and Government* (London: Jubilee Pamphlet, 1991), p. 21.

45. For more on this, see R. Jenkins, *Asquith* (New York: Harper Collins, 1988).

between 1918 and 1921[46] and a key socialist influence on him was the friendship and writings of Anglican Socialist R.H. Tawney, a fellow Labour Party member to whom he dedicated his book, *Christianity and the State*.[47] However, in addition to these socialist influences he was also influenced by the philosophical writings of T.H. Green.[48]

Stemming in part from Green's works, the British Idealists had taken a paternalistic view of the role of the state as being a protector of the economic, social, political and cultural fabric of the nation. Thus, from this perspective, the state retained an important function in the development and maintenance, via parliamentary democracy, of a system of rights and obligations that was conducive to the realisation of human self-actualisation, whilst safeguarding personal liberty. This perspective stemmed from a belief, held by Green, that personal liberty, in order to be realised, was more than merely the absence of restraint; hence, more than a negative definition of freedom could accommodate: 'The mere removal of compulsion, the mere enabling a man to do as he likes', Green argued, 'is in itself no contribution to true freedom.' Instead, Green argued for freedom 'in the positive sense; in other words, the liberation of the powers of all men equally for contributions to the common good'.[49] Hence, for Green, freedom was 'a positive desire or capacity of doing or enjoying something worth doing or enjoying'.[50] Therefore, without the *capacity* to do something worth doing or enjoying, freedom, for Green, was little more than a theoretical abstraction. To take just one field of human endeavour, Green argued in support of the 1870 Education Act in the following terms:

[46.] Kent, *William Temple*, p. 25. In this work Kent also argues that Temple was very influenced by Tawney, see pp. 16–17.

[47.] Temple, *Christianity and the State*. See the dedication on an unnumbered page before page vii.

[48.] Grimley, *Citizenship*, p. 45.

[49.] T.H. Green, *Collected Works*, Vol. III (1888) (Cambridge: Cambridge Library Collection, 2011), p. 372. Cited in Grimley, *Citizenship, Community and the Church of England*, p. 45.

[50.] Ibid., pp. 370–71. Cited in Grimley, *Citizenship, Community and the Church of England*, p. 45.

> Without a command of certain elementary arts and knowledge, the individual in modern society is as effectively crippled as by the loss of a limb or a broken constitution. He is not free to develop his faculties. With a view to securing such freedom among its members it is as certainly within the province of the state to prevent children from growing up in that kind of ignorance which practically excludes them from a free career in life, as it is within its province to require the sort of building and drainage necessary for public health.[51]

While Green set limits on state action, such as with respect to morality: 'it is the business of the state, not indeed directly to promote moral goodness, for that from the very nature of moral goodness it cannot do, but to maintain the conditions without which a free exercise of the human faculties is impossible',[52] he clearly saw a vital role for the state as an enabler of human freedom in a practical sense. His writings were to be influential on the thinking of Anglican Socialists such as Henry Scott Holland, as well as Temple.[53]

Temple was also influenced by other British Idealist writers such as Bernard Bosanquet and Thomas Arnold. Nevertheless, he was never an out-and-out British Idealist thinker, and his thinking on the state displays a level of scepticism about some of what he perceived as being their more idealistic views on the state, that the following quote alludes to: 'Hegel himself had bewilderingly treated the national State as a kind of incarnation of the Absolute. ... His English disciples did not follow him in his virtual deification of the State, but they were not far behind.'[54] However, Temple was clear that for so long as the human condition remains fallen: 'So there must be the restraint of law, as long as men have any selfishness left in them. Law exists to preserve and

---

[51] Ibid., pp. 373–74. Cited in Grimley, *Citizenship, Community and the Church of England*, p. 46.

[52] Ibid., p. 374. Cited in Grimley, *Citizenship, Community and the Church of England,* p. 46.

[53] Henry Scott Holland had been a student of T.H. Green while at Balliol College, Oxford where he had come under his influence. See Colloms, *Charles Kingsley*, p. 362.

[54] Temple, *Christianity and the State*, pp. 81–82.

extend real freedom.'[55] For Temple, then, parliamentary democracy afforded the right of elected representatives to enact laws, enforced by the state, which enhanced the total amount of freedom in society. As he put it:

> But the law which restrains any occasional homicidal impulse that I may have, by threatening penalties sufficiently disagreeable to make the indulgence of it seem to be not good enough, also protects my purpose of good fellowship against being violated by that same impulse. In such a case the restraint of the law increases the true freedom of all concerned.[56]

For Temple, therefore, in a parliamentary democracy, state enforced laws enhanced the sum of freedom in society. Unlike English pluralists (as described below), he did not see this as necessarily being at the expense of, or in contradiction to, vital components of civil society: 'Now actual freedom is the freedom which men enjoy in these various social units ... those intermediate groups – the family, the Church or congregation, the guild, the Trade Union, the school, the university, the Mutual Improvement Society.'[57] Indeed, he saw the state as a guardian of liberty that:

> will foster all such groupings, giving them freedom to guide their own activities provided that these fall within the general order of the communal life and do not injure the freedom of other similar associations. Thus the State becomes the Community of Communities – or rather the administrative organ of the Community – and there is much to be said for the contention that its representative institutions should be so designed as to represent the various groupings of men rather than (or as well as) individuals.[58]

However, for Temple, unlike for English pluralist writers, government departments responsible for education, health, social security and so

---

[55.] Temple, *Christianity and Social Order*, p. 68.

[56.] Ibid., p. 68.

[57.] Ibid., p. 70.

[58.] Ibid., pp. 70–71.

forth could legitimately operate within, and be an integral part of, this vision. This was particularly so when seeking to tackle the social ills of squalor, ignorance, want, idleness and disease, as William Beveridge had defined them, which will be considered in chapter two. His report of 1942 was to inspire and in large part define the reality of the Welfare State in the years that followed. Yet, Temple was at pains to say that this perspective on the state, and the role of government departments in the provision of welfare, was not a recipe for unfettered collectivisation or a negation of individual liberty:

> But modern democracy, though more in its continental than in its British forms, ... has been impatient of these intermediate groupings, and has moved towards 'individualism' or 'collectivism', as if there were no third alternative. But it seems scarcely too much to say that neither individualism nor collectivism is compatible with a truly Christian understanding of man or of life.[59]

Thus, it can be argued that Temple was less 'state collectivist' than writers in the British Idealist tradition, but more 'pro-statist' than those in the English political pluralist tradition. He thought that the Welfare State was capable of enabling major social improvements in the fields of housing, education, fairness in income, advances in industrial democracy, leisure, and freedom of worship. He set out a programme for action along these lines in the Appendix to *Christianity and Social Order*, which was influential in shaping political policy in the years that followed, such as the slum clearance initiatives in Britain in the post-war years. He also supported local councils as a way of spreading democratic representation and constraining any tendency towards over-centralisation of power in parliament, stating: 'But there is much to be said for the establishment of subordinate functional Councils with powers of action in their several provinces subject to Parliamentary veto.'[60]

Temple cannot, therefore, be fairly characterised as an out-and-out state collectivist; but neither was he as hostile to the modern state, and particularly the role of government in the provision of welfare, as John Neville Figgis and his later followers, including Milbank, were. This was

---

[59.] Ibid., p. 72.
[60.] Ibid., p. 71.

partly owing to the theology of the state that Temple had developed, which, as we have seen, ascribed a 'spiritual function' to the state and saw it as being a 'servant and instrument of God'.

However, a further aspect of Temple's thinking, as set out in *Christianity and Social Order* and often referred to as middle axioms, offers one approach for addressing the role the Church can play in the political affairs of the state. We shall now consider this, not least because Milbank's vision of a more interventionist role for the established Church – establishment being something that he supports[61] – as part of a move towards a post-liberal polity and society, challenges middle axiom thinking. Temple's thinking on middle axioms was also influential on shaping the thought of later Anglican Socialists in the Welfare Statist strand such as Ronald Preston and John Atherton, and their thinking is also briefly considered in what follows.[62]

Temple's Thinking on Middle Axioms

In *Christianity and Social Order*, Temple sets out how the Church should 'interfere' in society. He talks about three ways: (1) Church members fulfilling their 'moral responsibilities' within the social order; (2) Church members exercising their civil rights within the social order; and lastly, the one that relates to middle axioms, (3) the Church supplying 'a systematic statement of [social] principles' to aid Church members in doing (1) and (2).[63] In this way, Temple steers a clear path so that the Church of England is not seen as formulating political policy or allying itself with one particular political party or stance, although individual Christians may. In this regard, he had been influenced by the thinking of J.H. Oldham, who, in the preparatory material for the Oxford Conference on Church, Community and State held in 1937, described middle axioms as 'attempts to define the directions in which,

---

[61.] For example, he argues (with Adrian Pabst): 'For the Church, the key challenge is to make establishment work much better in terms of legislation and policies insofar as state decisions have contributed to the de-Christianisation of the nation.' Milbank and Pabst, *The Politics of Virtue*, pp. 230–40.

[62.] The author is indebted in what follows to Revd Dr Ian K. Duffield's expertise on middle axiom thinking.

[63.] Temple, *Christianity and Social Order*, p. 43.

in a particular state of society, Christian faith must express itself'.[64] It is a view Temple embraced:

> Religion may rightly censure the use of artistic talents for making money out of men's baser tastes, but it cannot lay down laws about perspective or the use of a paint-brush. It may insist that scientific enquiry be prompted by a pure love of truth and not distorted (as in Nazi Germany) by political considerations. It may declare the proper relation of the economic to other activities of men, but it cannot claim to know what will be the purely economic effect of particular proposals. It is, however, entitled to say that some economic gains ought not to be sought because of the injuries involved to interests higher than economic.[65]

For Temple, then, 'the Church is concerned with principles and not with policy',[66] and 'the Christian citizen applies them; and to do this he utilizes the machinery of the State'.[67] He therefore saw a positive role for the Church in influencing the political direction of the state when moral principles had relevance. However, he circumscribed the extent and type of such interventions because technical complexities/expertise (economic, financial, scientific, aesthetic, administrative etc.) went beyond the Church's capacity, stating: 'A policy always depends on technical decisions concerning the actual relations of cause and effect in the political and economic world; about these a Christian as such has no more reliable judgement than an atheist, except so far as he should be more immune to the temptations of self-interest.'[68]

Temple's thinking on middle axioms is less than entirely clear as he eschews the language and, arguably, does not distinguish clearly enough between principles, aims, objectives and strategies. However, he identifies six objectives at the end of *Christianity and Social Order* that can be seen as middle axioms. Stephen Spencer, a leading British expert on Temple, describes the six objectives in this way: 'These points are

---

[64] Cited in D.P. McCann, 'A Second Look at Middle Axioms', *The Annual Society for Christian Ethics*, Vol.1 (1981), p. 76. See also J.H. Oldham, *The Church and Its Function in Society* (London: G. Allen & Unwin Ltd, 1937).

[65] Temple, *Christianity and Social Order*, p. 32.

[66] Ibid., p. 43.

[67] Temple, *Citizen and Churchman*, p. 83.

[68] Temple, *Christianity and Social Order*, p. 40.

examples of "middle axioms", which are broad practical objectives that show how abstract theory impinges on practical problems and issues.[69] These six objectives are set down in full below:

1. Every child should find itself a member of a family housed with decency and dignity, so that it may grow up as a member of that basic community in a happy fellowship unspoilt by underfeeding or overcrowding, by dirty and drab surroundings or by mechanical monotony of environment.
2. Every child should have the opportunity of an education till years of maturity, so planned as to allow for his peculiar aptitudes and make possible their full development. This education should throughout be inspired by faith in God and find its focus in worship.
3. Every citizen should be secure in possession of such income as will enable him to maintain a home and bring up children in such conditions as are described in paragraph 1 above.
4. Every citizen should have a voice in the conduct of the business or industry which is carried on by means of his labour, and the satisfaction of knowing that his labour is directed to the well-being of the community.
5. Every citizen should have sufficient daily leisure, with two days of rest in seven, and, if an employee, an annual holiday with pay, to enable him to enjoy a full personal life with such interests and activities as his tasks and talents may direct.
6. Every citizen should have assured liberty in the forms of freedom of worship, of speech, of assembly, and of association for special purposes.[70]

In the Appendix to *Christianity and Social Order*, Temple then takes a further step beyond the objectives/middle axioms when he sets down what he calls 'A Suggested Programme' that identifies 'ways' for 'the realisation of our six-fold aim [i.e. objectives, i.e. middle axioms]'. He suggests the following eight elements of a programme to fulfil the six general objectives. These eight elements are summarised below:

1. Decent housing should be built near where workers worked.

[69.] S. Spencer, *William Temple: A Calling to Prophecy* (London: SPCK, 2001), p. 69.
[70.] Temple, *Christianity and Social Order*, pp. 96–97.

2. Family allowances should be paid to mothers for each child after the first two.
3. Wages should be sufficient for a family of four.
4. Milk and a good meal a day should be provided at school.
5. Education should be the primary occupation of everyone up to the age of 18.
6. The state should eradicate unemployment through public works, as and when it arises.
7. Labour should be represented on the directorates through the Unions.
8. Every citizen should have two days rest in seven, and an annual holiday with pay.[71]

Clearly, these are written in a more prescriptive, 'policy-specific' style that goes beyond Temple's positioning on middle axioms. Temple makes clear that he considered them as being what he 'personally', as an individual Christian, believed to be necessary, and offered them 'as suggestions for criticism rather than for adoption' and, indeed, begged the readers to consider them in that spirit. This reflects an important understanding by him that middle axioms do not remain fixed and require translation into policy; they represent a living, breathing, changing tradition that, inevitably from time to time, will require updating or reformulating.

Ronald Preston's and John Atherton's Thinking on Middle Axioms

Ronald Preston, a leading post-war Anglican authority on middle axiom thinking, also saw them as provisional and requiring continuous reworking according to context.[72] Preston, though disliking the term 'middle axiom', defended this thinking throughout his life,[73] seeing it as integral to the functioning of an established church. In fact the term 'middle way' (a classic Anglican kind of formulation) perhaps characterises his approach more accurately, which is the title of an

---

71. Ibid., pp. 99–115. This summary is listed in Spencer, 'William Temple and the "Temple Tradition"', p. 100.
72. See R. Preston, 'Middle Axioms in Christian Social Ethics', *Crucible: The Christian Journal for Social Ethics*, January/February 1971, pp. 9–15, and R. Preston, *Religion and the Persistence of Capitalism* (London: SCM Press, 1979).
73. Preston, 'Middle Axioms in Christian Social Ethics'.

important collection of his writings.[74] In this book he talks about a 'rough and ready process'[75] by which church bodies establish a 'fairly wide consensus'[76] by operating at a 'middle level between generalities which are not specific enough to have precise content and detailed policies on which the evidence is likely to be uncertain'[77] because of the 'ambiguous nature'[78] of most issues. Before his death in 2001, Preston was a leading member of the William Temple Foundation, established in 1944 in Temple's memory, and Temple's and Preston's thinking on middle axioms has largely held sway in the Church of England throughout the post-war period. John Atherton, a great admirer of Temple's and Preston's thinking and also a member of the William Temple Foundation until his death in 2016, was also of the view that middle axioms were transient, and this is reflected in his collaborative work of 2011 with Chris Baker and John Reader,[79] in which a list of newly formulated middle axioms relating to a rapidly changing welfare landscape is set down. In line with Temple's and Preston's thinking, the list is prefaced with the words: 'Seven guidelines for today: on having a sense of direction for attaining greater wellbeing for all'.[80]

Criticisms of Temple's Thinking on Middle Axioms

There have been several post-war thinkers in the Church of England who have been critical of this form of thinking, some of whose concerns are discussed later in this book (e.g. David Nicholls and John Milbank). For example, Alan Suggate offers a succinct but helpful discussion of 'middle axioms' in his article on William Temple in a collection of essays that appeared in 2014.[81] Suggate notes two particular criticisms of Temple's approach: (1) 'in the framing of middle axioms' there is a

---

[74.] See R.J. Elford and I.S. Markham (eds), *The Middle Way: Theology, Politics and Economics in the Later Thought of R.H. Preston* (London: SCM Press, 2000).

[75.] Ibid., p. 269.

[76.] Ibid., p. 268.

[77.] Ibid., p. 267.

[78.] Ibid., p. 268.

[79.] J. Atherton, C. Baker and J. Reader, *Christianity and the New Social Order: A Manifesto for a Fairer Future* (London: SPCK, 2011), pp. 121–29.

[80.] Ibid., p.121.

[81.] A.M. Suggate, 'William Temple', in P. Scott and W.T. Cavanaugh (eds), *The Blackwell Companion to Political Theology* (Oxford: Blackwell, 2004), pp. 165–79.

danger of 'a comfortable accommodation of Christianity to the powers that be'; and (2) the method is 'too abstract and deductive' in his view.[82] Suggate acknowledges, however, that: 'Temple recommended a dialectical movement between one's understanding of the faith and one's experiencing of living in the world. Principles are guides to action, but are themselves tested, clarified, and, if necessary, revised in the light of experience of living.'[83] Certainly, Temple saw 'middle axioms' as guides to *action* – hence not as ideas in the abstract. Indeed, it was the focus he placed on the need for their *application*, set within a well-argued accompanying contextual analysis, which ensured that his study of 1942 was taken seriously by 'the powers that be', both within and beyond the Church of England.

More recently, John Hughes offers an interesting summary of Temple's intellectual legacy (including his thinking on middle axioms) and the challenges it has faced since the early 1980s, stemming in particular from the writings of MacIntyre, Hauerwas, O'Donovan and Milbank.[84] He describes these thinkers as sharing a common purpose, which is to offer critiques of enlightenment liberalism out of which Temple's thinking on middle axioms had emerged, and locates this trend as being within a wider post-modern intellectual turn. The upshot of this new paradigm of thinking is that it has, once again, raised important questions about the extent to which the Church should 'interfere' in the political affairs of the state, and the most appropriate ways of 'interfering' when it decides that it should.

Temple's and Preston's thinking on middle axioms, though not universally accepted, has held sway in Anglican theological circles ever since. However, as we shall see in this study, this is a view which is antithetical to the vision held by some Anglican Socialists writing in the Christendom strand, not least John Milbank. For these writers, middle axiom thinking is an unwelcome reflection of the extent to which – in the post-war period – the Church of England has allowed itself to become increasingly depoliticised. This has resulted in unacceptable limits being placed on its ability to influence the shaping of governmental policy, not least apropos the provision of welfare, in a way that they would like to see diminished if not ended. Hence, we need to consider their approach as part of their wider theo-political perspective on the Church and state.

[82.] Ibid., p. 177.

[83.] Ibid.

[84.] J. Hughes, 'After Temple? The Recent Renewal of Anglican Social Thought', in Brown (ed.), *Anglican Social Theology*, pp. 74–101.

The Christendom Strand

Anglican Socialists in the Christendom strand have often been influenced by English political pluralist thinking and have sometimes played a significant part in its development and dissemination. They offer a critique of unlimited power vested both in an individual or a political state regardless of whether that power has been vested via a popular democratic mandate at an election. For these writers, such power, exercised by way of a hierarchy of authority, is seen as a threat, both to the existence of individual freedom and the autonomous associations that individuals freely form when freedom of association exists. One of these writers is John Neville Figgis, who in his work of 1913, *Churches in the Modern State*, develops most fully his thinking on the state. It is fervently English political pluralist in its Anglican Socialist perspective and, although its primary focus is on the relationship between Church and State, its wider relevance as a work in the history of political thought has rightly not gone unnoticed. For, in this work, he crystallises so much that has since become central to the English political pluralist frame of reference, particularly on the strengths and weaknesses of representative, parliamentary democracy, both as a concept and an actuality. The following summary of its salient arguments is offered as a way of illuminating the contribution Figgis has made to it.

John Neville Figgis' Thinking on the Modern State

Figgis was highly sceptical of any political dispensation that vested political sovereignty in one individual, such as in the form of an absolutist monarchy, and also of a constitutional monarchical or republican dispensation that incorporates representative, parliamentary government as part of an over-centralised, statist system of rule. Thus, Figgis argues in *Churches in the Modern State*: 'What we actually see in the world is not on the one hand the State, and on the other a mass of unrelated individuals; but a vast complex of gathered unions, in which alone we find individuals, families, clubs, trade unions, colleges, professions, and so forth.'[85] It is in these associations that individual freedom is attained and retained. In an earlier work published in 1907, Figgis similarly argues:

[85.] Figgis, *Churches in the Modern State*, p. 70.

What is needed nowadays is that against an abstract and unreal theory of state omnipotence on the one hand, and an atomistic and artificial view of individual independence on the other, the facts of the world with its innumerable bonds of associations and the naturalness of social authority should be recognised and become the basis of our laws, as it is of our life.[86]

Figgis was of the view that an 'unreal theory of state omnipotence' was a throwback to Hegel's idealist/authoritarian notions of state sovereignty, which he opposed. Yet, he was also critical of 'an artificial view of individual independence' of the kind he associated with Thomas Hobbes' atomistic vision – a scheme he thought placed too little emphasis on the importance that voluntary associations/groups can and should perform in human affairs.[87] Likewise, he was as unimpressed by the nineteenth-century liberal thinking of Jeremy Bentham and John Stuart Mill, which he saw as too individualistic and thus insufficiently associative, as he was of the Fabian statist collectivism later championed by Beatrice and Sidney Webb.[88] For Figgis, by contrast, the purpose of a state was to enable people to form and engage in voluntary associations, mediating as necessary between them, and not to seek to make claims to representing the 'public interest' or 'general will' or 'common good'. Indeed, for Figgis, the state existed 'to control and limit within the bounds of justice, the activities of all minor associations whatsoever'.[89] This is a view that Nicholls, an expert on Figgis, was later to describe in the following terms: 'What most of the pluralists rejected was the idea that the state should interfere with groups in order to protect the interests of members, and impose upon the group the kind of polity which it thought best.'[90] For Figgis, the Reformation and the emergence of the modern state had done just that, concluding:

[86.] J.N. Figgis, *From Gerson to Grotius* (Cambridge: Cambridge University Press, 1907), p. 206. Cited by Grimley, *Citizenship*, pp. 70–71.

[87.] A useful introduction to the thinking of Thomas Hobbes is R. Tuck, *Hobbes: A Very Short Introduction* (Oxford: Oxford University Press, 2002).

[88.] For more on the thinking of the Webbs, see L. Radice, *Beatrice and Sidney Webb* (London: Palgrave Macmillan, 1984).

[89.] Figgis, *Churches in the Modern State*, p. 251.

[90.] Nicholls, *The Pluralist State*, p. 7.

nor is there any of that system of checks and balances which are the result of medieval life, and preserve freedom at the expense of efficiency – no it is the omnicompetent, universal, all absorbing modern State, the mortal God, the great Leviathan of the later teachers ... not power divided, but power concentrated and united [that had come into being].[91]

Not only was it for Figgis, but later also for V.A. Demant, M.B. Reckitt and other early-twentieth-century Christendom Anglican Socialists. This support for a view that the role of the state should be little other than a mediator between groups was underpinned by a favourable historical perspective they shared on how social life had existed in the Middle Ages. Figgis published *Churches in the Modern State* in 1913 and died in 1919, three years before the publication of a book by a group of churchmen, including M.B. Reckitt, P.E.T. Widdrington, A.J. Carlyle, A.J. Penty and N. Carpenter, that was to have a major impact on Anglican Socialists writing in the Christendom strand. That book was called *The Return of Christendom* and in some respects Figgis's writings can be seen as a precursor to the views expressed in it. A brief summary of its core thesis as it relates to the modern state follows.

The 'Return of Christendom' Vision

In one of the chapters, Fr Paul Bull states: 'The disease of our age is disintegration of human life due to organization apart from God'; and: 'The Church to-day has lost the millions because she has failed to sanctify politics and economics through a pietistic and individualistic interpretation of the Gospel.'[92] Essentially, the Christendomists held to a view that the pre-Reformation, pre-capitalist, Catholic medieval society, partly characterised by its merchant and craft guilds, was truer to the creative and associational instincts and needs of human beings, than, as Reckitt argues in another chapter, 'the subjection of the community to capitalist Industrialism',[93] which he saw as being

---

[91.] J.N. Figgis, 'Lecture III on Marsilius', Mirfield MSS, Notebook 3, cited in Nicholls, *The Pluralist State*, p. 28.

[92.] P. Bull, 'The Kingdom of God and the Church Today', in A Group of Churchmen, *The Return of Christendom* (New York: The Macmillan Company, 1922), pp. 217–44, p. 218.

[93.] M. Reckitt, 'The Idea of Christendom in Relation to Modern Society', in ibid., pp. 1–28, p. 2.

antithetical to the 'mediaeval standards of Vocation and Fraternity'.[94] The division of labour, which factory production, via the Industrial Revolution, had brought about, was thus seen by these writers as alienating the workers from any sense of intrinsic work satisfaction, and a contributor to the 'moral hideousness of capitalism',[95] as Reckitt described it. However, crucially, the Christendomists were also highly critical of the way the Church, as they perceived things, had, via the Protestant Reformation, ceded too much ground to the state in bringing this about, with Reckitt bemoaning the fact that: 'The Church, however, has not yet revealed herself as the enemy of plutocracy.'[96] Hence, a key goal of the Christendomists was for the Church to claw back power and influence from the modern state in the quest for greater perceived relevance in society, as, in the words of Fr Bull: 'the Kingdom of God is that principle which alone can weave up the life of man into a perfect synthesis'.[97] He later summed up this aspect of the Christendom perspective as follows:

> That a false presentation of Christianity has disintegrated Christendom, and left the vast forces which largely control the life of man unconsecrated to the service of God. The evil tradition, which is not yet abandoned, that Christianity has nothing to do with politics and economics has banished God from 95 per cent. of the life of man. For politics and economics regulate homes, housing, schools, education, wages, sanitation, industry, and commerce, with all the relationships these involve. If this 95 per cent. of the life of the people is dissociated from God and religion, what wonder it is if they feel that God doesn't count in the battle of life.[98]

The contrast between this view and the one held by Temple, for example, that sought to establish limits for Church engagement in the modern state, is thus apparent and, as we shall see, is crucial for grasping an understanding of the difference in perspective on state-provided welfare held by Welfare Statist Anglican Socialists and Christendom Anglican Socialists.

[94.] Ibid.

[95.] Ibid.

[96.] Ibid.

[97.] Bull, 'The Kingdom of God and the Church Today', p. 219.

[98.] Ibid., pp. 224–25.

Figgis, and later other Anglican Socialists writing in the Christendom strand who had been influenced by *The Return of Christendom*, interpreted the Church of England as one of the associations whose congregations people voluntarily choose to enter, and much of *Churches in the Modern State* is a trenchant critique of the way he saw the rise of state sovereignty as a threat to religious liberty and the autonomy of religious associations. He was sceptical of the concept of a national church, seeing establishment as a constraint on the Church's sovereignty; instead, he advocated the need for the Church of England to see itself more as an integral part of a wider Church community, comprising several denominations and enjoying a greater level of autonomy from state direction, that would enable it to focus more on serving the needs of the poor than those of the rich, even if this meant that the Church would have to give up 'attempting to dictate the policy of the State in regard to the whole mass of its citizens'.[99] Figgis was not advocating that Christians should withdraw from playing a role in politics; rather, he was arguing that the Church of England should play less of a role in return for greater freedom from state influence, stating: 'We cannot eat our cake and have it.'[100]

A point worth noting is that, while Temple rejected Figgis' anti-establishment perspective on the Church of England – in Temple's eyes, it relegated its significance to that of any other church in voluntary society, which was anathema to his sense of its national identity – he nevertheless recognised, as we have seen in his thinking on middle axioms, that there were limits to which it could legitimately seek to influence the policy of the state. In this respect, then, it can be argued that Temple was closer to Figgis' thinking on the limits of Church interference in the state's political affairs, than some of the Christendomists that came after Figgis, not least Nicholls and Milbank, who have argued for a much greater level of Church interference in the state's political affairs than Figgis' perspective advocates.

[99.] Figgis, *Churches in the Modern State*, p. 113.
[100.] Ibid., p. 112.

In Summary

Figgis 'was opposed to a conception of an omnipotent state set against a mass of individuals who are its members – "the great leviathan" made up of little men, as in Hobbes's title-page'.[101] This is consistent with Figgis' statement that St Thomas Aquinas:

> does not make that cardinal error of political arithmetic, which sets the State on the one hand against the mass of individuals on the other; but in his strong regard for the family and other social unions he regards the individual as belonging to the State, although he belongs to smaller social unions which exist in their own right and not by the mere fiat of an autocrat.[102]

Figgis did not, however, envisage the abolition of a public state as either viable or desirable despite the threat it posed to liberty as he saw things. He envisaged its main function as being to make laws that would strengthen the role and popular sovereignty of the voluntary associations individuals freely entered into, such as the Church, in a scheme he described as a 'semi-federalist polity'.[103] Thus, for Figgis, as for all English pluralists, neither individualism nor statist collectivism provided a sound basis on which to construct a political system; rather, a political system had to be based on voluntary associationism, with group activity having pre-eminence over individualist and statist-collectivist alternatives.

These ideas resonated with V.A. Demant, an admirer of Figgis, whose Christendom thinking we now consider.

The Christendom Thinking of V.A. Demant

V.A. Demant, an Anglican Socialist writing in the Christendom strand, delivered his influential Henry Scott Holland Lectures in 1949, later published as *Religion and the Decline of Capitalism* in 1952.[104] Though known more for his contribution to Christendom thinking than to English political pluralism, he was influenced by the English pluralist

---

101. Nicholls, *The Pluralist State*, p. 82.
102. J.N. Figgis, 'Lecture on Aquinas', Mirfield MSS, Notebook 2. Cited in Nicholls, *The Pluralist State*, p. 82.
103. Figgis, *Churches in the Modern State*, p. 81.
104. Demant, *Religion and the Decline of Capitalism*.

movement of the early twentieth century, as well as by the Guild Socialist thinking of the same period, and shared some of Figgis' views on the threat that state sovereignty can pose for voluntary associations in civil society, as well as much of his thinking on the Reformation. Unlike Figgis, however, Demant had knowledge of how an over-collectivist state could result in a totalitarian outcome of the kind witnessed in the Soviet Union and Germany under the leadership of Stalin and Hitler. For Demant, this reinforced the dangers of the Church ceding too much power to the modern state, to a point when:

> the omnicompetent state rides in as the moral and cultural preceptor and takes the place of the Church. That is what rightly worries Professor Hayek who wrote, in *The Road to Serfdom*: 'The state ceases to be a piece of utilitarian machinery intended to help individuals in the fullest development of their individual personality and becomes a "moral" institution – where "moral" is not used in contrast to "immoral" but describes an institution which imposes on its members its views on all moral questions.'[105]

Indeed, for Demant: 'That is one reason why the state takes on a sacred character.'[106] For him, the antidote to the threat of omnicompetent statist collectivism was, in significant part, a return to the pre-Reformation, Christendom vision, to bring about a decline of the secular, capitalist modern state and reverse the reasons for its rise. Like Tawney, who, in his Henry Scott Holland lectures of 1922, later published as *Religion and the Rise of Capitalism* (1926),[107] had attributed the rise of capitalism – at least in part – to the Protestant Reformation, so had Demant. For Tawney, Christian history had led him to conclude that the post-Reformation 'abdication by the Christian Churches of one whole department of life, that of social and political conduct' was what in significant part had led to the emergence of an 'acquisitive society'.[108] In agreement with this thinking, Demant, in his lectures, argued:

[105.] Ibid., p. 104.

[106.] Ibid.

[107.] R.H. Tawney, *Religion and the Rise of Capitalism* (1926) (London: Penguin Books, 1938).

[108.] R.H. Tawney, *The Acquisitive Society* (1921) (London: Fontana, 1961), p. 183. Cited in C. Bryant, *Possible Dreams* (London: Hodder & Stoughton, 1996),

the success of Puritanism meant the triumph of the new commercial morality which held good among monied men; capitalists had established their right to secure a return for their money, and there was no authority to insist upon any correlative duty when they organized industrial undertakings and obtained control over the means of production.[109]

What is more, for Demant: 'Capitalism was a part of the whole movement known as liberalism. … It was this liberalism which dispensed with "the sacred" as a real element in existence and gave the "secular" all the religious valuations previously accorded to the divine realm.'[110] The result was that: 'Associative impulses were weakened, to be replaced by collective cement of cash or state.'[111] This had led to a situation in which, for Demant: 'The supervening bonds of contract only, which tended to make men related only as economic atoms, powerfully burdened the ministerial work of the Church.'[112] For some churchmen this had led to a view that, in the words of Scott Holland: 'The State must take up her neighbourly responsibility'[113] and, for Temple, as has been argued, to thus become a welfare state. For others: 'This faith that "the State principle" would restore the social bonds which a hypertrophied market principle had weakened … was not so straightforward.'[114] The reason Demant attributes to this is:

the principle of the omnicompetent state and the myth of the self-sufficient individual are both twins of the same parentage, that of naturalist humanism which distils from human life in its biological, community and spiritual setting, the two abstractions of individual and state which reason can encompass.[115]

---

pp. 189–90.

[109] Demant, *Religion and the Decline of Capitalism*, p. 19.

[110] Ibid., p. 37.

[111] Ibid., p. 38.

[112] Ibid., pp. 37–38.

[113] Cited in ibid., p. 55.

[114] Ibid.

[115] Ibid., p. 57. For more on Milbank's thinking on this, see D.M. Bell, 'Postliberalism and Radical Orthodoxy', in C. Hovey and E. Phillips (eds),

This view is shared by John Milbank. For Milbank, writing as an Anglo-Catholic in the Christendom strand, naturalist humanism (that is, scientific method combined with social and ethical values) embodies the separation of nature from grace[116] that occurred in late medieval theological tradition. This, he believes, enabled the rise of the modern, Western secular state and capitalism, via the Protestant Reformation, with a resultant diminished role for the Church in society and, specifically, in politics. Thus, only by way of a recovery of patristic and Thomist ontological thinking that is devoid of any separation of nature from grace can a truly authentic and viable political theology emerge that is post-liberal and Catholic. This theme will be further developed in Part Two. However, for Demant (and later for Milbank), the outcome of the rise of naturalist humanism was, in part, a 'state [that] can never be an object of emotional attachment which could replace a man's roots in home, property, neighbourhood and craft association'.[117] Nor could the omnicompetent, secular, modern state be permitted to ride in, 'as the moral and cultural preceptor' that takes 'the place of the Church'.[118]

The Cambridge Companion to Political Theology (Cambridge: Cambridge University Press, 2015), pp. 110–32.

[116] Thus establishing a dualism that had not existed previously in Christian theology. For Milbank, it was this dualism that in large part spawned the de-politicisation of the Christian Church in early modern Europe, marginalising its presence and influence in the *body politic* to a point where secular politics came to increasingly prevail over what had been a superior Catholically Christocentric intellectual and cultural epoch. Thus, Milbank sees this as 'the turning point in the destiny of the West'. See J. Milbank, *The Word Made Strange: Theology, Language, Culture* (Oxford: Blackwell, 1997), p. 44. Indeed, for Milbank, this new cultural reality (the autonomy of the secular) increasingly came to consider any recourse to transcendence (the supernatural) in the political sphere as an unwelcome intrusion in the state's political affairs. For Milbank, moreover, the *ideal* would be to bring about a dissolution of this act of dualistic 'ontological violence', via proclaiming the post-secular, thus enabling the Christian Church to regain its rightful place in a new Christendom, mediating grace and embodying the 'kingdom of God in embryo', though he is, to a degree, pragmatic about how this could be achieved.

[117] Demant, *Religion and the Decline of Capitalism*, p. 95.

[118] Ibid., p. 104.

It is thinking like this which made Demant so wary of the rise in the 1940s of the welfare state as a possible solution to the immorality of capitalism and its injustices, stating: 'that when the state principle is invoked as a remedy for the sickness of a society over-weighted by market and contract relationships, then the real disorder is more effectively concealed'.[119] By the 'real disorder', Demant meant what he saw as being the marginalisation of the Church, in relation to the modern, secular state in post-Reformation, liberal-capitalist society, and the absence of 'a common allegiance to the religious and moral axioms of Christendom'.[120] This is a view that is central to Milbank's perspective on the liberal-capitalist state, welfare and the Church, and it is why it can be located in the Christendom strand of the tradition, which he readily acknowledges:

> Indeed, there has always been a debate within Anglicanism between the statist Temple tradition on the one hand, and the 'Christendom' perspective of John Neville Figgis through to V.A. Demant and T.S. Eliot – deriving variously from the Oxford Movement, Radical Tory evangelicalism, non-statist Christian socialism and Catholic distributionism – on the other. Within this 'Christendom' perspective, it is the Church itself that is the real site of the redeemed society, of true human collaboration. In this respect the Church should operate as the fulcrum for the growth of civil society.

He goes on to say: 'Rowan Williams, the Radical Orthodoxy group (to which I belong) and increasingly many of the current Anglican episcopal bench, represent the latter "Christendom" legacy.'[121]

Milbank's Christendom thinking will be further considered in chapter two. Before, then, however, we need to briefly consider the revolutionist strand.

[119.] Ibid., p. 102.

[120.] Ibid., p. 98.

[121.] J. Milbank, 'The Big Society Depends on the Big Parish', ABC Religion & Ethics, 30 November 2010. Available at: http://www.abc.net.au/religion /articles/2010/11/30/3080680.htm (accessed on 3 March 2015), p. 3.

The Revolutionist Strand

Anglican Socialists from within the revolutionist strand have tended to be influenced by the writings of Leon Trotsky, who believed that capitalism, in its various nation-state settings, had to be overthrown by way of force in the form of a proletarian-led revolution. Lenin, in 1917, described this as necessary for establishing a 'dictatorship of the proletariat'.[122] A period of 'democratic centralism', as defined by Lenin in 1902,[123] would then be necessary to enable a bourgeois state to be transformed as part of the move to a society formed around workers' councils. These workers' councils would then become the cornerstone of a socialist society, where common ownership of the land and industrial resources would exist, enabling levels of direct democracy to flourish that would be far superior to the parliamentary representative models that existed in Western, liberal-capitalist democracies. Moreover, while it was appropriate in the period leading up to the proletarian revolutions for workers' vanguard parties to put forward transitional demands, as a means of influencing bourgeois parties to implement benefits that would stimulate the class consciousness of workers (such as state welfare programmes), for Trotsky, and for his later followers, these were never seen as anything other than temporary measures, to be overthrown when the time was ripe as part of the workers' revolution and the transition to socialism.[124]

This form of Trotskyist revolutionary socialist perspective is thus in stark contrast to the Welfare Statist approach advocated by Temple whereby, as we have seen, the state gradually becomes more of a welfare state than a 'Power-State' via parliamentary legislative sovereignty and the social programmes it affords on education, health, social security etc., on behalf of the population that have elected representatives to parliament to bring this about. It is also different to the Christendom perspective advocated by Figgis *et al.*, which has sought for the state's role in society to be tailored to enabling people to form and engage in voluntary associations – one being a revitalised church – with the state merely mediating as necessary between these groups. Of course,

---

[122.] Lenin, *The State and Revolution* (1917).

[123.] V.I. Lenin, *What Is to Be Done?* (1902) (Oxford: Oxford University Press, 1963).

[124.] For more on this, see L. Trotsky, *History of the Russian Revolution* (1930) (Chicago: Haymarket Book, 2008) and *The Revolution Betrayed* (1936) (Mineola, NY: Dover Publications, 2004).

neither the Welfare Statist nor Christendom perspectives advocate revolution by force, or anything resembling 'democratic centralism' via establishing a 'dictatorship of the proletariat' and the complete removal of the capitalist state apparatus as being necessary for a transition to socialism.

There are references to Trotsky in the writings of revolutionist Anglican Socialists such as Kenneth Leech, for example: 'I write as a revolutionary socialist who has learnt much from Marxist analysis, particularly in its Trotskyist form.'[125] One study of International Trotskyism also argues that Conrad Noel had lent support to the British Provisional Committee for the Defence of Leon Trotsky and had signed a letter defending Trotsky's right to asylum and calling for an international inquiry into the Moscow Trials conducted by Stalin between 1936 and 1938.[126] However, unlike Figgis and Temple, neither Leech nor Noel's writings contain *a developed theory of the state*, nor, for that matter, unlike Trotsky's, *a developed theory of the state and revolution*.

What is more, though undoubtedly committed revolutionary socialists, it cannot be assumed that either writer *wholly* endorsed the perspective on the state and revolution developed by Trotsky, as their writings do not provide confirmation of such an out-and-out endorsement. Also of relevance is that, whilst in the context of the post-2008 financial crash, discussions and analysis within Anglican Socialism concerning welfare in England and the Church of England's role in its provision were vibrant and influential on the shaping of events, it was noticeable that, whereas defenders of the Welfare Statist model, such as Steven

---

[125.] K. Leech, *Politics and Faith Today: Catholic Social Vision for the 1990s* (London: Darton, Longman & Todd, 1994), p. 2. Leech did not regard William Temple as being a socialist. See K. Leech, 'The Christian Left in Britain (1850–1950)', in R. Ambler and D. Haslam (eds), *Agenda for Prophets: Towards a Political Theology* (London: Bowerdean Press, 1990), p. 68. He was an admirer of the radical socialist thinking of Stewart Headlam. For more on Headlam, see S. Headlam, *The Guild of St Matthew: What It Is and Who Should Join It* (London: Guild of St Matthew, 1895).

[126.] R.J. Alexander, *International Trotskyism, 1929–1985: A Documented Analysis of the Movement* (Durham, NC: Duke University Press, 1991), p. 451.

Shakespeare,[127] and of the Christendom alternative, such as Milbank,[128] had been vocal and forthright in their views, any remaining defenders of the revolutionist strand were noticeably absent from these debates. With the death of Kenneth Leech in September 2015, it may be that the last significant standard-bearer of that strand of Anglican Socialism has left the stage, although there remains in existence a small Society of Sacramental Socialists as an offshoot of the Jubilee Group. Therefore, that strand will not feature any further in the analysis that follows.

Conclusion

There are three distinct strands of Anglican Socialist thinking on the modern state that have shaped their advocates' views on the role it should perform in the transition to a Christian socialist society. They have also shaped their views on the role the Church might play in that process, not least with respect to its interface with the state's welfare arm. Moreover, two of these strands remain relevant for locating and understanding the debate that took place in the Church of England after the financial crash of 2008 concerning welfare provision and the role the Church of England should perform in its delivery. Should its approach be one characterised primarily as shaped around a defence of the Welfare State and consistent with the thinking of Temple as, by and large, it had been up to 2010, or should it be one characterised by a move towards a more localist, community-based, voluntarist, Christendom model of welfare delivery, with the Church of England playing a greater role in the provision of welfare and a smaller welfare state as argued by Milbank? To answer that question some further historical and theoretical analysis of the period from 1945 to 2010 is necessary in chapter two (hence, before the launch of the 'Big Society' project which will be considered in Part Three) with respect to the setting-up of the Welfare State and to the rise and fall of the post-war welfare state consensus.

[127.] S. Shakespeare, *Affirming Common Wealth: A Response to Milbank*, ABC Religion & Ethics, 10 December 2010. Available at: http://www.abc.net.au /religion/articles/2010/12/10/3090394.htm (accessed on 27 August 2017).

[128.] Milbank, 'The Big Society Depends on the Big Parish'.

Chapter Two

Anglican Socialism and the Rise and Fall of the British Welfare State Consensus

Introduction

In this chapter I provide a brief historical analysis of the post-war Welfare-Statist 'Keynesian' consensus that lasted until circa 1976. The writings of Anglican Socialist R.H. Tawney from within the Welfare Statist strand will also be analysed, including the influence he had on shaping that consensus. The challenge to that consensus via the rise and consolidation of neoliberalism in the period since, will then be examined. This is necessary for contextualising and analysing the Church of England's approach to welfare provision since 1945. The writings of David Nicholls, an Anglo-Catholic author in the Christendom strand, will also be analysed because his works on the Church, the modern state and welfare have been influential within Anglican Socialism – including on the thinking of Milbank; a familiarity with his perspective is thus helpful for understanding contemporary debates within the Church of England and the Labour Party on welfare, and for historically locating and understanding Milbank's contribution to them.

The Welfare State Consensus: 1945–76

In his first speech as Prime Minister to the House of Commons,[1] Winston Churchill called for 'blood, toil, tears and sweat' as necessary

---

[1] W. Churchill, 'Blood, Toil, Tears and Sweat': First speech to the House of Commons as Prime Minister, 13 May 1940. Available at: http://www

to defeat the Nazi threat. Total war required nothing less, as Britain's contribution to winning the Second World War owed as much to the efforts of the whole population as to the military. Total war also required a level of state-directed economic and social activity of a kind previously unseen, including state-directed labour deployments on a wide scale. These events had for John Maynard Keynes (at the time working for the Treasury) reinforced a belief that state economic stimulus and planning could achieve real economic, political and social benefits.[2]

To get a flavour of the mood of the times: *The Times* editorial on 1 July 1940, stated:

> If we speak of democracy, we do not mean a democracy which maintains the right to vote but forgets the right to work and the right to live. If we speak of freedom, we do not mean a rugged individualism which excludes social organisation and economic planning. If we speak of equality, we do not mean a political equality nullified by social and economic privilege. If we speak of economic reconstruction, we think less of maximum production (though this job too will be required) than of equitable distribution ... the new order cannot be based on the preservation of privilege, whether the privilege be that of a country, a class or an individual.[3]

There is a strong echo in this quote of William Beveridge's view that a people's war demanded a people's peace,[4] and of a desire to avoid what had happened after the First World War, when those returning from battle had frequently to endure prolonged periods of unemployment, inadequate healthcare provision, housing and educational opportunity

---

.winstonchurchill.org/resources/speeches/1940-the-finest-hour/blood-toil-tears-and-sweat (accessed on 25 August 2016).

[2.] D. Fraser, *The Evolution of the British Welfare State* (New York: Palgrave Macmillan, 2009), pp. 245ff.

[3.] Cited in A.R. Morton (ed.), 'The Future of Welfare', Occasional Paper No. 41, Centre for Theology and Public Issues, University of Edinburgh, 1997, p. 12.

[4.] As Beveridge stated in 1942, public interest in what happened after the war 'represents simply a refusal to take victory in war as an end in itself; it must be read as a determination to understand and to approve the end beyond victory for which sacrifices are being required'. W.H. Beveridge, *The Pillars of Security* (London: George Allen & Unwin, 1942), pp. 107–8. Cited by Fraser, *The Evolution of the British Welfare State*, pp. 247–48.

for their children. In his report of 1942, *Social Insurance and Allied Services*,[5] a work influenced by the thinking of Temple,[6] Beveridge – though an agnostic in faith matters and a Liberal 'collectivist', not a socialist politically – identified five giant evils in society requiring remedy via state legislation and, in significant part, ongoing state welfare provision: squalor, ignorance, want, idleness and disease. His solution was a social security scheme that he described as follows:

> The principle of the Social Security Scheme is to ensure for everyone income up to subsistence level, in return for compulsory contributions, expecting him to make voluntary provision to ensure income that he desired beyond this. One consequence of this principle is that no means test of any kind can be applied to the benefits of the Scheme. Another is that the Scheme does not guarantee a standard of life beyond subsistence level.[7]

Beveridge defined seven needs to be covered by the scheme:[8]

- childhood (by way of state-provided family allowances);
- old age (by way of state pensions);
- disability (by way of state disability and injury benefits);
- unemployment (by way of state unemployment benefit);
- funeral expenses (to be met by a state funeral grant);

---

5. W.H. Beveridge, *Social Insurance and Allied Services* (London: HMSO, 1942).

6. Beveridge had been friends with Temple and Tawney whilst an undergraduate at Balliol College, Oxford, and their friendship had remained strong. See Lawrence Goldman, 'Founding the Welfare State: The Collective Biography of William Beveridge, R.H. Tawney and William Temple', a lecture given at the Institute of Historical Research on 7 April 2016. Available at: https://www.history.ac.uk/podcasts/franco-british-history-external/founding-welfare-state-collective-biography-william (accessed on 19 June 2019).

7. W.H. Beveridge, *Papers by W.H. Beveridge to Inter-Departmental Committee on Social Insurance and Allied Services*, 11 December 1941. Cited by Fraser, *The Evolution of the British Welfare State*, p. 359.

8. Ibid. For more on Beveridge and his report of 1942, see the biography by J. Harris, *William Beveridge: A Biography* (Oxford: Oxford University Press, 1988). See also N. Timmins, *The Five Giants: A Bibliography of the Welfare State* (London: Harper-Collins, 1995).

- loss of gainful occupation other than employment, e.g. bankruptcy, fire, theft (to be met by a state grant);
- marriage needs of a woman, e.g. widowhood, maternity, separation (to be met by a state widow's pension and state grants for the other categories).

He was clear that no satisfactory scheme of social security could be devised except on the following three assumptions:[9]

- children's allowances for children up to the age of fifteen or in full-time education up to the age of sixteen;
- comprehensive health and rehabilitation services for prevention and cure of disease and restoration of capacity for work; and
- maintenance of employment, that is to say avoidance of mass unemployment.

Hence, Beveridge's Social Security Scheme offered a possible solution to the problem of want; but he was clear that the other four giants also needed slaying, as part of a comprehensive set of state welfare reforms. Thus, for Beveridge, as historian Derek Fraser aptly puts it: 'true freedom lay in freedom *from* want, *from* disease, *from* ignorance, *from* squalor and *from* idleness'.[10] For Beveridge, then, as it had been for T.H. Green and, later, for Temple, *true* freedom was not an abstract notion but a tangible, measurable outcome for citizens delivered, in significant part, by way of state intervention and, specifically, after 1944/45, by way of state welfare provision. All that was needed was a government that shared his vision and had the political mandate and will to bring it about. The Attlee government broadly fitted that bill, though Beveridge was to disagree strongly with Attlee on the extent to which his government removed the role of the friendly societies in the post-war provision of welfare.[11] This is an aspect of the implementation of his report of 1942 which will be

---

[9.] Beveridge, *Social Insurance and Allied Services*, pp. 120–22. Cited by Fraser, *The Evolution of the British Welfare State*, p. 361.

[10.] Fraser, *The Evolution of the British Welfare State*, p. 255.

[11.] He had put in his 1942 report that the friendly societies should be allowed to continue to administer state-provided sickness benefits under the new arrangements; something that Attlee saw as impractical and rejected. For more on this, see J. Harris, 'Voluntarism, the State and Public-Private Partnerships in Beveridge's Social Thought', in M. Oppenheimer and N. Deakin (eds),

further examined in chapter four when considering his report of 1948, *Voluntary Action*, and in chapter five when considering the Church of England's handling of the 'Big Society' project.

The Attlee Administration (1945–51) and the Welfare State

The British Welfare State has been described as having twin pillars: the social security system and the National Health Service. Under the Attlee administration, via several major pieces of legislation such as the Family Allowance Act 1945, the National Insurance Industrial Injuries Act 1946 and the National Insurance Act 1946, the range of social security provision was considerably extended, in line with key recommendations of the Beveridge Report. In addition, the National Health Service Acts of 1946, 1947 and 1948 paved the way for the establishment of a National Health Service across all parts of the United Kingdom. In July 1948, this was brought about, with cradle-to-grave healthcare coverage free at the point of delivery and for all. The Education Act of 1944 was largely implemented by the Attlee government and provided for a raised school leaving age of fifteen and a reformed system of secondary education. The National Assistance Act of 1948 established a National Assistance Board to assume national responsibility for those in need who had previously been dealt with by the local Public Assistance Committees. The New Towns Act of 1946 led to a substantial expansion of housing provision via the creation of fourteen new towns across Britain, followed by the Housing Act of 1949 that enabled local authorities to acquire houses for renovation and improvement with a subsidy from the Exchequer.[12]

With respect to Beveridge's goal of achieving and maintaining full employment, high levels of unemployment having been the scourge after the First World War, Attlee's administration tackled this head on, by adopting an economic policy that was heavily state controlled and directed. Ports, canals, railways, airways, coal, gas and electricity, as well as the Bank of England, were taken under state control. Keynesian management of the economy was the economic tool deployed, with a combination of increases in taxation, especially for the better-off,

---

Beveridge and Voluntary Action in Britain and the Wider British World (Manchester: Manchester University Press, 2011), p. 10.

[12.] For more on the Attlee Administration and its legislative programme, see K. Morgan, *Labour in Power 1945–1951* (Oxford: Oxford University Press, 1985). For more on the wider economic and social context in which Attlee governed, see P. Hennessy, *Never Again: Britain 1945–1951* (London: Penguin, 2006). See also Timmins, *The Five Giants*.

and use of the peace dividend derived from reductions in defence expenditure from five billion pounds in 1945 to less than one billion in 1950,[13] to fund the new welfare services. In the two decades following the end of the war, unemployment rarely rose above two per cent[14] and thus Beveridge's target of less than three per cent as constituting full employment was achieved. Overall, this response by the Attlee administration to slaying the five giants was seen by many as broadly commensurate with the scale of the task and also as impressive in terms of its delivery of the goals that inspired it. Thus, it came to significantly define the political landscape in the decades that followed up to 1976; a period of government that has since been described as one of 'welfare consensus'.[15]

The Period of Welfare State Consensus: 1951–76

One historian, Derek Fraser, describes this period as one when: 'The support for the welfare state was part of a broader "social democratic" policy consensus, which also included the adoption of Keynesian economics, a commitment to full employment and a high level of government intervention, expenditure and planning.'[16] In support of this, Fraser cites Conservative Chancellor Rab Butler as saying, in response to an article in *The Economist* in 1954 that had drawn similarities between his approach and that of his predecessor, Labour's Hugh Gaitskell: 'Both of us, it is true, spoke the language of Keynesianism but we spoke it with different accents and a differing emphasis', leading to the coining of the term 'Butskellism' that described this consensual approach.[17] However, the Labour governments during this period, whilst adopting a Keynesian approach to economic policy with more economic planning and state intervention than had existed in the pre-war economy, saw the Welfare State more as a way of advancing a social democratic agenda. In this regard, as shall be argued below, they were influenced in part by

---

[13.] J. Weeks, '1945 and 2015: They Really Don't Match', *Compass: Together for a Good Society*, 28 June 2013. Available at: http://www.compassonline.org.uk/1945-and-2015-they-really-dont-match/ (accessed on 24 October 2017).

[14.] Ibid.

[15.] See Fraser, *The Evolution of the British Welfare State*, p. 287.

[16.] Ibid. There was a Conservative administration from 1951 to 1964 and from 1970 to 1974. Labour administrations existed in the remaining periods from 1964 to 1970 and from 1974 to 1979.

[17.] R.A. Butler, *The Art of the Possible* (London: Penguin, 1973), p. 163. Cited by Fraser, *The Evolution of the British Welfare State*, p. 289.

the writings of Tawney and the need, as he argued, for greater *equality* in society – this being a key democratic socialist aim for him and his followers.

From this perspective, the British National Health Service was one example of how this could be achieved. Universal, cradle-to-grave in its coverage, free at the point of delivery and classless in its access, it embodied much that those from within the Welfare Statist strand of the Anglican Socialist tradition, such as Temple and Tawney, had dreamed of. For here was a state-funded and state-run institution derived from a popular mandate[18] and from which tangible benefits to health care were being realised on a scale previously unknown to the industrial working class (and to many in the middle class, too). This had led to a point where it was electorally (and hence politically) non-viable for any government not to be seen to be in support of it.[19] However, by the 1970s serious tensions over the funding of the Welfare State were to arise, not least owing to a significant deterioration in the British economy. In the words of Richard Crossman, writing in December 1970, there was 'a cracking sound in the political atmosphere, the sound of the consensus breaking up'.[20]

The Callaghan Administration's Response to the Oil Crisis
In the early 1970s the British economy entered a period of economic downturn. With the quadrupling of oil prices in the mid-1970s, leading to a major dip in economic growth, the Callaghan Labour government made substantial cuts to public expenditure in return for an IMF loan. Callaghan would tell Labour Party members in a speech in Blackpool

---

[18.] Attlee's government secured a majority of over 150 seats. See K. Jefferys (ed.), *War and Reform: British Politics during the Second World War* (Manchester: Manchester University Press, 1994), p. 155.

[19.] Thus, 'One-Nation' Tories, such as Harold Macmillan, saw the National Health Service and the wider Welfare State as a necessary part of the economic, social and political landscape, not least because it co-existed with a period of economic and social improvement famously described by Macmillan in July 1957, as a time when 'most of our people have never had it so good'. See H. Macmillan, speaking at a Tory Party rally in Bedford in July 1957. Available at: http://news.bbc.co.uk/onthisday/hi/dates/stories /july/20/newsid_3728000/3728225.stm (accessed on 25 August 2008).

[20.] Cited in A. Sampson, *The Changing Anatomy of Britain* (London: Hodder & Stoughton, 1982), p. 75, and in D.B. Forrester, *Christianity and the Future of Welfare* (London: Epworth Press, 1985), p. 25.

delivered in 1976: 'we used to think you could spend your way out of a recession. … I tell you in all candour that option no longer exists.'[21] Thus, Keynesian economics was no longer *de rigueur* in government circles and the scene was set for a sea change in government policy, not least with respect to the Welfare State, with the election of the Conservative Party to office under Prime Minister Margaret Thatcher's leadership on 4 May 1979. However, before we consider that period of history, it is necessary to briefly examine the thinking of a key Anglican Socialist whose influence on the events we have been considering was significant, and was to remain so in the period since, as a perspective on the Welfare State.

R.H. Tawney Writing in the Welfare Statist Strand

R.H. Tawney's influence on post-war Labour Party thinking and practice was significant as evidenced, for example, in a remark by Hugh Gaitskell: 'Looking back quite objectively, I think he was the best man I have ever known.'[22] Like Temple, he went on to become a major figure in the Welfare Statist strand of the Anglican Socialist tradition. Though essentially an economic and social historian of considerable reputation, he published two books on socialist theory in the inter-war years, *The Acquisitive Society* (1921) and *Equality* (1931), that for many in the Anglican Socialist tradition and the Labour Party, then and since, have been seen as foundational for a defence of the Welfare State and for democratic socialism.

For Tawney, equality of opportunity and some degree of equality of economic outcome were not a challenge to personal freedom but, instead, were essential for it and for a democratic socialist society to exist. In defending the Welfare State in his epilogue to *Equality*, written in the 1952 edition, he stated: 'Those who hold that the resulting gains have been purchased by the sacrifice of liberty are under an obligation to state precisely the liberties held to have been injured or destroyed.

[21.] J. Callaghan, 'Leader's Speech, Blackpool 1976'. Available at: http://www .britishpoliticalspeech.org/speech-archive.htm?speech=174 (accessed on 25 August 2016).

[22.] H. Gaitskell, 'Address at a Memorial Service for R.H. Tawney at St Martin-in-the-fields, on Thursday, 8 February 1962'. Cited in D. Reisman, *State and Welfare: Tawney, Galbraith and Adam Smith* (London: Macmillan, 1982), p. 89.

Social policy has been specially concerned with health, education and security.'[23] In defence of this position, he goes on to list improvements in the infant mortality rate, the height and weight of schoolchildren, the disappearance of ailments previously afflicting them, improvements to educational opportunities and the virtual elimination of unemployment. He then states:

> It is not suggested that all these actions are due to the action of the State; but in most of them public intervention has played some part, and in several a decisive one. It is difficult to argue that they have been either prejudicial to freedom or without significance for it; nor would it be easy to show that their beneficial effects in diminishing inequality have been outweighed by incidental evils resulting from them.[24]

Tawney's defence of the Welfare State is thus clear: public intervention via the state can and should be a key part of the overall effort to improve the health and well-being of the populace and reduce the levels of inequality in society.

Essentially, Tawney, though initially sympathetic to guild ('non-statist') forms of socialism in the 1920s, by 1930 had come to believe that a more progressive taxation system was a key mechanism for achieving greater redistribution of wealth and opportunity in society, and thus equality, arguing for 'the pooling of its surplus resources by means of taxation, and the use of the funds thus obtained to make accessible to all, irrespective of their income, occupation, or social position, the conditions of civilization which, in the absence of such measures, can be enjoyed only by the rich'.[25] For Tawney, state-run welfare services funded from general taxation or National Insurance were examples of *redistribution in practice* and of ways of enhancing equality of opportunity and outcome, and hence democratic socialism and the Christian morality he believed underpinned it. As he argued:

> By taking money where it can be most easily spared, and spending it where it is most urgently needed, it produces the maximum of social benefit with the minimum of economic disturbance. By concentrating surplus resources, directing

---

23. Tawney, *Equality*, p. 232.

24. Ibid., p. 233.

25. Ibid., p. 122.

them to objects of primary importance, and applying them, as in the case of the services of health, housing, and education, under expert advice and in accordance with a specialized technique, it makes possible the attainment of results which no body of individuals, even though they spent ten times the sums involved, could achieve for themselves by their isolated action.[26]

Like Temple, however, Tawney was by no means insensitive to the dangers of statist collectivism, not least with respect to democracy and socialism. Thus, with regard to Soviet collectivism, he stated: 'Dams, bridges, power-plants and steel-works, however admirable, are not a substitute for human rights.'[27] In his 1952 Epilogue, he describes totalitarian regimes as being those 'which have suppressed the primary liberties, and also those which give short shrift to demands for equality ... and repudiate equality with the same ritual thunder as liberty'.[28] However, whilst recognising these dangers, Tawney's perspective on the state is unambiguously at variance with the more negative one held by writers in the Christendom strand such as Milbank. The following quote from him crystalises the reasons why:

> The idea that there is an entity called 'The State', which possesses, in virtue of its title, uniform characteristics existing independently of the varying histories, economic environments, constitutional arrangements, legal systems, and social psychologies of particular states, and that these characteristics necessarily combine the manners of a Japanese customs officer with the morals of a human tiger, is pure superstition. ... The State is an important instrument; hence the struggle to control it. But it is an instrument, and nothing more.[29]

For Tawney, then, the state did not *embody* uniform characteristics: for it was 'an instrument, and nothing more'. This was consistent with Temple's view that: 'The State is, in practice, the people who administer

---

[26.] Ibid., p. 136.

[27.] Ibid.

[28.] Ibid., p. 227.

[29.] R.H. Tawney, *The Attack and Other Papers* (London: George Allen & Unwin, 1953), p. 97.

it.'[30] Thus, any characteristics it had were those that had been given to it. For Tawney, moreover, even in a liberal-capitalist context, the modern state, via parliamentary, representative democracy, with the checks and balances both constitutionally and electorally this afforded on the potential for the abuse of power, it was possible for it to be an instrument capable of enhancing freedom via democratic control over (and deployment of) its administrative apparatus, in the interests of furthering equality and thus the cause of democratic socialism by way of incorporating state-provided welfare programmes. In this respect his view of the state chimed perfectly with that of Temple, who had argued: 'The State was made for men and women, not men and women for the State.'[31]

By contrast, for Milbank, the modern, liberal-capitalist state *possesses* uniform characteristics pertinent to it – these often being defined by its secularity. Indeed, its character is that of a preserver of a modernist, liberal-capitalist, socio-economic and theo-political reality – and, specifically, of the financial and economic power elites that largely define and maintain it – even when incorporating welfare appendages as it did after 1945. For these in themselves, being redistributive and not pre-distributive in origin and character, do not fundamentally alter the underlying hegemonic structural and cultural arrangements that maintain capitalism and its dominant economic elites. For Milbank, only a return to Catholic values (as he interprets them) and a much more elevated role for the Church in human affairs and a commensurately diminished one for the modern, liberal-capitalist, secular state and its welfare appendages, could achieve the Blue Socialist, post-liberal outcome that he champions, and which will be considered in Part Two.

Thus, whilst Tawney and Milbank have a similar historical perspective on religion and the rise of capitalism, this being in significant part a result of the Protestant Reformation and its overturning of patristic and Thomist values *inter alia* on price and usury, it is clear that Tawney was not a Christendomist. He stated in his work of 1920: 'The tradition of universal allegiance which the church – to speak without distinction of denomination – has inherited from an age in which the word "Christendom" had some meaning, is a source not of strength but of weakness.'[32] Rather, he saw a potential for the modern state to

---

[30.] Temple, *Citizen and Churchman*, p. 38.

[31.] Ibid., p. 27.

[32.] Tawney, *The Acquisitive Society*. Cited in M. Brown, 'The Church of England and the Common Good', in N. Sagovsky and P. McGrail (eds), *Together for*

be an enabler in the delivery of a Christian socialist vision of society via the welfare state model, underpinned by a system of parliamentary, representative democracy such as existed in Britain, and shaped by a Labour government of the likes of the Attlee administration, with a popular mandate commensurate to its task.

One final but important point to mention about Tawney's perspective, before we consider the collapse of the welfare state consensus, is that he also criticised those other reformers who, he felt, had gone astray for being preoccupied with relieving distress via a welfare state. Tawney was of the view that what workers 'want is security and opportunity', and hence not merely 'assistance in the exceptional misfortunes of life, but a fair chance of leading an independent, fairly prosperous life, if they are not exceptionally unfortunate'.[33] Personal aspiration for living a reasonably prosperous way of life, for Tawney, was thus a legitimate aim in a democratic socialist society and would best be enabled via the increased equality that a welfare state could provide.

The Collapse of the Welfare State Consensus: 1976–2010

It has been argued earlier that the collapse of the welfare state consensus began in the mid-1970s, and thus was inherited by Margaret Thatcher's government. However, her administration was to accelerate its decline. The moment she became Prime Minister on 4 May 1979 began a period of Conservative government that would span three parliaments and last for eleven and a half years. Her administration was radical in its rejection of social democracy as an ideology of government, and thus much of the socialist philosophical underpinning of the welfare state consensus. Indeed, her view was that the British people 'had given up on socialism – the thirty-year experiment had plainly failed – and were ready to try something else. That sea change was our mandate.'[34]

---

the *Common Good: Towards a National Conversation* (London: SCM Press, 2015), p. 130.

[33] R.H. Tawney, *R.H. Tawney's Commonplace Book* (1912), ed. with an Introduction by J.M. Winter and D.M. Joslin (Cambridge: Cambridge University Press, 1972), p. 13.

[34] M. Thatcher, *The Downing Street Years* (London: HarperCollins, 1993), p. 10.

A major study of poverty in the United Kingdom published by Peter Townsend in 1979 had demonstrated that: 'By the state's own definition ... there were between 15 and 17.5 million who were in or near poverty.'[35] Hence, according to this study, poverty remained a major problem in Britain that the Welfare State had not managed to eradicate. What is more, Frank Field, a Labour Party MP and Anglican Socialist who later contributed substantially to the Blue Labour initiative considered in chapter three, published a study in 1981 arguing that, although some redistribution of wealth had resulted from the Welfare State, it had not had a positive impact on the condition of the poor, but had been more of a transfer of income from the very rich to the prosperous.[36]

Other criticisms of the Welfare State at that time, related to a view that it had spawned an underclass that was state-dependent and thus without incentive. This had led Keith Joseph, a key ally of Margaret Thatcher, to conclude that: 'the only lasting help we can give to the poor is helping them to help themselves; to do the opposite, to create more dependence, is to destroy them morally, whilst throwing an unfair burden on society'.[37] There was also evidence of welfare fraud within the system and increased bureaucracy in the system's administration. Thatcher, in her memoirs, concludes:

> The final illusion – that state intervention would promote social harmony and solidarity or, in Tory language, 'One Nation' – collapsed in the 'winter of discontent' [1978/79] when the dead went unburied, critically ill patients were turned away from hospitals by pickets, and the prevailing mood was one of snarling envy and motiveless hostility.[38]

Thatcher's period in office coincided with the emergence of the 'New Right' – a group of thinkers who were anti-Keynesian, anti-welfare state, anti-public ownership of industry and thus against the mixed economy,

---

[35] P. Townsend, *Poverty in the United Kingdom* (London: Allen Lane and Penguin Books, 1979), p. 895. Cited by Forrester *Christianity and the Future of Welfare*, p. 46.

[36] F. Field, *Inequality in Britain: Freedom, Welfare and the State* (London: Collins, Fontana, 1981), pp. 19 ff.

[37] Cited by R. Lowe, *The Welfare State in Britain Since 1945*, 2nd edn (London: Macmillan Press, 1999), p. 307.

[38] Thatcher, *The Downing Street Years*, p. 8.

preferring instead a return to more *laissez-faire* economics, a more minimalist role for government in economic affairs and a substantially reduced state sector, which we now consider.

The New Right's Perspective on the Welfare State

The foundations of the New Right can in part be traced at least as far back as the classical economic theories expounded by Adam Smith in *The Wealth of Nations* (1776).[39] Smith had argued that free exchange is a transaction from which both parties to it benefit, otherwise they would not voluntarily enter into it; or, as Milton Friedman, an American guru of the New Right, was later to put it – neoliberalism is underpinned by the 'elementary proposition that both parties to an economic transaction benefit from it, provided the transaction is bilaterally voluntary and informed'.[40] From this perspective, then, put in its most unadulterated form, any restrictions on freedom of trade (such as state intervention, regulations, laws etc.) will reduce the well-being of individuals, by denying or diminishing their opportunity to improve their situation unhindered via the exchange mechanism referred to above. As such, the function of the state should not be to restrict and tax trade to support welfare projects and other social programmes, but to extend the freedom of trade within and beyond national borders. Thus, as F.A. Hayek, a key intellectual influence on the New Right, argued with respect to parliamentary democracy: 'Agreements by the majority on sharing the booty gained by overwhelming a minority of fellow citizens or deciding how much is to be taken from them is not democracy. At least it is not that ideal of democracy which has any moral justification.'[41] This thinking was influential on a key think tank of the New Right, the *Institute of Economic Affairs* and its offshoot, the *Social Affairs Unit*, which published works such as *Wither the Welfare State* (1981) and *Breaking the Spell of Welfare* (1981) which used such

---

[39.] A. Smith, *An Inquiry into the Nature and Causes of the Wealth of Nations* (1776) (Oxford: Oxford University Press, 2008).

[40.] M. Friedman, *Capitalism and Freedom* (Chicago: University of Chicago Press, 1962), p. 55. Cited by S. Clarke, 'The Neoliberal Theory of Society', in A. Saad-Filho and D. Johnston (eds), *Neoliberalism: A Critical Reader* (London: Pluto Press, 2005), p. 50.

[41.] F.A. Hayek, *New Studies* (London: Routledge & Kegan Paul, 1978), p. 165. Cited by R. Hattersley, *Choose Freedom: The Future for Democratic Socialism* (London: Michael Joseph Press, 1987), p. 71.

arguments to attack the post-war Welfare State project.[42] We shall see in Part Two that this thinking is considered by Milbank as antithetical to the Blue Socialist perspective which he champions as an alternative to it, even though both are highly critical of the Welfare State and its redistributive philosophical underpinnings.

The thinking of the New Right also chimed with the mandate Thatcher believed she had been given: to reduce public expenditure, rein in the role of the state, and thus enable a reduction in personal taxation and greater incentivisation in the economy, as well as to reduce what she saw as the scourge of welfare dependency.[43] Thus, under her leadership, much of the post-war Attlee administration's legacy was systematically undermined. State control over significant aspects of the economy was reduced via a series of privatisations of state assets (e.g. gas, water, electricity and steel). The 1982 Social Security and Housing Benefit Act included reductions to social security benefits by removing earning-related supplements and, from 1982 onwards, pensions were increased in line with prices rather than earnings. Unemployment at this time had also risen from three per cent in 1974 to twelve per cent by 1982/83, which for some people represented an end to the post-war Keynesian consensus that unemployment should never again be permitted to rise to pre-war levels,[44] even though it reflected serious changes in the economy. Further changes were made via the Social Security Act 1986 which included changes to the Social Fund (money for use in emergencies for claimants which now became a loan rather than a grant). In addition, local authority control over housing was weakened by legislation that allowed council tenants to buy council houses and the move to providing social housing via housing associations. Local authority control over education was also reduced by allowing schools to opt out of state control and become grant maintained.

In 1990, the National Health Service and Community Care Act created an internal market in the NHS via the so-called purchaser/provider split. In this scheme of things, health authorities were meant to

---

[42.] A. Seldon, *Wither the Welfare State*, Occasional Paper 60 (London: Institute of Economic Affairs, 1981), and D. Anderson, J. Lait and D. Marsland, *Breaking the Spell of the Welfare State* (London: Social Affairs Unit, 1981).

[43.] For more on the Thatcher government's policy and legislative programme, see Thatcher, *The Downing Street Years*. See also E. Evans, *Thatcher and Thatcherism* (London: Routledge, 2018), and E. Filby, *God and Mrs Thatcher: The Battle for Britain's Soul* (London: Biteback Publishers, 2015).

[44.] See Fraser, *The Evolution of the British Welfare State*, p. 307.

purchase services from health providers, so as to introduce an element of competition into the service with a view to achieving improvements as a result. Some hospitals were encouraged to become self-governing, though still in the NHS, but with more autonomy as regards directives from the Department of Health. GP fundholders were also established to enable GPs to purchase services directly for their patients, albeit primarily from within the NHS. The sum of these changes to the NHS were not to alter the state provision of health care free at the point of delivery. However, they did begin a process of marketisation within the NHS that was later to be further developed under various administrations: John Major (1990–97), Tony Blair (1997–2007) and Gordon Brown (2007–10). When John Major became Prime Minister in 1990, he brought about further, less ambitious reforms on similar lines, which incrementally carried on much of what came to be called the 'Thatcher Revolution', with a particular focus on target setting as a means of managing and demonstrating delivery of output from the services provided by the Welfare State. He lost the general election of May 1997 and so the stage was set for a period of Labour government that was to last until May 2010 under the banner of 'New Labour'.

New Labour and the Welfare State

In 1995, Frank Field wrote the following about the Welfare State: 'Britain's present welfare system has the worst of both worlds: it is broken backed, yet its costs escalate. In its efforts to support it actually restrains the citizen offering disincentives rather than incentives, and educating people only about the need to exploit the system.'[45] When Tony Blair won office in 1997, Field was encouraged to 'think the unthinkable' and he contributed substantially to the thinking as set out in the Green Paper, *A New Contract for Welfare* (1998). At this time, Field was not an out-and-out, anti-welfare statist thinker, but he felt that it required substantial reform. His thinking was influential in the promotion of 'third-way' thinking of the kind that Anthony Giddens' book, *The Third Way*, had done much to champion.[46] Third-way thinking was aimed

---

[45] F. Field, *Making Welfare Work: Reconstructing Welfare for the Millennium* (London: Institute of Community Studies, 1995). Cited by Fraser, *The Evolution of the British Welfare State*, p. 314.

[46] A. Giddens, *The Third Way: The Renewal of Social Democracy* (London: Polity Press, 1998). See also J. Forde, 'The Third Way: Industrial Partnerships

at being neither socialist nor free market, but instead would channel a middle-way between the two. As Blair put it in 1997: 'we have reached the limits of the public's willingness simply to fund an unreformed welfare system through ever higher taxes and spending'.[47] The focus was now to be 'Welfare to Work' rather than welfare dependency, with youth unemployed being given options either to undertake subsidised work, education or training, work for an environmental task force or undertake voluntary work, and not just expected to be entitled to receive unemployment benefit from the state.

In the years that followed, there were further initiatives concerning unemployment under Blair and later under the Gordon Brown premiership.[48] They also decided to keep most of the structural reforms to the NHS that had occurred by way of the National Health Service and Community Care Act 1990, including the purchaser/provider split and hence the internal market, GP involvement in healthcare purchasing, and NHS Trusts. Therefore, the landscape of the NHS was pretty much as it had been under the previous Tory administration, though with significant increases in funding in Blair's second and third terms.[49]

Under the premiership of both Tony Blair and Gordon Brown there was the same stress on performance indicators that there had been under Major's administration, as well as major private-sector involvement in large new-build projects funded by private firms under what was, essentially, a mortgage arrangement, that came to be called the Private Finance Initiative, that had been begun by the Conservatives under Major. Continuity in the education policy of the previous Conservative administrations was also evident and, in certain respects, was even

---

in the NHS', (Unpublished MA dissertation, University of Huddersfield, 2000).

[47.] T. Blair, *Hansard*, HC Deb., 14 May 1997, Vol. 294, col. 65.

[48.] For example, in 2008, incapacity benefit was replaced by an Employment Services Allowance and a revised Jobseekers' Allowance. As Gordon Brown said in the White Paper of 2008: 'we have put not just rights but the responsibilities that match them at the head of our welfare reforms … a system that offers more support but that expects more in return'. Cited by Fraser, *The Evolution of the British Welfare State*, p. 316.

[49.] For more on the Blair and Brown governments' policy direction and key pieces of legislation, see F. Faucher-King and P. Le Galès, *The New Labour Experiment: Change under Blair and Brown* (Stanford: Stanford University Press, 2010), and D. Coates and P. Lawler (eds), *New Labour in Power* (Manchester: Manchester University Press, 2000).

more radical in its departure from the post-war 'statist' solutions. Under Gordon Brown's premiership, 450 more city academies, of the kind that had previously been established under Blair, were created to enlarge the already significant number of schools that had opted out of local authority control, with funding of new buildings coming through PFI initiatives (several of these being faith schools). Pensions were also reformed under Labour. In 2005 the commission set up to review pensions announced that the retirement age would eventually have to increase to 68, arguing that, with the rising number of elderly living longer, the costs of the previous system were too burdensome on the remaining working population. Also, more housing association properties were built and more council houses were sold off under Labour.

For some critics of Labour's third-way approach,[50] this amounts to evidence that, rather than reversing the 'Thatcher Revolution', Labour, under Blair and Brown, had consolidated it, and thus further weakened the Welfare State and the post-war welfare state consensus. In support of this view, they point to subsequent statements by Blair, for example, in an interview with the BBC: 'My job was to build on some of Thatcher's policies.'[51] From Gordon Brown's perspective,[52] in 2008 the Welfare State was still intact but had been modernised along the lines of greater public and private sector partnership, and its future had been secured. So, it was able to withstand the financial crash and the impact this would have on government policy. Yet, for a third group, the Welfare State was seen as being in decline and in need of being substantially replaced with another vision for the twenty-first century and, partly out of this revisionist thinking, emerged the Blue Labour/Red Tory political phenomenon that is analysed in Parts Two and Three. Blue Labour and Red Tory thinking on welfare was developed in significant part by John Milbank, and theo-politically underpinned in significant part by Radical Orthodoxy, a grouping founded by Milbank in the late 1990s. Milbank was to influence the shaping of events that followed, not least with respect to the role the Church of England was to play in them.

However, before we address Milbank's Blue Socialist thinking and his contribution to the Blue Labour/Red Tory political phenomenon, a brief summary of David Nicholls' thinking on the Church, welfare and

---

[50] See B. Jordan, *Why the Third Way Failed: Economics, Morality and the Origins of the 'Big Society'* (Bristol: Policy Press, 2010).

[51] T. Blair, interview with the BBC, 8 April 2013. Available at: http://www.bbc .co.uk/news/uk-politics-22073434 (accessed on 26 August 2016).

[52] G. Brown, *My Life: Our Times* (London: Bodley Head, 2017).

the state is necessary. Milbank's affinity with English political pluralism has, in part, been shaped by David Nicholls' writings, as he has since acknowledged, stating that Nicholls 'was a great friend' whom he knew as part of the Jubilee Group and that he had also 'debated with him when he was part of the Christendom Trust'. In 2014 Milbank was of the view that, in an 'era of a crisis of the nation state', Nicholls' work was 'extraordinarily prophetic' and that he is now 'closer to his [Nicholls'] positions than when he was alive'.[53]

David Nicholls' Writings in the Christendom Strand

The publication of V.A. Demant's *Religion and the Decline of Capitalism* in 1952 marked a high point in the Christendom strand, after which there was a decline in interest until the early 1970s. After the publication in 1922 of the *Return of Christendom*, the Christendom Group had been formed, led by Maurice Reckitt, with a view to providing a vehicle for developing and promoting the ideas contained in that book. A quarterly journal was subsequently established, edited by Reckitt, called *Christendom*, which existed between 1931 and 1950. Matthew Grimley has argued that English political pluralism 'had its heyday before 1914, when it had offered a convincing and timely critique of the pretentions of the Idealist state. But it was a philosophy less suited to Britain after the First World War.'[54] Yet, it would be wrong to suppose that its influence on some later thinkers, particularly Christendomists, was negligible, as his own work attests.[55] In his study of the Moot Circle – a group of around thirty to forty Christian intellectuals that met in the Home Counties or Oxford under the chairmanship of J.H. Oldham in the years between 1938 and 1947 – Grimley argues it 'is an interesting case-study for students of civil society in Britain because it shows the resurgence in twentieth-century thought of a mediaeval concept of civil

---

[53] J. Milbank, 'Associationism, Pluralism and Post-liberalism: The Theo-political Legacy of David Nicholls and Current British Politics'. A lecture delivered in 2014 in Oxford to the David Nicholls' Memorial Trust. Available as a podcast at: http://www.dnmt.org.uk/ (accessed on 15 August 2015).

[54] Grimley, *Citizenship*, p. 102.

[55] M. Grimley, 'Civil Society and the Clerisy: Christian Elites and National Culture, c. 1930–1950', in J. Harris (ed.), *Civil Society in British History: Ideas, Identities, Institutions* (Oxford: Oxford University Press, 2005), pp. 231–47.

society'.[56] For Grimley, this 'older strain of civil society shared with some modern readings an emphasis on the autonomy of groups against the state'.[57] For example, thinkers in the Moot Circle, such as Demant and the Roman Catholic theologian Christopher Dawson, had been influenced by Guild Socialism in their youth 'and retained a pluralist suspicion of state power'.[58] T.S. Eliot, another member of the group, had similar pluralist misgivings about an over-statist inclination to try to remedy the limitations of liberal democracy.[59] Demant was also a key influence on Eliot, particularly his thinking on culture.[60]

After a low point for English political pluralism from the mid-1950s to the late 1960s, when this thinking had largely disappeared from public view, on 31 March 1971 the *Christendom Trust* was established with Reckitt as leader, Demant as secretary and David Nicholls as a founding member and chair from 1992 until his death in 1996.[61] In 2006 Kenneth Leech described Nicholls as: 'an old-style guild socialist, opposed to state socialism'.[62] Owing in significant part to the works of Nicholls, in the 1970s there was a revival of interest in English political pluralism within sections of Anglican Socialism and, to a degree, an awakening of interest in it within the universities.[63] Nicholls' writings, in the main, are more academically detached in style than were those of his predecessors writing within the Christendom tradition. His training as a political scientist, historian and theologian enabled him to approach his subject area in that way. Paul Hirst has rightly described the English pluralist writers as not comprising 'a comprehensive and coherent academic school' but instead

---

56. Ibid., p. 232.

57. Ibid.

58. Ibid., p. 239.

59. Ibid., p.232. Eliot, like several members of the Moot Circle, was also influenced in his writings by Roman Catholic thinking on subsidiarity which had, in part, been shaped by pluralist thinking. See Grimley, 'Civil Society and the Clerisy', p. 240, and see Pius XI, *Quadragesimo Anno*, an encyclical issued by the Pope on 15 May 1931. Available at: https://w2.vatican.va/content/pius-xi/en/encyclicals/documents/hf_p-xi_enc_19310515_quadragesimo anno.html (accessed on 5 January 2017).

60. Grimley, 'Civil Society and the Clerisy', p. 242.

61. D. Nicholls' obituary, *The Times*, 22 June 1996.

62. See K. Leech, 'Farewell to the Days of Birettas and Cassocks', *Church Times*, November 2006.

63. For example, Hirst, *The Pluralist Theory of the State*, is in some ways indebted to Nicholls, as confirmed by Hirst in his acknowledgements (not paginated).

'writing for popular and political effect'.[64] This need not diminish the value and significance of their work, of course, as Hirst acknowledges. What this more popular style of writing did result in, though, was a lack of profile for their work in the universities.

David Nicholls' writings on English political pluralism were, to some degree, to redress this. Works such as *Church and State in Britain since 1820* (1967), *Three varieties of Pluralism* (1974) and *The Pluralist State* (1975)[65] did much to help distil and define the thinking of the English pluralist writers, particularly Figgis, on whom he had completed a PhD thesis. His wide academic training and historical knowledge also enabled him to place their contribution to political theory and theology, within the wider historical and political context from which it had emerged and was partly shaped. In this regard, his work *Deity and Domination: Images of God and the State in the Nineteenth and Twentieth Centuries* (1989) is a major work in both the fields of political theology and the history of ideas and, specifically, the way God and the state have been seen by key writers of political theory and Christian theology in the nineteenth and twentieth centuries, not least by Temple.

However, it is in his essay writing that one gets to see a more unbridled side to his thinking that is unambiguously sympathetic to the English political pluralist frame of reference. Thus, in one of his essays on Christianity and politics, he argues: 'The population of a modern state cannot, however, legitimately be said to have the kind of coherence and organic structure that is assumed in talking about its wishes.'[66] What Nicholls means by this becomes apparent in the following statement:

> representative government may be seen to encourage a subtle form of irresponsibility. Millions of adults hand over to a few hundred so-called representatives the right to make decisions on their behalf, while for the following five years these millions pursue in good conscience their own interests and pleasures.[67]

[64.] Ibid., p. 15.

[65.] D. Nicholls, *Church and State in Britain since 1820* (London: Routledge, 1967), *Three Varieties of Pluralism* (London: Macmillan, 1974), *The Pluralist State*.

[66.] D. Nicholls, 'Christianity and Politics', in R. Morgan (ed.), *The Religion of the Incarnation: Anglican Essays in Commemoration of Lux Mundi* (Bristol: Bristol Classical Press, 1989), p. 176.

[67.] Ibid.

This is a system of government that is too centralist and thus insufficiently democratic for Nicholls. It is a view he shared with the other English pluralists. Yet, he is more sceptical than they were (and Milbank has since been) of representative government as a means of delivering genuine democracy. Milbank is of the view that representative government has its place and could be made more representative via a substantially reconfigured role for the state and its relationship to the Church (as we shall see in Part Two). For Milbank, this would be part of a wider series of reforms along the lines that writers in the Christendom strand have advocated. Nicholls was not, however, 'asserting that only individual persons can properly be said to have wishes, or make decisions. Certain voluntary human groups may develop sufficient of a common life and purpose to make it possible to speak of their wishes or decisions, but the modern state is not one of them.'[68]

Consistent with this thinking, in a short critique of Temple's perspective on the state along these lines, he argues: 'It is difficult to make sense of Temple's ideas on state sovereignty and it would not be unfair to say that his political theory is generally a somewhat incoherent amalgam of notions inherited from his undergraduate days.'[69] The outcome of Temple's thinking on the state is described by Nicholls in the following terms:

> God and State – conceived of in terms of a conjunction of sovereignty and benevolence or welfare – are then features of the liberal capitalism of many western countries in our day. In these countries class conflict has been contained by paternalistic legislation, mitigating the harsher consequences of the capitalist system, combined with a subtle manipulation of political and cultural institutions.[70]

For Nicholls this was not a satisfactory outcome, as containing class conflict had not removed it or its causes – these being in significant part the product of capitalism. What was also not a satisfactory outcome for Nicholls, was the circumscribed role that Temple had argued the Church should adopt towards the state in his thinking on middle axioms. In Nicholls' view: 'By insisting that Christians, as

---

[68.] Ibid.

[69.] D. Nicholls, 'William Temple and the Welfare State', *Crucible: The Christian Journal for Social Ethics*, October-December 1984, p. 165.

[70.] Ibid., p. 168.

such, should be concerned with principles rather than with policies he ensured that nothing they said, as such, would be likely to have much immediate effect.'[71]

It is views such as these on welfare and, indeed, on the interface between Church and state, that Milbank was to further develop in the 1980s onwards. Influenced by the thinking of Nicholls, as well as by the other Christendom writers previously mentioned, Milbank's contribution to contemporary theology, whilst rooted in that Anglican Socialist strand, has nevertheless been broader and more complex than this label can fully encompass.[72] Before we further engage with his thinking, however, some conclusions to chapter two can be drawn.

Conclusion

Two dominant strands of economic thinking have characterised the history of the welfare state consensus and its collapse. These have been Keynesianism and neoliberalism. Keynesianism, with its emphasis on more governmental planning and state intervention in the economy, chimed with the ambitious implementation timeframe the Attlee administration had set itself for reconstructing the post-war economy and for delivering on the Beveridge report. In Britain, Keynesianism was the order of the day and remained so until the mid-1970s. However, since circa 1976, neoliberalism has been the dominant economic theory or paradigm underpinning much of the Conservative and Labour administrations' approaches to the funding and management of the Welfare State. Thus, the Blair/Brown New Labour/Third Way administrations can be seen as having significantly accommodated neoliberalism in their policies and practices.

There is a fundamental difference between how Milbank sees the modern, liberal-capitalist state as possessing uniform characteristics (these often being secular), in contrast to how Welfare Statist Anglican Socialists such as Tawney have seen it as not embodying uniform characteristics but, rather, as nothing more than an instrument. Thus, for Tawney, even in a liberal-capitalist context, the state was capable of accurately reflecting the will and needs of the populace via the ballot box, not least with respect to the provision of welfare. This is a crucial

---

[71.] Ibid., p. 164.

[72.] For example, his incorporation of post-modern thinking into his systematic theology reflects other influences.

difference between these two strands of Anglican Socialism. We shall see in Part Two and Part Three that it partly explains why Milbank considers liberal democracy as having significant limitations in what it can achieve in advancing the kingdom of God on earth, preferring instead a reformed, post-liberal system of governance with the Church of England playing a more prominent role in the affairs of the nation, as well as in the provision of welfare. David Nicholls' work on the Church and state, particularly during the late 1960s and 1970s, was important in the way it made the English political pluralist perspective more widely known and understood within the university setting and beyond. He also influenced Milbank who has since described his work as 'extraordinarily prophetic'.

In Part Two it will be argued that Milbank's Blue Socialism offers: (a) a post-liberal alternative to both Keynesianism and neoliberalism and that this thinking, were it adopted by either a Red Tory- or a Blue Labour-style administration, would have profound implications for the way welfare is provided in Britain; and (b) a vision of a post-liberal society that would have major implications for the role the Church of England would play in the provision of welfare and for its relationship with the state *per se.*

Part Two

John Milbank's Blue Socialist Thinking and his Perspective on the British Welfare State

Chapter Three

John Milbank Writing in the Christendom Strand

Introduction

In Part One, John Milbank's thinking on welfare and the Church was located within the Christendom strand of Anglican Socialist tradition. This chapter will identify and analyse key elements of what he calls Blue Socialism. After a brief summary of seven key terms, I shall focus on his perspective on the modern, liberal-capitalist state and welfare provision, including key historical and theoretical influences that have shaped it. Some lines of criticism of his Blue Socialist thinking will then be developed, and a summary of his alternative 'civil economy' vision to that of Keynesian 'statism' and neoliberalism will be provided. This will enable me in the next chapter, to evaluate his perspective on the British Welfare State in relation to the voluntary sector, and the Church of England's post-war contribution to the provision of welfare, and his proposed Blue Socialist, post-liberal alternative vision of the role he argues the Church of England should perform in the provision of welfare.

To begin I describe seven key terms, the first of which is the neologism Blue Socialism that characterises Milbank's perspective.

Key Terms

Blue Socialism

Blue Socialism was first described in 2008 by Milbank as 'socialism with a Burkean tinge', and his interpretation of it therefore needs to be understood in this way.[1] At first blush this would seem an unlikely juxtaposition, as Edmund Burke has been and remains a key theoretical underpinning for 'One Nation' Conservative thinking, with his belief in the importance of safeguarding the traditional institutions of state and civil society, and the maintenance of continuity in the social structures that define a society's economic, social, cultural, political and religious character. Yet, Milbank is of the view that some of these values are by no means antithetical to a viable Christian socialist polity – indeed he thinks they are integral to one. So, for Milbank, Blue Socialism is a political philosophy that seeks to fuse aspects of traditional Christian socialist thought with aspects of Burkean 'One Nation' Conservative thinking, offering an alternative to Keynesian 'statism' and to neoliberalism. This thinking will be explored in more depth later in the chapter.[2]

Blue Labour

Blue Labour was a term coined by political theoretician Maurice Glasman in a speech made in April 2009 in Conway Hall, Bloomsbury.[3] Glasman defined Blue Labour as a rejection of neoliberal economics, whilst also being highly critical of the Keynesian welfare consensus of the post-war years, which he considered as too statist an approach to advancing democratic socialism. Instead, Blue Labour would offer, 'a new politics of *reciprocity, mutuality* and *solidarity*'.[4] A project group was subsequently established around the Blue Labour banner in the

---

[1.] Milbank, *The Future of Love*, p. xvii.

[2.] Blue Socialism and its political offshoot, Blue Labour, contribute to a wider theoretical context than Milbank's writings fully convey. A key document is M. Glasman, J. Rutherford, M. Stears and S. White (eds), *Labour Tradition and the Politics of Paradox: The Oxford London Seminars, 2010–2011*(London: Lawrence and Wishart, Ebook, 2011). It contains a wide range of contributions from leading Labour Party members that cover *inter alia* Blue Socialist criticisms of neoliberalism, globalism, statism and welfarism, setting these in their historical context both within and beyond the Labour Party.

[3.] For more on Glasman's thinking on Blue Labour, see 'The Good Society, Catholic Social Thought and the Politics of the Common Good', in I. Geary and A. Pabst (eds), *Blue Labour: Forging a New Politics* (London: I.B. Tauris, 2015), pp. 13–26.

[4.] A. Stratton, 'Labour: Now It's Kind of Blue', *The Guardian*, 24 April 2009.

Labour Party aimed at devising a political strategy that would enable their leader, Ed Miliband, to move the party beyond the New Labour/ Third Way thinking of Tony Blair's and Gordon Brown's leaderships. Blue Labour was later described by two of its leading advocates as having its roots more in High Toryism and the co-operative movement than in Victorian Liberalism,[5] and that it 'seeks to recover and renew the radical conservatism that defines England and resonates strongly with cognate traditions across the rest of the United Kingdom'.[6] Blue Labour thus became associated with being very critical of liberalism: both the 'social-cultural' and 'secular' liberalism it considered as influential on shaping the old welfare statist Labour left, and free-market liberalism associated with the right. Instead, it offered a more conservative approach to the importance of personal loyalty, family, faith, community and locality, whilst seeking to move beyond the Third Way centrist pragmatism of the Blair/Brown years.

The Blue Labour project was shaped in significant part by Christian influences, with Ian Geary, an executive member of Christians on the Left, and Simon Oliver, William Van Mildert Professor of Divinity in the Department of Theology and Religion at Durham University and a member of the Radical Orthodoxy grouping, being the main organisers of the Blue Labour seminars that took place around 2010–13, that helped to define some of its thinking.[7] Milbank had been a key influence and adviser to the Blue Labour project, and contributed substantially to the thinking underpinning the initiative, including publishing articles on Blue Labour. These were critical of the Welfare State as an approach to the provision of some aspects of welfare, preferring instead a more localised, community-based approach to their delivery, with the Church of England playing a key and enhanced role.[8] Jon Cruddas MP, and Labour Party policy co-ordinator under Ed Miliband's leadership, has said the following about Milbank's thinking:

---

5. Geary and Pabst (eds), *Blue Labour*, p. 4.
6. Ibid., p. 5.
7. Ibid. Cited in the 'Acknowledgements' section that is unpaginated.
8. See, for example, J. Milbank, 'Blue Labour, One-Nation Labour and Postliberalism: A Christian Socialist Reading'. Available as a PDF download at: http://theologyphilosophycentre.co.uk/papers/Milbank_BlueLabourOne NationLabourAndPostliberalism.pdf (accessed on 21 December 2021).

Over the last decade, his writings have combined a critique of secular liberalism and capitalism with an alternative political vision. Milbank's particular contribution centres on a Christian socialism that appears paradoxical in terms of current political divisions – blending demands for greater economic justice with a renewed sense of the importance of social tradition, locality and personal honour. He was one of the first to argue that right-wing economic liberalism and left-wing cultural liberalism are two halves of the same picture, and to propose instead a more associationist and teleological approach in both domains, focussed upon an attempt to achieve greater human flourishing. ... Building on Polanyi, Milbank has put forward original ideas about how to re-embed the global 'market-state' into the 'complex space' of intermediary institutions and the social bonds and civic ties they uphold – a vision that has, directly and indirectly, influenced the Labour Party's thinking about the 'Good Society' in general and welfare reform in particular.[9]

Along similar lines, Cruddas has said of Milbank's influence on the Blue Labour movement:

John Milbank is one of the main thinkers behind the emerging post-liberal politics in Britain. ... His thinking has influenced in equal measure the Red Tory project of Phillip Blond and the Blue Labour movement founded by Maurice Glasman. Blue Labour's work on an ethical market, a mutualist approach to welfare and a focus on vocationalism for all, rather than just equality of opportunity, has been considerably shaped by Milbank's work and so, through the impact of Blue Labour, has in turn influenced debates within the Labour Party, including the Policy Review.[10]

Likewise, Maurice Glasman:

[9.] See University of Nottingham, Impact Assessment (no author cited), 'Shaping the Ideology of Red Tory and Blue Labour'. Available as a PDF download at: http://impact.ref.ac.uk/casestudies2/refservice.svc/GetCaseStudyPDF/28886 (accessed on 13 March 2017).

[10.] Ibid.

Professor John Milbank has had a profound impact on the political position that has come to be known as Blue Labour. He spent some very important time with me and urged me to 'think paradoxically' and that has been a very significant feature of the academic and political work. A seminar was created at Oxford University called 'The Labour Tradition and the Politics of Paradox' which generated 120,000 downloads in a week when it was published as an ebook by Lawrence and Wishart. Since then, the ideas of Professor Milbank have informed a range of debates and policy initiatives within the Labour movement from welfare reform to foreign policy.[11]

These quotes evidence how Milbank's contribution to the Blue Labour project was considerable. In October 2015, after the election of Jeremy Corbyn as leader of the Labour Party, the Blue Labour project group merged with other elements on the right of the party to form the Labour Together Group (later to morph into the Future Britain Group), that has sought to offer an alternative perspective to the one being put forward by the more traditional Red Labour elements in the party, as defined below. However, the thinking underpinning the Blue Labour project remains highly relevant, both within the Labour Party and wider afield, not least concerning possible approaches to welfare provision in England in the twenty-first century.[12]

Red Labour
Since 2009 Red Labour has been used as a term to describe those in the Labour Party who reject key aspects of the Blue Labour approach, such as its evaluation of the Welfare State. They identified with Corbyn's far left socialist leadership and argue for a Keynesian approach to governmental economic management as an alternative to neoliberalism, based on the need, as they see it, for a substantial fiscal stimulus support to fund major infrastructure and other projects, and replenish underfunding of the Welfare State and local government.[13]

[11.] Ibid.

[12.] For an introduction to Blue Labour thinking, see Geary and Pabst (eds), *Blue Labour*, and R. Davis, *Tangled Up in Blue: Blue Labour and the Struggle for Labour's Soul* (London: Ruskin Publishing, 2011).

[13.] For more on this see O. Wright, 'Red, Purple or Blue: Which Kind of Labour Are You?', *Independent*, 26 September 2011.

Red Tory

Although there is a tradition of Red Toryism that has its origins in Canadian politics,[14] for this study the term refers to the ideas developed by Anglican political theologian, Phillip Blond, in his book: *Red Tory: How Left and Right Have Broken Britain and How We Can Fix It*, published in 2010. The book's acknowledgements demonstrate his indebtedness to Milbank: 'my most commensurate thanks and deepest debt go to John Milbank without whose time, dedication and sheer editorial enthusiasm this book would not have appeared'.[15] Furthermore, Blond is a member of the Radical Orthodoxy grouping and was a PhD student under Milbank's supervision whilst at Peterhouse College, Cambridge, in the early 1990s. Milbank is also chair of trustees for Blond's think tank, ResPublica.[16]

Blond has said of Milbank's influence in that think tank:

> In terms of my own work as Director of ResPublica (one of Britain's most influential think-tanks) where John [Milbank] is Chair of Trustees, I always discuss my own and our public and policy-led approach with him. It would not be an exaggeration to say that inasmuch as I have influenced British public life with ideas on anything like Red Tory, The Big Society and Military Academies – I have always drawn on John's work and advice when formulating ideas and policy.[17]

Red Toryism attempts to fuse economic equity (that is, the principle that an economy must achieve an apportionment of its resources and goods that is considered fair by the people who operate within it) with social conservatism, and is highly critical of the Welfare State and the welfare dependency Blond argues it produces. It is also highly critical of neoliberalism (what Blond calls the free-market economy) and instead calls for a reduced role for the state and the market in society, and, in their place, the strengthening of local communities and economies and the need to bring about a restoration of the family as the source of

---

[14.] See C. Taylor, *Radical Tories: The Conservative Tradition in Canada* (Toronto: Anansi Press, 2006).

[15.] P. Blond, *Red Tory*, p. ix.

[16.] See the ResPublica website at: http://www.respublica.org.uk/our-people /trustees/ (accessed on 10 April 2018).

[17.] University of Nottingham, 'Shaping the Ideology of Red Tory and Blue Labour'.

social stability. Hence, it has a strong community-based and voluntarist focus to some of the alternatives it offers to statist forms of social and economic delivery.

These ideas, though not identical to those advanced by the Blue Labour project,[18] have much in common with them, and thus with Milbank's thinking, particularly concerning welfare, voluntarism and the Church. They will be covered in Part Three when we examine the influence that they had on shaping the 'Big Society' project, and that Milbank's support for the project had on shaping the Church of England's approach to welfare in the aftermath of the financial crash of 2008.

The 'Big Society' Project

The 'Big Society' project was launched by the Conservative Party in the summer of 2010 as part of its election manifesto and lasted until around the end of 2013. At its outset, it was described by David Cameron as follows:

> The start of a deep and serious reform agenda to take power away from politicians and give it to people. That's because we know instinctively that the state is often too inhuman, monolithic and clumsy to tackle our deepest social problems. We know that the best ideas come from the ground up, not the top down. We know that when you give people and communities more power over their lives, more power to come together and work together to make life better – great things happen.[19]

The key aims of the 'Big Society' project were subsequently defined in a speech by Cameron in July 2010 at Liverpool Hope University:

1. Social Action. The success of the Big Society will depend on the daily decisions of millions of people – on them giving their time, effort, even money, to causes around them. So

---

18. Blue Labour developed a strategy called the 'Good Society', which contains much in common with 'Big Society' thinking. See Glasman, 'The Good Society, Catholic Social Thought and the Politics of the Common Good', pp. 13–26.

19. Briefing from the Prime Minister's Office, 18 May 2010, 'Government Launches the Big Society Programme'. Available at: https://www.gov .uk/government/news/government-launches-big-society-programme--2 (accessed on 2 December 2016).

government cannot remain neutral on that – it must foster and support a new culture of voluntarism, philanthropy, and social action.

2. Public Service Reform. We've got to get rid of the centralised bureaucracy that wastes money and undermines morale. And in its place we've got to give professionals much more freedom, and open up public services to new providers like charities, social enterprises and private companies so we get more innovation, diversity and responsiveness to public need.

3. Community Empowerment. We need to create communities with oomph – neighbourhoods who are in charge of their own destiny, who feel if they club together and get involved they can shape the world around them.[20]

Though the term was coined by Steve Hilton, then Director of Strategy for the Conservative Party, the 'Big Society' project was substantially underpinned by the thinking of Jesse Norman, an influential Tory Party MP and political thinker, and by the Red Tory thinking of Blond, who was an adviser to Cameron on it.[21] It was also a project that was viewed favourably by Milbank, as we shall see.

Radical Orthodoxy

Radical Orthodoxy can be defined as a post-modern, post-liberal theological grouping and is situated predominantly (though not exclusively)[22] within the British Anglo-Catholic tradition. It is highly critical of radical, liberal strands of Protestant theology, and sees orthodoxy as a more radical interpretation of the Christian tradition and its outworking. It has sought to fuse post-modern philosophical and theological perspectives with pre-modern, and thus is highly

---

[20.] See D. Cameron, 'Transcript of a Speech by the Prime Minister on the Big Society, 19 July 2010'. Available at: https://www.gov.uk/government /speeches/big-society-speech (accessed on 1 December 2016).

[21.] See, for example, J. Harris, 'Phillip Blond: The Man Who Wrote Cameron's Mood Music', *The Guardian,* 8 August 2009.

[22.] There are a small number of Roman Catholics who have contributed to Radical Orthodoxy thinking. See, for example, G. Loughlin, 'Erotics: God's Sex', in J. Milbank, C. Pickstock and G. Ward (eds), *Radical Orthodoxy* (London: Routledge, 1999), pp. 143–62.

critical of the paradigm of modernism. It has much in common with Christendom thinking, particularly with regard to its perspective on the Middle Ages and the Reformation, and its highly critical interpretation of Protestantism as being a major reason for the rise and consolidation of capitalism, something that it opposes. Considerable elements of its thinking can be traced to Milbank's book of 1990, *Theology and Social Theory*, and Milbank remains a key founding member of the Radical Orthodoxy group of thinkers.[23] Thus, a key intellectual influence running through Red Tory and Blue Labour thinking has been the theology of the Radical Orthodoxy grouping.

Liberalism

Milbank (and Adrian Pabst – see below) defines liberalism as the 'the social-cultural liberalism' of the left and 'the economic-political liberalism' of the right.[24] He sees these as being two sides of the same (modernist/rationalist) coin, arguing that: 'Far from representing genuine alternatives to one another, the two liberalisms are mutually reinforcing in that they fuse economic-political individualism with bureaucratic-managerial collectivism and social-cultural atomization – as Max Weber realised better than Karl Marx.'[25] Milbank's reference

---

[23.] Milbank, *Theology and Social Theory*. Not all members of the Radical Orthodoxy grouping think the same on all aspects of its theology. For example, with respect to the Christendom vision, Milbank argues: 'Only the Church has the theoretical and practical power to challenge the global hegemony of capital and create a viable political-economic alternative', thus very much in line with Christendom thinking. See Milbank, *The Future of Love*, p. xi. However, Graham Ward offers a minority opinion in the grouping, stating: 'Christendom is over; and with it Christian hegemony', because he finds Christendom thinking too 'restorationist', though he remains post-liberal, post-modern and post-secular in his outlook. See G. Ward, *Cities of God* (New York: Routledge, 2000), p. 257.

[24.] J. Milbank and A. Pabst, 'The Anglican Polity and the Politics of the Common Good', 2014. See the *Together for the Common Good* website at: https://togetherforthecommongood.co.uk/leading-thinkers/the-anglican-polity-and-the-politics-of-the-common-good (accessed on 13 December 2021).

[25.] J. Milbank and A. Pabst, 'The meta-crisis of liberalism: "The downward spiral"', *The European*, 13 April 2015. Available at: https://www.theeuropean.de/en/john-milbank/10019-the-meta-crisis-of-liberalism (accessed on 30 December, 2021).

to Weber partly relates to his affinity for the perspective developed in Weber's *The Protestant Ethic and the Spirit of Capitalism*,[26] in which he identified Protestant (particularly Calvinist) thinking on work and the merits of financial gain, as being conducive to the emergence of capitalism.

From Milbank's perspective, liberalism (the theoretical credo underpinning capitalism) has been the dominant (though not exclusive) economic, political, social and cultural ideology in the West since the Reformation. What is more, for Milbank, the 'triumph of liberalism more and more brings about the "war of all against all" (Hobbes) and the idea of man as self-proprietary animal (Locke) that were its presuppositions'.[27] In an article published in 2015 and co-authored with Adrian Pabst, an Anglican political theologian in the Radical Orthodoxy grouping, he attributes this tendency as partly responsible for why liberalism is now in a state of meta-crisis, contending:

> Just as liberal thought redefined human nature as isolated individuals who enter into formal contractual ties with other individuals (instead of the ancient and Christian idea of social, political animals), so too liberal practice has replaced the quest for reciprocal recognition and mutual flourishing with the pursuit of wealth, power and pleasure.[28]

For Milbank and Pabst:

> It subjects the real economy of productive activities to relentless commodification and speculation, while at the same time separating symbolic significance, equated with pure exchange value, from material space which is seen increasingly as just an object for arbitrary division, consumption and destruction. As a result, it renders ecological damage constitutive of our fundamental economic processes.[29]

These ideas will be further analysed in what follows, not least because Milbank's definition of liberalism, so central to his overall perspective

---

[26.] See M. Weber, *The Protestant Ethic and the Spirit of Capitalism* (1905) (London: Create Space International Publishing Platform, 2013).

[27.] Milbank and Pabst, 'The meta-crisis of liberalism: "The downward spiral"'.

[28.] Ibid.

[29.] Ibid.

on Blue Socialism, modernism, secular politics, the liberal-capitalist state, and welfare and the role of the Church in its provision, is far from being immune to challenge.

John Milbank's Contribution to the Christendom Strand

It is no coincidence that Milbank dedicated his magnum opus, *Theology and Social Theory*, to 'surviving members of the Christendom Trust'.[30] His affinity for their ideas is evident in much of his writing on political theology, as he readily acknowledges: 'I stand on the whole within the tradition of non-statist Christian Socialism which regards modern statism as involving the support of the very rich, a guarantee of their finances, and an enabling additional support through "welfare" of their dispossessed workforce.'[31] In common with the other Christendomist writers previously discussed, Milbank perceives the modern, liberal-capitalist state as a secular entity encroaching into areas previously within the purview of the Church. Thus, he argues that, since 'the 19th century, there has been a tendency to hand over the incarnational mission of the church to the state. In other words, to see the state as the more complete realisation of the Church's social mission than the Church itself.'[32] Whilst he acknowledges that 'in certain respects such an advance is crucial' and that 'we can't stop at charity', he nevertheless goes on to say:

> there is a profound question mark over the whole tradition which William Temple exemplified. It is a rather Hegelian one that tends ultimately to surrender things to the state, as if the political lay beyond the social [and] ... the temptation to advocate legislation often means losing focus on interpersonal

---

[30.] Milbank, *Theology and Social Theory*, where it is stated immediately prior to the contents pages: 'For Alison, and the surviving members of the Christendom Trust'.

[31.] Milbank, *The Future of Love*, pp. xvi-xvii.

[32.] J. Milbank, 'What a Christian View of Society Says about Poverty', from a series of briefings by the Contextual Theology Centre and The Children's Society, December 2011. Available at: http://www.theology-centre.org.uk/wp-content/uploads/2013/04/windsor-consultation-milbank.pdf (accessed on 20 August 2015), pp. 2–3.

relationships, and losing focus on the notion that you treat
recipients of charity as human beings.[33]

The resemblance in Milbank's thinking on the modern, liberal-capitalist
state to that held by Figgis, Reckitt, Demant and Nicholls (see Part One) is
thus apparent and is what in significant part accounts for his scepticism
about the state as a provider of welfare. Furthermore, from Milbank's
perspective, this Hegelian, statist trajectory has profound theological
implications. For it runs counter to his view that the Church, not the
state, represents the 'kingdom of God in embryo'. Thus, he says 'the
Church is trying to be the kingdom in embryo. The Church itself is the
site of the true society. It is the project that brings in everything: there
are no easy boundaries between the secular and the sacred.'[34] This is not
to suggest, however, that Milbank, in his contribution to the Blue Labour
project or in his more recent book, co-authored with Adrian Pabst, on
post-liberalism and the politics of virtue,[35] is advocating an out-and-
out Christian theocracy as either achievable or viable at this moment
in history, as a solution to the contemporary theo-political challenges
that the Church of England faces. Nevertheless, it is one reason why he
wants to see an enhanced role for the Church of England in society and
politics, as well as a diminished role for the state, in preference to greater
levels of institutional subsidiarity. He adduces examples of how this
might be achieved, via augmented local government and more localised
decision-making autonomy for schools, colleges, universities and NHS
hospitals, for example.[36]

[33.] Ibid.

[34.] Ibid., p. 2.

[35.] Milbank and Pabst, *The Politics of Virtue*.

[36.] Whilst this study focuses on Milbank's and Pabst's writings on post-
liberalism, it is a term that can be interpreted with different levels of emphasis
and meaning. George A. Lindbeck's *The Nature of Doctrine: Religion and
Theology in a Post-liberal Age* (Louisville, KY: Westminster John Knox Press,
1984) is a key work in this field. He takes a cultural/linguistic approach to
religion and theology that emphasises the importance of religious narrative
as a framework for apprehending reality through the story of a given
community. This approach can be seen as an alternative to the emphasis that
modernist thinkers have placed on reason (Descartes) or experience (Locke)
as the epistemological foundations for belief. Post-liberal theologians, such
as Lindbeck and Stanley Hauerwas, have often been critical of capitalism,
challenging the pre-eminence that Enlightenment thinkers such Locke

However, as the lineage of Milbank's thinking on Church and state can, like the thinking of Figgis, Reckitt, Demant and Nicholls before him, in significant part be attributed to his perspective on how life was in the Middle Ages and how it changed via the Reformation, it is to these that we must next turn our attention. What follows will therefore be a summary analysis of Milbank's perspective on the Reformation and the rise of capitalism, followed by a section identifying some alternative perspectives. This should enable us to see more clearly why he holds the views he does about the Welfare State *vis-à-vis* the voluntary sector, and the Church of England's post-war role in the provision of welfare, which will be developed, analysed and evaluated in chapter four.

From 'Socialism of the Gift' to 'Commodity Exchange Subject to Contract'

Milbank's interpretation of how life was in the Middle Ages is pivotal to his Christian socialist thinking. His account is rich with praise for the virtues he argues were present and later diminished as a result of the Reformation:

> In the Middle Ages, charity was a reciprocal 'state', not just an 'action': its purpose was to effect *real* reconciliation with a visible neighbour, and not to ensure oneness or 'generosity' to a stranger. Even the beggar who received your alms could *return* your love by praying for your soul, and all charity was a public exchange binding one with 'fraternity'. Thus there were founded work and trade guilds, monasteries and universities, which were both free *and* associative, and therefore … the most genuine kind of community … the arrival of these modes of organisation coincided with the emergence of a town-based market economy, and they represented a certain way of making exchanges, or of organising freedom as collective freedom. They *were* in a sense proto-socialist,

have placed on individual rights and freedoms for shaping the economic and political order, instead placing more emphasis on a need for communal structures and collective engagement. A useful introduction to post-liberal theology that covers their work and the work of others is R.T. Michener, *Postliberal Theology: A Guide for the Perplexed* (London: T&T Clark, 2013).

and not simply *destined* to disappear. If they did disappear, then this was a contingent result of the collapse of a certain cultural consensus.[37]

The medieval 'cultural consensus' he is referring to is a Catholic 'proto-socialist' one, as he interprets it, underpinned by a Catholic theology of social reciprocity, in which he argues there existed a charitable ethos where exchange was based on more than a profit motive: instead, it embodied the notion of 'socialism of the gift', in some respects resembling earlier so-called primitive societies, that, he argues, did 'not make our divisions between public contract and private gift'.[38] Thus, Milbank describes Catholic medieval society as a place where:

> religion, organicism and community seem to belong together. ... This concerns the *economy* of primitive societies. As anthropologists have for a long time told us, so-called primitive societies do not make our divisions between public contract and private gift, nor between the free active subject and the inert object. Hence, for these societies a thing exchanged is not a commodity, but a gift, and it is not *alienated* from the giver but expresses his personality, so that the giver *is* the gift, he *goes with* the gift. Precisely for this reason a *return* on the gift is always due to the giver, unlike the modern 'free gift'. Yet this gift is still a gift and not a commodity subject to contract, because it returns in a slightly different form at a not quite predictable time, bearing with it also the subjectivity of the counter-giver.[39]

For Milbank, then, for a Christian socialist ethos and post-liberal society to exist, there has to be significantly more than a profit motive to any social exchange; rather, it must also embody a Catholic notion of 'the gift' (that is, a Catholic understanding of social reciprocity based, as it must be, on the need for respect to exist between each party to the exchange,

---

[37.] J. Milbank, 'Socialism of the Gift, Socialism by Grace', 2007. Available at Wiley Online Library, p. 542.

[38.] Ibid., p. 538. Milbank's thinking on 'Socialism of the Gift' is heavily indebted to the earlier anthropological writing of Marcel Mauss, as he acknowledges. See M. Mauss, *The Gift: Forms and Functions of Exchange in Archaic Societies* (1925) (Eastward, CT: Martino Fine Books, 2011).

[39.] Milbank, 'Socialism of the Gift', p. 538.

and a shared recognition of the *mutual* benefit that should come from it, resulting in the receiver's inclination to want to reciprocate the gift). Thus, he argues: 'In every exchange, something other than calculation of profit and loss must enter.'[40] Although this runs antithetically to the emphasis, he believes capitalist, free-market economies place *profit* as being the key motivator/driver/necessity underpinning the exchange of goods and services in a capitalist defined marketplace, he argues pre-Reformation, Catholic society demonstrated that the human condition is well capable of embodying such an ethos.

In support of this, he alludes to how artisans in the Middle Ages (and, in some contexts, since) made goods as expressions of creative endeavour – artistic, technical, cultural – as well as for their functionality/utility; and, also, with regard both to the price they could secure for them in the marketplace *and* the intrinsic pleasure they derived from making them in that way, and that the artisans hoped the purchasers would derive from the goods having been made in that way. Likewise, he refers to how doctors historically and contemporaneously, even in capitalist contexts, 'do not *normally* and as a rule pursue money alone, because they would despise themselves and others would despise them if they did'. Rather, the doctor 'goes with what he does, becomes the gifts he bestows'.[41] Yet, like Marx (whose labour theory of value owed much to the thinking of Thomas Aquinas),[42] he deplores the alienation (estrangement) he believes workers in capitalist economies and societies often experience from the commodities they produce or the services they provide. This is a result of a requirement for them to be made and delivered for exchange in a context that is often subservient to, and characterised by, a modernist, liberal-capitalist, individualist, free-market driven, utilitarian, secularised and, as he sees it, immoral ethos, that is based on little other than the *profit* motive.[43] From Milbank's perspective, the Catholic 'proto-socialist'

[40.] Ibid., p. 544.

[41.] Ibid.

[42.] Marx's labour theory of value holds to the same principle as that held by Aquinas: that the just price equals the seller's cost. See R.W. McGee, 'Thomas Aquinas, A Pioneer in the Field of Law and Economics', *Western State University Law Review* 18, no. 2 (1990), pp. 471–83.

[43.] For more on Marx's theory of alienation ('Estranged Labour'), see K. Marx and F. Engels, *Economic and Philosophic Manuscripts of 1844* (sometimes referred to as the Paris Manuscripts), first published in 1927. Available at: https://www.marxists.org/archive/marx/works/1844/manuscripts/labour .htm (accessed on 26 October 2016).

ethos of the Middle Ages, underpinned by its Catholic theology of social reciprocity that emphasised 'gift exchange' in economics, was, to a significant degree, theologically and politically mutated as a result of the Reformation, that gave rise to what he describes as 'our historical tragedy ... [the] replacement of the gift with contract – which means the treating of all and everyone as a stranger'.[44] Indeed, it was the Reformation, he argues, which brought about the rise of its antithesis – capitalism; that is, an economic system that embodied the replacement of gift with contract, this being in part a result of the abandonment of the Catholic doctrine of the just price and the prohibition of usury, to which we now turn.

The Catholic Doctrine of the Just Price and the Prohibition of Usury

To get a sense of the theological paradigm shift to which Milbank refers, it is worth briefly revisiting the thinking of Temple, who states: 'The two main pillars of medieval theological economics were the doctrine of the Just Price and the Prohibition of Usury.'[45] Contrast the rejection of interest charged on a loan in the works of Aquinas (1225–74) – his writing in line with the patristic equation of usury with greed (believing that charging interest would be a violation of natural law) – to that later developed by Jean Calvin (1509–64), whereby interest could be charged on a loan (except when lending to the poor),[46] and we begin to see the theological underpinning for Milbank's view that Protestantism was in significant part responsible for the rise and consolidation of capitalism. This was a view also held by Temple, who, following Weber and Tawney, had concluded: 'Calvin had unwittingly opened the way for the coming of Economic Man.'[47] Whereas Aquinas had believed that 'the just price equals the seller's cost' – that is, that it should correspond with the labour and costs to the producer of making the commodity or of providing the service to the purchaser – after the Reformation, thinkers such as Adam Smith came to argue that the just price of goods and services equals the one that the free-market determines based on supply

---

[44.] Milbank, 'Socialism of the Gift', p. 539.

[45.] Temple, *Christianity and Social Order*, p. 53.

[46.] M. Wykes, 'Devaluing the Scholastics: Calvin's Ethics of Usury', *Calvin Theological Journal* 38, no. 1 (2003), pp. 27–51. Available at: http://web .mit.edu/aorlando/www/SaintJohnCHII/CalvinUsury.pdf (accessed on 1 December 2016).

[47.] Temple, *Christianity and Social Order*, p. 54.

and demand determinants.[48] From Milbank's perspective, it is difficult to imagine how capitalism could have emerged as an economic system, without interest being charged on loans and profit being charged as part of the price of goods and services where the market mechanism could accommodate it. This necessitated the abandonment of the Catholic doctrine of the just price and the prohibition of usury – this also being a key theme running through Tawney's analysis of religion and the rise of capitalism, which Milbank professes to endorse (see below).[49] However, recognising that does not, for some historians of the Reformation, mean that this change in theological perspective was (even in part) the *cause* of the rise of capitalism; from their perspective it was more a case of the Protestant religion having been *usurped* by the rising capitalist class to serve its own ends. Thus, Max I. Dimont argues:

> Though Protestantism had begun as a strictly religious reform movement, the people behind the new economic forces seized the Reformation and bent it to their own economic needs. ... As the modes of production changed, the people responsible for these changes searched for a state that would legalize what they were doing and for a religion that would sanctify it. They adopted the Protestant religion and made it embrace the capitalist state. The two went hand in hand like bride and groom.[50]

Unsurprisingly, however, given Milbank's perspective, he is far more sympathetic to the interpretation of the rise of capitalism that he ascribes to Tawney's study:[51] 'Here I would argue that High-Church Anglican and socialist historian R.H. Tawney was after all essentially right: the process has to do with religion – with Christianity and late medieval and early modern developments within Christian theology and practice.'[52]

[48.] Smith, *The Wealth of Nations*.

[49.] Tawney, *Religion and the Rise of Capitalism*, pp. 52–55.

[50.] M.I. Dimont, *Jews, God and History* (1962). Cited in S. Becker, S. Pfaff and J. Rubin, 'Causes and Consequences of the Protestant Reformation'. Available at: https://pdfs.semanticscholar.org/d680/a29a28682b933d75e35d5aec902c843 ab770.pdf (accessed on 18 January 2017), p. 2.

[51.] Tawney, *Religion and the Rise of Capitalism*.

[52.] J. Milbank, 'Can the Market Be Moral? Peace and Prosperity Depends on a Reimagined Socialism', ABC Religion & Ethics, 24 October 2014.

A key strand of Tawney's analysis was that, stemming in significant part from Calvin's theology, Puritanism had developed:

> a creed which transformed the acquisition of wealth from a drudgery or a temptation into a moral duty [and] was the milk of lions. It was not that religion was expelled from practical life, but that religion itself gave it a foundation of granite. ... The good Christian was not wholly dissimilar from the economic man.[53]

However, a distinction can be drawn between Tawney's analysis of religion and the rise of capitalism and the argument being made by Milbank as set out below, which places much more emphasis on the changing interpretation of 'the Fall of Man' as an explanation for the rise of capitalism, which Milbank appears to acknowledge, by prefacing his argument with the words 'in considerable extension of Tawney'.[54] For, whereas Tawney's analysis sees the nexus between religion and the rise of capitalism as being *bi-directional* – that is, one that emphasises how events shaped ideas and ideas shaped events, Milbank's appears to place far greater primacy on ideas being the shaper of events. For example, Tawney argues that the Church's diminishing influence in economic and political affairs played a part in capitalism's ascendancy:

> side by side with the expansion of trade and the rise of the new classes to political power, there was a further cause, which, if not the most conspicuous, was not the least fundamental. It was the contraction of the territory within which the writ of religion was conceived and run.[55]

Hence, for Tawney, the diminishing role the Church played in society as a result of the upheaval caused by the Reformation was part of a wider socio-economic dynamic, *with the expansion of trade also being key*, that could partly explain the rise of capitalism.

Available at: http://www.abc.net.au/religion/articles/2014/10/24/4114040 .htm (accessed on 23 October 2016), pp. 3–4.

[53.] Tawney, *Religion and the Rise of Capitalism*, p. 251.

[54.] Milbank, 'Can the Market Be Moral?', p. 4.

[55.] Tawney, *Religion and the Rise of Capitalism*, p. 272.

Contrast this with the perspective held by Milbank, which emphasises the role ideas played in that process to the apparent marginalisation of so many of the other contributing factors evident in Tawney's analysis, such as an expansion of foreign commerce resulting from growth in the money-market. Milbank argues: 'In keeping with, but in considerable extension of Tawney, one can say that Protestant theology inherited and developed a *dis-connection of reality* – a nominalist denial that all effects analogically echo their causes in a great chain of being leading back to God.'[56] For Milbank, this 'dis-connection of reality' embodied 'a poor reading of the Bible, which saw in it an excessive paganism and wished rather to celebrate an entirely inscrutable, self-willed God who has created the world as an arbitrary set of disconnected things, linked only by mechanism'.[57] It was this thinking that, for Milbank, could largely account for the rise of capitalism. For it had meant that: 'Human beings are then thought to operate on this natural order, no longer in the first place with respect to justice towards all creatures, including human beings, but in the image of a self-willed God as mere dominators and manipulators of dead, meaningless processes.'[58] What is more, for Milbank, it was this Protestant (and flawed Catholic Jansenist) misinterpretation of 'the Fall' that was the religious underpinning of capitalism's rise and subsequent consolidation. As he puts it:

> another important root of modern liberalism, traceable for example in Adam Smith, derives from an extreme 'Augustinian' theology in both Calvinistic and Jansenistic versions. For this theological outlook (which was not that of Augustine himself), original sin is so extreme that human beings must be considered to be by nature 'totally depraved'.[59]

For Milbank, then, the fact that prior to his *Wealth of Nations* (1776), Adam Smith had written his *Theory of Moral Sentiments* (1759),[60] in which he had argued for some moral underpinning as necessary for capitalism to work effectively, does not in any way negate the fact that

---

[56] Milbank, 'Can the Market Be Moral?', p. 4.

[57] Ibid.

[58] Ibid.

[59] Milbank, 'Blue Labour, One-Nation Labour and Postliberalism', pp. 1–2.

[60] A. Smith, *The Theory of Moral Sentiments* (1759) (London: Penguin Classics, 2010).

free markets, operating as the means by which the price of goods is determined and driven by the profit motive and Smith's 'invisible hand' mechanism as the reconciler of supply with demand, are, by their very nature, lacking in moral direction and outcome.[61] In Milbank's words: 'Belief in the "invisible hand" – as the only remaining economic and social bond – has left us with both rampant individualism and excessive abstraction.'[62] For Milbank, the result of this flawed thinking on 'the Fall', has been nothing less than the spawning of a theo-political disaster in the form of a modernist (hence rationalist), individualist, liberalist, capitalist credo crystallised in the writings of Protestant thinkers, such as Grotius, Hobbes and Locke of the seventeenth century, which Milbank considers as basically 'secular and materialistic'.[63]

In Summary

Liberalism, for Milbank, is an ideology founded on a flawed Protestant perspective on human nature (on 'the Fall of Man'), that celebrates individual desire in a way that makes human association or relationship one based on distrust, 'since it is held that it is bound to be perversely motivated'.[64] As he puts it: 'liberalism assumes that we are basically self-interested, fearful, greedy and egotistic creatures, unable to see beyond our own selfish needs and instincts'.[65] For Milbank, the implications of this thinking on the characterisation and consolidation of capitalism as an economic, political, social, cultural and theological epoch have been immense. As he argues, because of this flawed interpretation of 'the Fall', and thus of human nature, in capitalist societies, 'order must either be imposed by an absolute ruler, or distilled from the balancing of vice with vice. Inherent justice therefore vanishes in favour of technological procedures for coordinating and turning into profit or political power our worst human instincts, the lowest common human denominators.'[66]

[61.] Milbank, 'Blue Labour, One-Nation Labour and Postliberalism', pp. 1–2.

[62.] J. Milbank, 'Breaking the Faustian Pact: The End of Thatcherism and the Promise of Blue Labour', ABC Religion & Ethics, 30 April 2015. Available at: http://www.abc.net.au/religion/articles/2015/04/30/4226515.htm (accessed on 23 March 2016), p. 2.

[63.] Milbank, 'Blue Labour, One-Nation Labour and Postliberalism', p. 1.

[64.] Ibid., p. 4.

[65.] Ibid., p. 1.

[66.] Milbank, 'Can the Market Be Moral?', p. 4.

For Milbank, then, as it had been for Figgis, Demant and the authors of the *Return of Christendom*, the rise of the modern, secular state and its 'separation' from the Church as a result of the Reformation can in large part be explained as the means by which order was imposed in a capitalist context. That is, by a 'Hobbesian'-style 'absolute ruler' in the form of a secular, omnicompetent state; a capitalist state often characterised by the 'technological procedures for coordinating and turning into profit or political power our worst human instincts', only subsequently to be softened at the edges by way of the welfare appendages after 1945. As Milbank puts it: 'For what are the real motivations of the state after all (at least, after it has cast off any lingering odour of British Hegelianism)? Surely they are to secure its economic and military might, combined with the desire to keep the populace in order through a neo-pagan deployment of bread and circuses?'[67] Therefore, for Milbank, the modern Welfare State is, in significant part, the means by which the capitalist, ruling economic elites preserve their socio-economic hegemony. They do this by acquiescing in a centralised and limited parliamentary, representative system of government and by the redistribution of wealth via the handing out of 'crumbs from the table' to the oppressed populace by way of state-provided welfare programmes, in order to keep them quiescent. As Milbank puts it: 'The population is in turn bought off with "welfare" which blinds them to the injustices of the workplace and releases them from any active thought as to what the pursuit of true education, true health and true care for others might really involve.'[68]

For Milbank, moreover, the emergence and consolidation of the modern, secular, liberal-capitalist state has increasingly and regrettably marginalised the role of the Church in society to that of the private sphere. He thus argues: 'The new, secular *dominium* could not ... really tolerate a "political" Church as a cohabitant. Hence, it was first necessary, with Marsiglio and Luther, to produce the paradox of a purely "suasive" Church which must yet involve external state coercion for its self-government.'[69] Unlike Temple, whose theology of the state had afforded it a 'spiritual function' – it being a 'servant and instrument of God' – for Milbank, by contrast, the state is a secular product of modernism, with no spiritual functionality. Needless to say, he is critical of middle axiom thinking that imposes limits on the extent to which the Church should

---

[67] Milbank, 'The Big Society Depends on the Big Parish', p. 4.

[68] Ibid., p. 3.

[69] Milbank, *Theology and Social Theory*, p. 19.

intervene in the socio-political affairs of the state, whilst nevertheless acknowledging that: 'If theology is to have the right to speak in the socio-economic domain, then it has to earn such a right.'[70]

Milbank's views on the Reformation and the rise of capitalism are not shared by many writers and historians of the period, and I now consider a selection of these counter-perspectives.

Other Perspectives on the Reformation and the Rise of Capitalism

There are numerous alternative perspectives on the Reformation and the rise of capitalism to that held by Milbank. Although the following can offer no more than a sample, they are nevertheless illustrative of grounds for contestation of his perspective. One, relating to the chronology of events, was developed by Amintore Fanfani, who, in his work of 1935, argued: 'Europe was acquainted with capitalism before the Protestant revolt', and thus cannot adequately be explained as being a result of it.[71] This has been a theme other historians of the Reformation, such as Kurt Samuelson[72] and R. Stark,[73] have since further developed. These historians often point to how the first bank, for example, was established in Venice in 1157, leading to the expansion of banking in Italy, a Catholic country, in the late twelfth and thirteenth centuries, and hence prior to the 'Protestant Revolution' and the emergence of banking in Protestant countries. This is suggestive, they argue, of how the theology prohibiting usury was being undermined by a newly emerging commercial economy and its financial transactions in late medieval Italy. Indeed, it was this reality that had partly spawned what Tawney described as follows: 'There was plenty of the "capitalist spirit" in fifteenth-century Venice and Florence, or in South Germany and Flanders, for the simple reason that these areas were the greatest

---

70. Milbank, *The Future of Love*, p. 76.

71. A. Fanfani, *Catholicism, Protestantism and Capitalism* (London: Sheed & Ward, 1935), p. 183. Available at: http://www.strobertbellarmine.net/books /Fanfani--Catholicism_Protestantism_Capitalism.pdf (accessed on 22 January 2017).

72. K. Samuelson, *Religion and Economic Action* (Toronto: University of Toronto Press, 1993).

73. R. Stark, *The Victory of Reason: How Christianity Led to Freedom, Capitalism and Western Success* (New York: Random House, 2006).

commercial and financial centres of the age, though all were, at least nominally, Catholic.'[74] There is, then, a different emphasis in Tawney's analysis to that of Weber's, the latter displaying little appreciation of the difficulties the chronological sequencing of the historical events pose for his more theoretically based analysis.

Another alternative perspective was produced by Jacob Viner.[75] He argues that well into the eighteenth century, Scotland was a poor country, and his study attributes this in significant part to the economic teachings of the Scottish Calvinists, which he contends encouraged frugality and not acquisitiveness, and thus were antithetical to a capitalist spirit (ethos). His study of Scottish Calvinism, therefore, if one interprets it as being fairly typical of other strands of European Calvinism, is thus at odds with a view that Calvinism could have been a major reason for the rise of capitalism in Europe.

A different line of interpretation has been advanced by Marxist historians of the Middle Ages such as Rodney Hilton. Marxists argue that Catholic medieval Europe embodied a socially stratified society often characterised by class struggle between the exploited peasantry/serfs and the aristocracy, as evidenced by the Peasants' Revolt in England in 1381, which was largely the result of high taxes stemming from the conflict with France during the Hundred Years War. Indeed, according to this perspective, Catholic medieval society was more akin to a 'proto-capitalist' than to the 'proto-socialist' society of the kind described by Milbank.[76]

Also of relevance are studies into global history that argue that previous interpretations of the rise of capitalism have been too Eurocentric and thus incorrectly assumed that capitalism first arose in Europe and that the reasons for its rise were unique to the European context of the time, such as the 'Protestant Revolution'. For example, J.M. Blaut's work argues that there were trade routes between Asia, the Middle East, the northern half of Africa, right up to the southern edges of Europe in the Middle Ages, that meant that in each of these

---

[74.] Tawney, *Religion and the Rise of Capitalism*, p. 312.

[75.] See J. Viner, *Religious Thought and Economic Society* (Durham, NC: Duke University Press, 1978). A useful summary of this perspective is in S. Pierotti, 'Backup of the Protestant Ethic and the Spirit of Capitalism: Criticisms of Weber's Thesis'. Available at: http://dearhabermas.org/weberrelbk01.htm (accessed on 15 December 2021).

[76.] See, for example, R. Hilton, *Class Conflict and the Crisis of Feudalism: Essays in Medieval Social History* (1985) (London: Verso Books, 1991).

there was a 'process of increasing urbanisation and increasing long distance commodity movements which characterised the late middle ages throughout the hemisphere'.[77] He thus argues it is an error to draw comparisons with Europe, Africa, India or China in the way that earlier studies of the rise of capitalism often have. Instead, he contends that attention should be given to enclaves of 'proto-capitalism' that were evident in each global sphere.[78] This line of argument is also supported by several other studies into the rise of capitalism undertaken from a global perspective.[79]

One of these is the extensive study by Janet Abu-Lughod into the development of trade and economic output in the period before 1500 in 'the Orient'.[80] Another is by M.S. Alim, who argues:

> The historical evidence indicates that wages in India and Egypt were comparable to those in the historically advanced countries. ... The leading industrial countries in 1750 had only a modest lead over lagging countries in manufacturing output per capita. If Britain's industrial manufacturing output per head was 10, then China's was 8, India's 7, Brazil 6, France 9, Belgium 9, the US 4.

Hence, the thrust of his argument is that there was: 'a near parity of economic development of western Europe and China, India and the Middle East as late as 1800'.[81] Another global perspective is the epic 'bottom-up' account of the rise of capitalism produced by the Marxist historian, Chris Harman, which led him to conclude: 'It was not "European values" that created capitalism, but rather capitalism that created what we think of as European values. And capitalism did not arise because of some unique European occurrence, but as a

---

[77] See J.M. Blaut, *The Colonizer's Model of the World* (New York: Guilford Press, 1993), p. 165.

[78] Ibid., p. 157.

[79] See, for example, K. Pomeranz, *The Great Divergence: China, Europe, and the Making of the Modern World Economy* (Princeton, NJ: Princeton University Press, 2001).

[80] J. Abu-Lughod, *Before European Hegemony: The World System A.D. 1250–1350* (New York: Oxford University Press, 1989).

[81] M. S. Alim, 'How Advanced was Europe in 1760 After All?', *Review of Radical Political Economy* 32, no. 4 (September 2000), p. 625.

product of the development of the forces and relations of production on a global scale.'[82]

These global studies of the rise of capitalism have implications for Milbank's perspective on the Reformation and the reasons for the rise of capitalism that go far wider than the debate concerning the influence the 'Protestant Revolution' may have had. For they also impinge on his view that the emergence of the modern, Western state and its 'separation' from the Church that occurred in the early-modern period can in significant part be accounted for as being necessary for the rise of capitalism.

What this handful of counter-perspectives reveals is that it can be reliably argued that Tawney's analysis of religion and the rise of capitalism cannot possibly account *in toto* (and for some historians in large part) for the causes of such a complex and multifaceted phenomenon as capitalism's ascendancy. Yet, with respect to Tawney's analysis, there is a nuanced, *bi-directional* and balanced emphasis between the various contributing factors he argues were responsible, of which Protestant theology was only one (albeit a key one) which is less evident in Milbank's perspective. This is reflected in an essay Tawney wrote in 1930 on Weber's study, where he saw an interdependent causality in the relationship between the Protestant Reformation and the rise of early modern capitalism, stating:

> There was action and reaction, and, while Puritanism helped to mould the social order, it was, in its turn, moulded by it. It is instructive to trace, with Weber, the influence of religious ideas on economic development. It is not less important to grasp the effect of the economic arrangements accepted by an age on the opinion which it holds of the province of religion.[83]

This was wholly consistent with the view he had reached in his earlier work of 1926, when he stated: 'Religion influenced, to a degree which today is difficult to appreciate, men's outlook on society. Economic and

---

[82]. C. Harman, *A People's History of the World* (London: Verso, 1999). The quote is from Harman, 'The Rise of Capitalism', *International Socialism* 2, no. 102 (Spring 2004). Available at: https://www.marxists.org/archive/harman/2004/xx/risecap.htm (accessed on 23 January 2017), p. 2.

[83]. R.H. Tawney, 'Max Weber and the Spirit of Capitalism' (1930), in J.M. Winter (ed.), *History and Society: Essays by R.H. Tawney* (London: Routledge & Kegan Paul, 1978), p. 195.

social changes acted powerfully on religion.'[84] Tawney's analysis places more emphasis than Weber's had and, it would appear, than Milbank's does, on Protestantism having *adopted* the risk-taking, profit-making ethic of capitalism both theologically and culturally, as much as the other way round, saying: 'it seems a little artificial to talk as though capitalist enterprise could not appear till religious changes had produced a capitalist spirit. It would be equally true, and equally one-sided, to say that the religious changes were purely the result of economic movements.'[85] For Tawney: 'material and psychological changes went together, and of course the second reacted on the first'.[86] Moreover, he reconfirmed this interdependent causality in his preface to the 1937 edition of *Religion and the Rise of Capitalism*, stating: 'Puritanism helped to mould the social order, but it was also itself increasingly moulded by it.'[87] Nonetheless, his most eloquent summary of his thinking on interdependent causality in the shaping of history *per se*, and not just on religion and the rise of capitalism, can be found in his statement of 1949:

> The philosophy which sees the one constant dynamic in the pressure and pull of economic forces [economic determinism] is a just nemesis on the facile sentimentalism of historical interpretations which idealise the flower to the neglect of roots and soil [ideational determinism]. But such forces are not automatic agents. They become a power, not directly, but at one remove, when passed through the transforming medium of human minds and wills, which are not passive, but impose, in reacting to them, a pattern of their own. ... It is with the human response, not the material challenge, that the last word lies.[88]

Thus, for Tawney, as one historian succinctly puts it: 'At every cross-roads, after all, there are several paths to follow, and choice is in the circumstances unavoidable.'[89] However, the circumstances in which choice is exercised play a crucial role in shaping the options available

---

84. Tawney, *Religion and the Rise of Capitalism*, p. xii.

85. Ibid., p. 312.

86. Ibid.

87. Ibid., p. xiii.

88. R.H. Tawney, *The Western Political Tradition* (London: SCM Press, 1949), p. 17.

89. Reisman, *State and Welfare*, pp. 35–36.

to the chooser – choice and context go hand in hand. Tawney's book of 1926 rightly remains prominent within the body of work that has been amassed on this subject, not least because, for some historians, it has not been discredited by subsequent research, at least with respect to its central arguments. However, as with Milbank's interpretation of these events and their likely causes, it is but one of many compelling and often mutually contradictory interpretations.

Yet, it is Milbank's historical perspective on the reasons for the rise and consolidation of capitalism that is *foundational* for his thinking on so much that has followed, not least his perspective on welfare and the Church. However, there is another aspect to Milbank's thinking on Anglican Socialism that now needs to be analysed, as it will help to locate the nature of his contribution to the Blue Labour project and its critique of the welfare state model of delivery, and his affinity for much of the Red Tory critical perspective on the Welfare State advanced by Phillip Blond and covered in Part Three. For Milbank defines his Anglican Socialist perspective as: 'Blue Socialism', that is 'socialism with a Burkean tinge'.[90]

A Blue Socialism that is Beyond Left and Right?

Burke had, of course, famously written in his *Reflections*: 'To be attached to the subdivision, to love the little platoon we belong to in society, is the first principle (the germ as it were) of public affections. It is the first link in the series by which we proceed towards a love to our country and to mankind.'[91] The importance that Burke attached to loving the 'little platoons' that we belong to in society resonates with Milbank's sense of the importance of small associations and other intermediate groups in society. These often define a sense of the local (the provincial) that is so important to his Christian social anthropology (that is, his Catholic sense of what community relations should embody). It immediately suggests that the more traditional positioning of socialism since the French Revolution as being an ideology of 'the Left' is seen as less than adequate for Milbank, for the reasons set out below.[92]

[90.] Milbank, *The Future of Love*, p. xvii.

[91.] E. Burke, *Reflections on the Revolution in France*, 2nd edn (1790) (London: J. Dodsley, 1955), p. 69.

[92.] Milbank, *The Future of Love*, p. xvii.

Milbank sees some areas of common ground between the 'High Tory' Anglican tradition and the 'High Socialist' Anglican tradition when compared to either liberalism or secular strands of socialism. He argues that these put Blue Socialism beyond what has traditionally been seen as left and right:

1. Both have historically been opposed to liberalism and thus can be seen as being 'counter-enlightenment'.[93]
2. Both have strands within their respective traditions that have been wary of statist paths to tackling social problems at the expense of community-based initiatives.[94]
3. Neither has argued in favour of overtly rationalist or, in the case of Marxism, scientifically materialist accounts of history or society, based on supposedly objective empirical knowledge.[95]
4. Crucially, both embody a sense of the reality of sin in human affairs, thus avoiding, as Milbank sees it, the danger of utopian tendencies in secular liberalism (such as displayed by Jean-Jacques Rousseau,[96] for example) or secular socialism (such as displayed by Marx and Engels).

[93.] Ibid., p. xvi.

[94.] For example, Neoliberalism and Guild Socialism.

[95.] For more on this, see H.B. Mayo, 'Marxist Theory and Scientific Methods', *The Canadian Journal of Economics and Political Science* 18, no. 4 (November 1952), pp. 487–99. Available at: https://www.jstor.org/stable/138368?seq=1#page _scan_tab_contents (accessed on 3 November 2016). See also Milbank, *The Future of Love*, p. xvi.

[96.] Milbank's view of Rousseau is: 'there is another "romantic" variant of liberalism that was invented in the late 18th Century by Jean-Jacques Rousseau. ... [He] inverted Thomas Hobbes by arguing that the isolated, natural individual is "good", lost in contemplative delight at the world around him, satisfied with simple pleasures and provisions. He is not yet egotistic, because that vice arises from rivalry and comparison. However, Rousseau took the latter to be so endemic a motivation once the individual is placed in a social context, that he transferred pessimism about the individual into a new pessimism about human association. ... This led to a scepticism about the role of corporate bodies beneath the level of the state.' See Milbank, 'Blue Labour, One Nation Labour', p. 2. See Milbank, 'Blue Labour, One Nation Labour and Post-liberalism', p. 2.

5. Both have distinctly Christian moral underpinnings, unlike secular versions of liberalism, such as that espoused by Jeremy Bentham,[97] and of socialism, such as that advocated by Marx and Engels.[98]

Therefore, for Milbank, aspects of both of these anti-liberal political traditions can and should inform the thinking necessary for forging a new paradigm of socialist theory and praxis for the twenty-first century along the lines he calls 'Blue Socialism'. He sees this Blue Socialism as a possible political path towards the goal of achieving a post-liberal world; one that, from his perspective, would be underpinned by a Catholic theo-political outlook,[99] with the Church of England playing a more prominent role in the affairs of the nation, including in the provision of welfare, as part of a strategy Milbank and Pabst describe as: 'Restoring the State as also the Church'.[100]

Blue Socialism being a relatively new term on the political horizon is thus an evolving body of thought. It has only partly been developed by Milbank and is a term, therefore, which can be understood with different levels of emphasis. However, there are common elements to this thinking that attempt to fuse Burkean 'One Nation' Conservative thinking with 'non-statist' socialist thinking within sections of the Labour Party which, as we have seen, Milbank has helped to shape, of which the following are key:

1. It is highly critical of neoliberalism, both with regard to its economic and philosophical underpinning and its global socio-political consequences since the late 1970s.[101]

[97.] See, for example, J. Bentham, *Defence of Usury; Shewing the Impolity of the Present Legal Restraints on the Terms of Pecuniary Bargains in a Series of Letters to Adam Smith* (1787), in which he defends usury on the grounds of what he terms liberty, that is: 'the liberty of making one's own terms in money-bargains'. Available at: http://socserv2.mcmaster.ca./~econ/ugcm /3ll3/bentham/usury (accessed on 2 November 2016).

[98.] For their critique of religion, see, for example, K. Marx and F. Engels, *The Communist Manifesto* (1848) (London: Progress Publishers, 1966).

[99.] See Milbank and Pabst, *The Politics of Virtue.*

[100.] Ibid., pp. 230–40.

[101.] Geary and Pabst (eds), *Blue Labour*, pp. 28ff.

2. It is highly critical of the overreliance by post-war Labour governments on the state as a vehicle for advancing democratic socialism via the welfare state model. Indeed, in this regard, its thinking would chime more with that of Demant, in his assertion that: 'the state can never be an object of emotional attachment which could replace a man's roots in home, property, neighbourhood and craft association'.[102]

3. It is highly critical of the Welfare State as a means of providing welfare, seeing it as too centralist (thus insufficiently associational in comparison with the voluntary sector), excessively bureaucratic, impersonal and over-prescriptive in its universalist approach to the provision of welfare. By contrast, it advocates an alternative approach to the provision of welfare, based increasingly on empowering intermediate-level community groups and associations in society (a key one being the Church), with more responsibility for areas that since 1945 have been seen more as the preserve of the Welfare State, including education, health, support to the unemployed, shelter for the homeless and poverty avoidance generally.[103]

4. It is critical of the overreliance it considers New Labour placed on market mechanisms as a means of reconciling supply and demand in the interests of the citizen, including the management of state welfare functions. Instead, it prefers to engage with ideas from Guild Socialism and continental corporatism (that is, increased government intervention in the economy underpinned by moral precepts such as just price thinking) as possible alternative options.[104]

5. It places a greater emphasis on the importance of family, faith and flag as being key Blue Socialist foundational values, in contrast to how they have traditionally been considered as

---

[102.] Milbank, 'The Big Society Depends on the Big Parish' and 'The Blue Labour Dream', in Geary and Pabst (eds), *Blue Labour*, pp. 27–49. See also, Demant, *Religion and the Decline of Capitalism*, p. 95.

[103.] This theme is covered extensively in Geary and Pabst (eds), *Blue Labour*.

[104.] On guilds and continental corporatism see Milbank and Pabst, *The Politics of Virtue*, pp. 150–51.

> Conservative ones: emphasising reciprocity, mutuality and solidarity as key for shaping this new vision.[105]

6. It considers the traditional internationalist positions often adopted by British post-war Labour governments on domestic and geopolitical matters, including immigration control, may have been insufficiently nuanced, and thus at the expense of a national sense of pride that citizens want to feel about their cultural identity and national achievements.[106]

As this book is focused on Milbank's influence on reshaping the Church of England's strategy on welfare, it is not necessary to analyse each of these elements, though element number three will be covered in chapter four on the aspects that directly relate to the focus of this study.

The Influence of Catholic Social Teaching on Milbank's Blue Socialism

Catholic social teaching has been a significant theoretical influence on some of those developing Blue Socialist thinking and is particularly prominent in Milbank's most recent work with Adrian Pabst on 'the politics of virtue'.[107]

Two key elements of Catholic social teaching, commended by Milbank and Glasman as being consistent with Blue Socialist thinking, are as follows:[108]

---

[105] Stratton, 'Labour: Now It's Kind of Blue'. Also see M. Merrick, 'The Labour Family', in Geary and Pabst (eds), *Blue Labour*, pp. 235–52.

[106] D. Goodhart, 'Globalisation, Nation States and the Economics of Migration', in Geary and Pabst (eds), *Blue Labour*, pp. 121–40.

[107] Milbank and Pabst, *The Politics of Virtue*, pp. 70, 86, 135 and 142. As Milbank puts it elsewhere: 'However, one needs also to recognize a wider family resemblance with many variants of Christian social teaching which characteristically stress subsidiarity (the distribution of money and power to appropriate levels, not necessarily the lowest) and the break-up of central sovereignty through the operation of intermediary associations.' Milbank, *The Future of Love*, p. xvii.

[108] Glasman, 'The Good Society, Catholic Social Thought and the Politics of the Common Good', p. 20.

1. A theory of labour value (stemming in large part from the works of Aquinas)[109] that sees labour as more than merely physical space and time, in contrast to the way many see the impersonal neoliberal market mechanism, thus placing more emphasis on the experience, skill, expertise and human dignity required to produce a commodity or provide a service when determining its exchange value.

2. A body of thought based around the concept of subsidiarity that places great emphasis on the principle that a central authority (which can be interpreted as the state) should perform only those tasks which cannot be performed at a more local level.[110]

It can be argued Catholic social teaching thus offers a potential alternative both to unmediated statist collectivism and unfettered non-statist individualism by way of what Glasman describes as: 'The reintroduction of institutional mediation' – this being the 'task of contemporary statecraft'.[111] Indeed, in this regard, the Blue Socialist perspective on the role of the state appears to be close to that of the English political pluralist tradition – to mediate between groups and associations in civil society.

[109.] T. Aquinas, *Aquinas Ethicus: or, the Moral Teaching of St Thomas: A Translation of the Principal Portions of the Second Part of the Summa Theologica*, with notes by Joseph Rickaby SJ (London: Burns & Oates, 1892), Vol. 2. Available at: http://oll.libertyfund.org/pages/aquinas-on-usury (accessed on 4 November 2016). The Roman Catholic labour theory of value is a central tenet of Catholic social teaching and is covered in Leo XIII, *Rerum Novarum: Encyclical of Pope Leo XIII on Capital and Labor*, issued 15 May 1891. Available at: http://w2.vatican.va/content/leo-xiii/en/encyclicals /documents/hf_l-xiii_enc_15051891_rerum-novarum.html (accessed on 5 January 2017).

[110.] On subsidiarity, see Pius XI, *Quadragesimo Anno: Encyclical of Pope Pius XI on Reconstruction of the Social Order*, issued 15 May 1931. Available at: https://w2.vatican.va/content/pius-xi/en/encyclicals/documents/hf_p-xi _enc_19310515_quadragesimo-anno.html (accessed on 5 January 2017). Essentially, subsidiarity is the principle that central institutions, such as those comprising the modern state's administrative apparatus, should only perform those functions that cannot be performed at a more local level.

[111.] Glasman, 'The Good Society, Catholic Social Thought and the Politics of the Common Good', p. 20.

Criticisms of Milbank's Blue Socialism

In what follows I provide five criticisms of Milbank's Blue Socialist thinking as it relates to the categorisations he uses, which are illustrative of the wider problem with his Blue Socialist outlook – an outlook that underpins much of his thinking on the provision of welfare.

One of these is a distinction he draws between two branches of the socialist tradition. First, the Fabian and Marxist strand, which he categorises as 'the social/cultural liberalism of the left' and the other side of the same coin as 'the economic-political liberalism' of the right.[112] Second, the contrasting Christian 'conservative romantic' socialist strand derived in part from High Anglican/Tory lineage (John Ruskin, Charles Kingsley, F.D. Maurice, J.N. Figgis *et al.*),[113] that he considers as being more authentically ethical and thus antithetical to liberalism. Yet, it can be argued that Marxist and Fabian strands of socialism (themselves so different from one another in so many respects) were more a reaction *against* the strands of liberal economic, political, individualist philosophy that emerged in the seventeenth, eighteenth and nineteenth centuries (their scepticism of Adam Smith's unfettered free marketism being just one example), and hence cannot plausibly be seen as the other side of the same coin as the economic-political liberalism of the right. For Milbank's definition of liberalism is so broad as to include thinkers as diverse as Hobbes, Smith, Rousseau and Marx, all categorised with the same liberal 'umbrella' term. Thus, the question immediately arises: how can Hobbes, for example, be credibly categorised in the same way as Marx? Hobbes' more negative view of human nature underpins the need for a social contract theory that affords legitimacy of authority of the state over the individual, in preference to the alternative barbaric and anarchic state of nature. Marx had a more optimistic view of human nature and a vision of a stateless communist society, without need for any hierarchical forms of authority. The answer, for Milbank, is that they both represent strands of modernist, liberalist thinking underpinned by *rationalist* philosophical assumptions.[114] However, it can be queried whether that is sufficient to categorise them in a way that underrepresents their obvious differences as political philosophies.

[112.] Milbank, *The Future of Love*, pp. 242–63.

[113.] Milbank and Pabst, 'The meta-crisis of liberalism: "the downward spiral"'.

[114.] Milbank and Pabst, *The Politics of Virtue*. This theme is covered at length as a basis for their definition of liberalism.

A second line of criticism, again relating to categorisation, is that socialism, both as a philosophical and historical tradition, has tended to place a desire to achieve greater levels of *equality* in society – often by way of establishing human rights via the passage of legislation – as a key priority. By contrast, Burke argued that: 'Political equality is against nature. Social equality is against nature. Economic equality is against nature. The idea of equality is subversive to order, it is a monstrous fiction.'[115] Indeed, he placed great emphasis on 'an entailed inheritance derived to us from our forefathers, and to be transmitted to our posterity'.[116] In this regard, his scathing critique of the French Revolution[117] is an attack on abstract rights over inherited rights and has since been seen as a key plank of Conservative political thought, and thus to be in direct opposition to the socialist pursuit of greater levels of equality in society. Yet, Burke's perspective on equality is in significant part the underpinning for Milbank's 'Blue Socialism with a Burkean tinge', with its unambiguous critique of statist redistribution that evidently is not confined to material wealth, but also pertains to legislative state-established and enforced human rights, of which Milbank has been unambiguous in his criticism – seeing them as a product of liberalist individualism.[118] For this reason Burke's perspective on equality and rights does not sit easily with those who identify democratic socialism with the pursuit of greater levels of equality as a human right (such as those in the Tawney tradition) by way of advancing an egalitarian model of social justice via the passage of legislation, and, often, in part delivered via a welfare state model of redistribution.

A third line of criticism relating to categorisation pertains to Milbank's novel attempt to fuse Burke's *anti-rationalist* thinking with socialism, a strand of political philosophy that has been shaped more by an Aristotelian affinity for *rationalist* solutions to societal woes.[119] Indeed,

---

[115.] Cited by M. Freeman, *Edmund Burke and the Critique of Political Radicalism* (Oxford: Blackwell, 1980), p. 21.

[116.] For his discussion on rights, see Burke, *Reflections on the Revolution in France* (1790), pp. 29–33.

[117.] Burke, *Reflections*.

[118.] Milbank and Pabst, *The Politics of Virtue*, pp. 13–67. See also Milbank, 'Against Human Rights'. Available at: http://theologyphilosophycentre.co.uk /papers/Milbank_AgainstHumanRights.pdf (accessed on 14 December 2021).

[119.] See Aristotle, *Prior Analytics Book 1* (c. 350 BCE), Clarendon Aristotle series (Oxford: Oxford University Press, 2009).

it is Burke's preference for experience and tradition over rationalistic theorising as the guide for political governance, that is a key reason why his thinking has been the bedrock for so much Conservative political philosophy ever since. For example, Michael Oakeshott's Conservative critique of rationalism owes much to Burke, as he acknowledged; that is, his rejection of the idea that you can impose a plan on people and make state institutions the primary vehicle for delivering a better society.[120] By contrast, socialism has often emphasised the need for rationalistic planning in economic, political and social spheres. This has been in the interests of the perceived *collective* needs of society as a whole, and especially those of the working class. Indeed, it is this emphasis on planning that has often been seen by socialist writers in the Marxist, Fabian and wider labour traditions, as the best means of bringing about a society characterised by a fair and equitable distribution of its resources. Often this has been via collective control over of its means of production, distribution and exchange and thus the workings of the market or, alternatively, via a welfare statist model of delivery, premised on a mixed economy as per the Fabian model. This emphasis that socialism has placed on rationalism thus calls into question the extent to which Milbank's 'socialism with a Burkean tinge' can credibly be categorised as socialist. This is not, of course, to suggest that all socialist writers have placed *the same level of need* for rationalistic planning as necessary or desirable for a transition from a capitalist to a socialist society. George Orwell, for example, a writer whom Milbank admires,[121] was more cautious of this approach, perceiving the danger of a totalitarian outcome.[122] It is to suggest, however, that *a level* of rationalistic planning can be seen as essential to socialist thinking and *praxis*, in a way that is antithetical to Burke's philosophy.

[120.] See M. Oakeshott, *Rationalism in Politics and Other Essays* (York: Methuen, 1981).

[121.] Milbank, 'Blue Labour, One Nation Labour and Post-liberalism', pp. 4–5.

[122.] He insisted: 'My novel Nineteen Eighty-Four is not intended as an attack on socialism, or on the British Labour party, but as a show-up of the perversions to which a centralized economy is liable.' It was rationalistic, centralised, state planning of the economy that he railed against, not democratic socialist philosophy *per se*. The above quote is from a letter to F.A. Henson, 16 June 1949, cited in A.L. McKay, 'Wrong about Orwell Being on the Right', 28 August 2012. Available at: https://www.e-ir.info/2012/08/28/wrong -about-orwell-being-on-the-right/ (accessed on 25 November 2019).

A fourth line of criticism relates to the way Milbank categorises Blue Socialism as being a strand of the tradition that is centred on religious (essentially Christian) moral underpinning, *in contrast* to the way the post-war democratic socialist left, allegedly, 'increasingly understands itself as liberal, and frequently, in addition, as atheist and anti-religious', and that an opposition to the free market thus 'can only be "conservative"'.[123] The emergence of Red Labour since 2015 – particularly whilst under the leadership of Jeremy Corbyn – as a more dominant grouping in the Labour Party does not appear to accord with such a categorisation. It is not apparent how Red Labour supporters – unambiguously opposed to unfettered free market economics – regard themselves as being either liberal or anti-religious; neither is it apparent how that strand of Labour Party tradition has ever regarded itself as such.[124] Certainly, there are Red Labour supporters who do not have a religious affiliation or belief; but that does not imply they are anti-religious, with connotations of intolerance towards those with a religious belief, and Milbank has not provided any evidence to the contrary.

A fifth line of criticism relating to categorisation is Milbank's view, shared by other Blue Labour advocates, that Blue Socialism connects with an interpretation of British labour history that Pabst describes as one in which Labour roots had 'much less to do with Victorian liberalism than with High Toryism and the cooperative movement',[125] and that 'Labour has always been conservative in this sense of a genuine popular rootedness and belief in the best of the British legacy.'[126] This is also the perspective argued by Glasman:

> The founders of the labour movement understood the logic
> of capitalism as based upon the maximisation of returns on
> investment, and the threat this posed to their lives, livelihoods

---

[123] Milbank, *The Future of Love*, p. xv.

[124] For example, consider the Methodist influences on the emergence of trade unions and the British Labour Party. For a good introduction to this aspect, see N. Scotland, 'Methodism and the English Labour Movement 1800–1906', *Anvil* 14, no. 1 (1997). Available at: https://biblicalstudies.org.uk/pdf/anvil/14-1_036.pdf (accessed on 25 January 2017).

[125] A. Pabst, 'Blue Labour and the Politics of the Common Good', in Geary and Pabst (eds), *Blue Labour*, p. 4.

[126] Ibid., p. 5.

and environment, but they did not embrace class war, and clung stubbornly to an idea of a common life with their rulers and exploiters.[127]

Blue Socialist advocates such as Milbank, Pabst and Glasman thus invite us to interpret British labour history in a way that is problematic, owing to the popular labour struggles that 'High Toryism' tended to oppose. Take the Chartist Movement (1838–57) as one example of a predominantly working-class movement for political reform and increased democracy in Victorian Britain. Robert Saunders' study provides evidence of substantial fear held by the political Whig and Tory elites of the Chartism threat.[128] Likewise, the study into Chartism by Michael J. Turner focused on local politics in Manchester and concluded that the movement challenged and undermined the old Tory Anglican power elite which it opposed.[129] In a similar vein, the study by Emma Griffin, which forcefully argues that such a radical movement of millions of working men and women, with no experience of 'bourgeois' civic engagement, could not have happened without a growing sense of anti-establishment class consciousness, and a resultant growing and radical working-class solidarity.[130] These studies illustrate the difficulties of interpreting the Chartist struggle through the lens of the Blue Socialist perspective on British labour history; on the contrary, there is compelling evidence that Chartism was seen as dangerously subversive by the British establishment, including the Tory elite.

In a similar vein, it is not clear how one is to interpret a British labour struggle such as the 1889 London Dock Strike, key to the formation of the trade union movement, as being consistent with the values and aspirations of 'High Toryism'. Over 100,000 workers took part in that strike for better working conditions and fairer wages; a labour struggle

---

[127.] M. Glasman, 'Labour as a Radical Tradition: Labour's Renewal Lies in Its Traditions of Mutualism, Reciprocity and Common Good', *Soundings*, no. 46 (September 2010), pp. 31ff.

[128.] R. Saunders, 'Chartism from Above: British Elites and the Interpretation of Chartism', *Historical Research* 81, no. 213 (August 2008), pp. 463–84.

[129.] M.J. Turner, 'Local Politics and the Nature of Chartism: The Case of Manchester', *Northern History* 45, no. 2 (2008), pp. 323–45.

[130.] E. Griffin, 'The Making of the Chartists: Popular Politics and Working-Class Autobiography in Early Victorian Britain, *The English Historical Review* 129, no. 538 (June 2014), pp. 578–605.

that was summed up by John Elliot Burns, a key organiser of the dispute, in the following terms:

> Still more important perhaps is the fact that labour of the humbler kind has shown its capacity to organise itself; its solidarity; its ability. The labourer has learned that combination can lead him to anything and everything. He has tasted success as the immediate fruit of combination, and he knows that the harvest he has just reaped is not the utmost he can look to gain. Conquering himself, he has learned that he can conquer the world of capital whose generals have been the most ruthless of his oppressors.[131]

The outcome was not only a victory for the strikers but has generally been regarded as pivotal to the events that led to the formation of the Labour Party in 1900.[132] We begin to see, then, how even making brief reference to just two of the major movements of popular protest in nineteenth century British labour history, reveals the Blue Socialist perspective as being at variance with other substantial historical accounts and interpretations, as well as with their evidential underpinning.

What these five criticisms of Milbank's perspective reveal is that the novel categorisations adopted by him that underpin much of his Blue Socialist outlook result in a portrayal of British labour history and its philosophical influences, as well as the part played by Marxist, Fabian and, indeed, by some Anglican Socialists within these popular protests and struggles, that is inconsistent with much of the more mainstream historiographical interpretations and their evidential underpinning – this being just one example of a wider tendency in Milbank's overall interpretation of history. Of course, that, in itself, for some, may not invalidate his perspective on British labour history or, indeed, his approach to the study and writing of history *per se*; but it does mean that for one to be convinced of its interpretation requires accommodating

---

[131.] J. Burns, 'The Great Strike', *New Review* 1, no. 5 (October 1889), pp. 40–82. Cited in L. McCluskey 'foreword', *The Great Dock Strike of 1889* (London: Unite the Union, 2015), p. 54. Available at .https://markwritecouk.files.wordpress .com/2018/07/the-great-dock-strike-of-1889-web-booklet11-23272.pd (accessed on 29 December 2021).

[132.] A. Thorpe, *A History of the British Labour Party*, 3rd edn (London: Palgrave Macmillan, 2008).

his novel categorisations, which are by no means immune to challenge when one examines the historical evidence. However, it is Milbank's interpretation of history, and his critique of capitalism that is so indebted to it, that has, in significant part, led him to offer alternatives to it that are summarised below.

Milbank's Blue Socialist Alternative to Capitalism

The Blue Socialist, post-liberal, civil economy alternative to capitalism that Milbank has put forward via the Blue Labour project and since[133] is premised on the following – that there needs to be much greater emphasis on *pre-distribution* over statist *redistribution*. That is, 'an attempt to produce a just economy in the first place as a major vehicle of material equity',[134] rather than by way of statist re-distribution (e.g. welfare) initiatives, as a way of mitigating the worst effects of an unjust economy. From Milbank's perspective, a greater focus on *pre-distribution* would achieve 'the removal of many people from welfare dependence – something that neo-liberal policies only *create*'.[135] Milbank thus sees the civil economy option as offering an alternative both to Keynesian redistributionist 'statism' and to neoliberal anti-redistributionism. The emphasis it places on the need for *pre-distribution* over *redistribution* is critical for grasping his perspective for bringing about a diminished need for welfare in society *per se*, as well as for a diminished welfare statist model of delivery when it is still required, in preference to a Church provided one. He succinctly lists the following six components as necessary for a civil economy alternative in an essay on the Blue Labour project:[136]

1. The sharing of risk in all financial transactions – including house mortgages – between lenders and borrowers, investors and owners, shareholders and managers, employers and employees.
2. The rewriting of company law to demand statement of social purpose and profit sharing as conditions of trading.

---

133. Milbank and Pabst, *The Politics of Virtue*, pp. 37–49, 129–76.
134. Milbank, 'The Blue Labour Dream', in Geary and Pabst (eds), *Blue Labour*, p. 32.
135. Ibid., p. 33.
136. Ibid., p. 39.

3. A new public institutional 'trust' for the pooling of technological knowledge to replace the current patenting system.
4. Ethical as well as economic negotiation of wages, prices and share values amongst owners, workers, shareholders and consumers who would all be given real political and economic stakes in every enterprise.
5. Passing through vocational training and membership of various recognised professional vocational associations, encouraging an honourable ethos, being made conditions of entry to business practice.
6. A contributory welfare system whose mutualism would preclude any need for means-testing to ensure a safety net. Such a system would again enshrine reciprocity and have the further merit of encouraging people to take greater risks in business in the knowledge that, if they failed, not all their gains would be lost.

The result is a Blue Socialist, civil economy, post-liberal alternative that would lead to an outcome that Milbank and Pabst describe as follows:

> Overwhelmingly, it ties economic profit to ethical and social purpose, and seeks to ethicise exchange. In the same spirit, it replaces the separation of risk from reward with risk and profit-sharing models. In both respects, it publicly requires an economic pursuit of honourable practice and genuine benefit rather than just abstract wealth and power. It assumes that the seemingly 'other worldly' and soul-regarding pursuit of the truly good is, in fact, in natural alignment with the various goods of concrete flourishing (work, housing, food, hygiene, health) and higher fulfilment (work satisfaction, subtle cuisine, beautiful environment, educational development) that human beings everywhere naturally seek. For this reason, it believes that the real economic task is the shared coordination of all these pursuits in terms of a 'common good'.[137]

Indeed, for Milbank, his civil economy alternative would restore a link between politics and economics that he considers has been lost in the

---

[137.] Milbank and Pabst, *The Politics of Virtue*, p. 171.

contemporary neoliberal paradigm, which acts as an impediment to restoring a sense of the Christian concept of the common good and a means of delivering it.

Clearly, this is a wide-ranging and ambitious set of proposals that has significant theo-political implications. In the next chapter these will be analysed and evaluated as they relate to Milbank's critical perspective on the Welfare State, *vis-à-vis* the voluntary sector, and the Church of England's contribution to the provision of welfare in the post-war period. However, before then, there are a number of conclusions stemming from the analysis in this chapter.

Conclusion

Milbank's perspective on the Middle Ages, the Reformation, the Church and the modern state, and Protestantism and the causes of the rise of capitalism, sits within the Christendom strand of the Anglican Socialist tradition. In this respect at least, we can see how much of his thinking is derivative, owing a lot to those who came before him, particularly Figgis and Demant. We have seen how his criticism of state-provided welfare in a liberal-capitalist context stems from his view that the Church's role in its provision has been circumscribed by the rise of the modern, secular state and its 'separation' from the Church, and, more latterly, by the state's welfare appendages. The result has been an increasing relegation of the role of the Church to that of the private sphere – a process that Milbank thinks has been compounded by Temple's theology of the state and, most specifically, his thinking on middle axioms. As we saw in chapter two, this was a view that Nicholls also held and is core to Milbank's thinking that the Church of England must abandon that approach if it is to rediscover its original purpose, which is to be the 'kingdom of God in embryo' in a re-established but contemporary vision of a Catholic Christendom for a post-liberal era. In the next chapter this perspective will be revisited when we examine Milbank's Blue Socialist vision of a post-liberal alternative role for the Church of England in the provision of welfare in the twenty-first century.

In this chapter it has been argued that Milbank's historical perspective on religion and the rise of capitalism in Western Europe is open to challenge and, in contrast to Tawney's, places too much emphasis on ideas as being the shaper of historical events. This partly reflects Milbank's post-modern unease with positivist, *a posteriori* research methodologies and his scepticism of their epistemological merits – social science being one example[138] – which is also reflected in his thinking on the writing of history, which can be located in the anti-economic determinism school. For Milbank, the writing of history can legitimately be approached, at least in part, via an *a priori* commitment to adopting a 'romantic' perspective on history, to counter what he describes as liberalism's tendency to 'rewrite history in its own image'. It does this by 'augmenting our tendencies to pursue wealth and prestige instead of human and divine love'. The result is that 'history is retrospectively understood as "horrible"'. Instead, history should be written in a way that emphasises the 'positive human good', as 'life as such depends upon a bedrock of gift-exchange and it develops in time through the astonishing and gratuitous irruption of charisms'. Thus, for Milbank: 'It follows that a romantic view of history is more realistic than a cynical one.'[139] However, as shall be evidenced in the next chapter, an *a priori* commitment to adopting a 'romantic' view of history does not always result in a convincing interpretation of history. This is a point I shall return to in chapter six.

Also, I have argued that Milbank's Blue Socialist thinking that categorises political theorists with widely divergent perspectives as liberals, largely because their thinking has been shaped by post-medieval, modernist/rationalist philosophical assumptions, is less than convincing. It does not do justice to the sophistication and divergence of their political philosophies. Four other criticisms of Milbank's Blue Socialist thinking have also been provided that are illustrative of how, on theoretical and empirical grounds, it is open to challenge. Its marginalisation of growing working-class consciousness in England, characterised by growing hostility to the emerging industrial capitalist class since the late eighteenth century, as well as to aristocratic power and privilege, does not accord with other substantial archival-based studies of the history of popular labour protest in late-eighteenth-century and nineteenth-century England, such as E.P. Thompson's study of the *Making of the English Working Class* and several others.[140] The Chartist

---

[138.] Milbank, *Theology and Social Theory*, pp. 49–101.

[139.] Milbank, 'Blue Labour, One Nation Labour and Post-liberalism', p. 6.

[140.] See, for example, E.P. Thompson, *The Making of the English Working Class* (1963) (London: Pelican, 1972); E. Hobsbawm, *Labouring Men: Studies in the History of Labour* (London: Weidenfeld & Nicolson, 1964) and *Worlds of Labour: Further Studies in the History of Labour* (London: Weidenfeld & Nicolson, 2014). See also the interesting study of Chartism by M. Chase, *Chartism: A New History* (Manchester: Manchester University Press, 2007).

struggle (1838–57) and the 1889 London Dock Strike are two examples illustrative of this point. However, the above analysis provides a platform on which we can now analyse and evaluate Milbank's perspective on the Welfare State, as well as his Blue Socialist, post-liberal perspective on the role he thinks the Church of England should perform in the provision of welfare.

Chapter Four

John Milbank's Thinking on Welfare and the Church of England's Role in its Provision since 1945

Introduction

We saw in the previous chapter how John Milbank's Christendom perspective on history is foundational to his theo-political outlook. It is hardly surprising, then, that this perspective has also shaped his critical interpretation of the impact the British Welfare State has had on the voluntary sector, and on the Church of England in the provision of welfare. Therefore, before we analyse his endorsement of the 'Big Society' project in Part Three, and the influence his thinking had on shaping the Church of England's response to it, it is necessary for us to examine whether his perspective on the history of the Welfare State *vis-à-vis* the voluntary sector providers of welfare – including the Church of England – is consistent with the historical evidence. We also need to begin to assess critically his proposed Blue Socialist, post-liberal alternative vision of the role he argues the Church of England should perform in the provision of welfare. Therefore, the analysis that follows has been structured with these two purposes in mind. It will cover:

1. Milbank's critical perspective on the history of the Welfare State, *vis-à-vis* the voluntary sector providers of welfare, and the way he feels it was at the expense of those intermediary level welfare providers, such as church organisations, and resulted in a decline in church observance and affiliation in

Britain in the post-war period that he wants to see reversed. The analysis will cover the period up to the launch of the 'Big Society' project in mid-2010 – the period since then will be covered in Part Three.

2. His Blue Socialist alternative vision of the role he argues the Church of England should perform in the provision of welfare, as central to his case for establishing a new post-liberal polity for achieving the common good in England in the twenty-first century.

Before we embark on this evaluation, however, there will be a short section that clarifies the meaning of the term 'voluntary sector' and a section on Milbank's perspective on welfare and the Church.

Voluntary Sector

A difficulty with examining the interface between the British Welfare State and the so-called voluntary sector providers of welfare is that the latter can be described in different ways. This reflects the diversity in the sector regarding, *inter alia*: size; scope of activity; funding streams; whether local, national or international; whether faith-based or secular; and whether wholly or partly reliant on volunteers (this is not an all-encompassing list). Unsurprisingly, therefore, the terminology used to describe this sector has been varied: philanthropic, voluntary, community, intermediate, non-governmental and charity being six terms in current use. New Labour governments attempted to overcome this difficulty by using the term 'Third Sector' and ascribing it to those bodies which were neither state nor market (private) sector organisations, and this is a term that John Milbank has also used.[1] However, though this term has not completely disappeared from use, it has not featured much in political language since 2010. For this study I intend to use the term voluntary sector, as this is often used by social historians.[2] It can be defined as that which encompasses not-for-profit organisations such as: social enterprises; co-operatives; charities; mutuals; faith-based groups; churches; trade unions; and a variety of pressure groups. Voluntary sector organisations can have salaried employees but are often, at least in part, staffed by

---

[1] For example, Milbank, 'The Big Society Depends on the Big Parish', p. 2.

[2] For example, G. Finlayson, *Citizen, State, and Social Welfare in Britain 1830–1990* (Oxford: Oxford University Press, 1994).

volunteers. Their funding is usually via voluntary donations or state grants and is the sector between the state and the citizen that is separate to that of the private (market) sector.

John Milbank on Welfare and the Church

We saw in chapter three how Milbank is highly critical of Temple's perspective on the liberal-capitalist state and the role Temple envisaged for the Church in relation to it. He argues:

> Temple's 'middle axioms' approach … tends to divorce goal from means and thus be content to achieve an abstract end in the impersonal utilitarian way. … Only a revived Christendom can possibly resist this, because it is only in that structure that genuine western principles of constitutional liberty and equity have been forged – and atheism has inevitably eroded them.[3]

We saw that Milbank's thinking on 'gift-exchange' as the outworking of a Catholic theology of social reciprocity is foundational to his perspective on history. Unsurprisingly, it also features in his perspective on work in a contemporary context. For Milbank, 'gift exchange or social reciprocity … would transform politics and the economy away from abstract standards and values associated with the prevailing technocratic managerialism towards the dignity of the person and human flourishing within a common polity based on a shared *ethos* of work'.[4]

[3.] J. Milbank in his reply to an analysis of his work in a write-in printed immediately below the article by C. Baker, J. Atherton and J. Reader, 'A Case of Ecclesial Over-Optimism: A Response to Milbank's Return to Christendom's Social Vision', *Political Theology Network* (23 February 2012). Available at: http://www.politicaltheology.com/blog/a-case-of-ecclesial-over-optimism-a-response-to-milbanks-return-to-christendoms-social-vision/ (accessed on 20 April 2017).

[4.] J. Milbank and A. Pabst, 'Post-liberal Politics and the Alternative of Mutualising Social Security', in N. Spencer (ed.), *The Future of Welfare: A Theos Collection* (London: Theos, 2014). Available at: https://kar.kent.ac.uk/38380/1/The%20future%20of%20welfare%20-%20a%20theos%20collection.pdf (accessed on 19 April 2017), p. 91.

We see from this quote that Milbank's perspective on work is *highly values based*, consistent with Catholic social teaching, which, as we saw, sees labour as more than merely physical space and time. Labour has to be managed in a way that is consistent with the needs of persons *as persons*, both with respect to the giver and receiver in the gift exchange. For Milbank, then, any form of organisational thinking that does not place ethical values pertaining to the dignity of the person (e.g. caring, honesty, fairness, integrity, loyalty, confidentiality, reciprocity) and a desire for human flourishing at its core cannot be Catholic, and is unlikely to foster a vocational ethos.

Unlike Temple, who saw the modern state as having a 'spiritual function' and being 'a servant and instrument of God for the preservation of justice and the promotion of human welfare',[5] Milbank thinks that the Church is better equipped than the secular Welfare State to ensure that these values are at the core of the work necessary for the delivery of welfare. This is evident in his statement: 'to imagine that the state and not the Church is the proper supplier of mercy, education and health is, quite simply, a form of practical atheism, of sheer disbelief'; rather, it is 'only religion that is likely to care for the person *as person* – as someone possessed of an immortal spirit who is therefore "more" than any collectivist whole'.[6] For Milbank, then, the secularity of the modern, liberal-capitalist state and its welfare appendages means that it is not adequately equipped to care for the person *as person*: that is, as someone possessing a spiritual dimension that defines them in a way that secular, statist modes of welfare delivery cannot adequately cater for or properly address – only the Church can do that.

What does this mean in practical terms for the Church and its role in the provision of welfare in twenty-first century England? Milbank argues that, owing to its unique parochial system that 'helps to structure and coordinate local life in diverse ways', the Church of England provides 'a ready-made platform for a great extension of such involvement in the future'.[7] However, to maximise its potential it needs:

> a shift in direction away from the Temple legacy of long reports telling the government what to do ... to a more authentic radicalism in which the church gets involved in all kinds of processes of welfare, medicine, banking, education,

---

5. Temple, *Citizen and Churchman*, p. 26.
6. Milbank, 'The Big Society Depends on the Big Parish', p. 4.
7. Milbank and Pabst, *The Politics of Virtue*, p. 238.

the arts, business, technology, ecology and more, and seeks to transform them in the joint name of reciprocity and virtue.[8]

He concludes his argument with words that outline what he believes will be the result of this radicalism for the Church: 'More than ever this is what the church now needs to do. And this may also prove the secret to increasing church attendance – for providing the consequences of Eucharistic sharing will surely lead many more to share in the Eucharist itself.'[9]

Earlier in this book I identified the historical and ideological lineage of Milbank's view, that the modern, secular, liberal-capitalist 'omnicompetent' state, with its post-war welfare appendages, had marginalised the role of the Church in the provision of welfare. One consequence of this marginalisation, according to Milbank, has been that the Church has experienced a period of considerable decline, both with respect to affiliation and observance. As he puts it:

> If Britain has become more secularised over the past century or so, it has to do with two distinct yet complementary developments: first, the expansion of both state and market in hitherto autonomous, more mutually governed areas (including education, health, welfare, the family, etc.); secondly, the retreat of the Church from its traditional involvement in these social, charitable, educational and cultural activities. Taken together, they help to explain why the economy has been progressively disembedded from society and interpersonal relationships have been subsumed under either bureaucratic processes or commercial transactions (or indeed both at once).[10]

To reverse that decline, Milbank advocates a reclaiming of lost ground by the Church in the provision of welfare, in tandem with a reduced level of state-managed provision – hence his support for the 'Big Society' project in 2010 and his call for the Church of England to embrace it.

---

8. J. Milbank, 'Christian Vision of Society Puts Economics and Politics in Their Place', ABC Religion & Ethics, 8 December 2011. Available at: https://www.abc.net.au/religion/christian-vision-of-society-puts-economics-and-politics-in-their/10100960 (accessed on 14 February 2021), pp. 1–3.
9. Ibid.
10. Milbank and Pabst, 'The Anglican Polity and the Politics of the Common Good'.

That aspect of Milbank's thought will be addressed later in this chapter. Before then, I shall offer an evaluation of Milbank's perspective on the Welfare State, *vis-à-vis* the voluntary sector, for the period from 1945 to the launch of the 'Big Society' project in mid-2010.

John Milbank, the Welfare State and the Voluntary Sector: 1945–2010

Milbank describes the Welfare State in the following terms:

> the 1945 and the 1979 welfare settlements represent two sides of the same coin: the former shifted the emphasis towards nationalisation while the latter accentuated privatisation – but both promoted impersonal universalisation and predictability. In different ways, both relied on the strong state and centralised power at the expense of intermediary institutions and popular participation. Crucially, both further fragmented mutual organisation.[11]

So, Milbank perceives the Welfare State as an entity that promotes 'impersonal universalisation and predictability'. By this he means it offers an impersonal delivery of welfare to its recipients. He further contends this is partly the result of an overly prescriptive universality in the design of its interventions, meaning that they are not always sufficiently tailored (bespoke) and holistic in their design and delivery to meet the specific needs of individuals (emotional, spiritual, as well as physical and practical), in contrast to the way he considers voluntary sector providers of welfare often are. This is a view that, to an extent, chimes with writers such as Digby Anderson, Brian Griffiths, Roger Hadley, Stephen Hatch, Ivan Illich, Immanuel Jacobovits and Jonathan Sacks (this is not an exhaustive list),[12] who have been critical of the

---

[11.] Milbank and Pabst, 'Post-liberal Politics and the Alternative', p. 90.

[12.] See D. Anderson, *Come Back Miss Nightingale: Trends in Professions Today* (London: Social Affairs Unit, 1998), B. Griffiths, *Morality and the Market Place* (London: Hodder & Stoughton, 1982), R. Hadley and S. Hatch, *Social Welfare and the Failure of the State* (London: George Allen & Unwin, 1981), I. Illich, *Limits to Medicine* (New York: Marion Boyars, 1976), Immanuel Jacobovits, *From Doom to Hope: A Jewish View of Faith in the City* (London: Office of the Chief Rabbi, 1986) and J. Sacks, 'The Jewish Community

way they perceive the rise of the Welfare State and professionalism and managerialism in state welfare provision, as prone to running counter to values such as self-reliance, responsibility, duty, localism, virtue and charity, in deference to an overreliance on the judgement of professionals, and on an impersonal state bureaucracy (as they perceive it) as the provider of welfare.

We also see from this quote that Milbank sees the British Welfare State as being 'at the expense of intermediary institutions and popular participation', having encroached on areas of activity that were previously undertaken by the voluntary sector. Crucially, he sees it, whether under Labour or Conservative administrations, as a major cause of what he describes as 'fragmented mutual organisation'. By this he means it has regrettably fragmented the intermediate level groups and organisations in British civil society that had shouldered the burden of providing welfare prior to 1945 – church welfare organisations being one example – and thus has weakened them. These concerns will be evaluated in what follows under three categories:

1. *Governmental welfare policy and its interface with the voluntary sector before the launch of the 'Big Society' project*

Governmental welfare policy is only one aspect of the history of voluntary sector provision of welfare in Britain since 1945; it does not, therefore, tell the full story. Nevertheless, it is an important part of the story, as it will throw light on whether Milbank is accurate in his criticisms of the Welfare State in relation to the impact it has had on the voluntary sector's provision of welfare. I shall therefore consider it with respect to the post-war Labour and Conservative administrations.

2. *Increased governmental financing of the voluntary sector, and the impact it had on its delivery of welfare before the launch of the 'Big Society' initiative*

Milbank argues that the Welfare State changed in character from its original intended purpose in ways that he is critical of, with a greater level of statist, governmental control over the

---

Could Not Exist for One Day Without Its Volunteers', *Daily Telegraph*, 28 October 2012.

voluntary sector evident from the 1970s onwards, stemming in part from increased state sector financing of the voluntary sector, with negative consequences on the way it has provided welfare.

3. *The alleged retarding effect that Milbank argues the British Welfare State has had on church affiliation and observance*

Milbank endorses the perspective advanced by the historian Frank Prochaska,[13] who argues that the waning of Christianity in Britain and the growth of governmental involvement in the provision of welfare were closely intertwined. It is an interpretation that is open to challenge.

Welfare Policy and the Voluntary Sector: Labour's Approach
Those, such as Milbank, who take a negative view of the post-war Labour administrations' welfare policy and its interface with the voluntary sector often quote Richard Crossman, who, in a speech delivered in 1973, lends support to this line of thinking. Crossman had been Secretary of State for Social Services from 1968 to 1970 in Harold Wilson's administration, and his recollection of Labour's approach to welfare in the post-war years was that we all 'disliked the do-good volunteer and wanted to see him replaced by professionals and trained administrators in the socialist welfare state of which we all dreamed. Philanthropy to us was an odious expression of social oligarchy and churchy bourgeois attitudes.'[14] Certainly, there is some evidence that, within the post-war Labour Party's rank and file, there existed elements that disliked the voluntary agencies, seeing them as inadequate to the task of achieving the democratic socialist society to which they aspired, and these views did not disappear overnight as a result of the creation of the Welfare State.[15] However, they were not, and never have been, the views held by a majority in the party's leadership, and historians, such as Nicholas Deakin and Justin Davis Smith, have adduced evidence to suggest that a more nuanced picture

---

[13.] See, for example, F. Prochaska, *Christianity and Social Service in Modern Britain: The Disinherited Spirit* (Oxford: Oxford University Press, 2006).

[14.] R. Crossman, 'The Role of the Volunteer in the Modern Social Service: Sidney Ball Memorial Lecture, 1973', in A.H. Halsey (ed.), *Traditions in Social Policy* (Oxford: Blackwell, 1976), pp. 259–85.

[15.] Finlayson, *Citizen, State, and Social Welfare in Britain 1830–1990*, p. 297.

of the history of Labour's post-war welfare policy and its interface with the voluntary sector to that displayed by Crossman is both necessary and defensible.[16]

In chapter one it was noted that Temple had considered the need for a balance between state sector and intermediate sector contributions to the provision of welfare, and saw them as complementary. Indeed, Temple envisaged a welfare state as becoming 'the Community of Communities – or rather the administrative organ of the community'[17] – not a replacement for the community. From Temple's perspective, then, there was no reason why state and voluntary sector provision of welfare could not coexist and be mutually advantageous. The same view was also held by Beveridge, whose work of 1948, *Voluntary Action*, makes clear.[18] This report primarily concerned itself with two themes. One was to recognise and promote the value of philanthropic organisations and their contribution to making life better for the less fortunate in society, such as unmarried mothers, prisoners, the disabled, and in support of national heritage, the arts and the environment. This was something that Attlee's welfare state policies had neither discouraged nor impeded but had done little to actively promote. The other was to argue for more of what Beveridge called 'mutual aid'. Mutual aid was what he described as 'consciousness of common need' that 'leads to combined action to meet that need, to helping oneself and one's fellows together'.[19] For Beveridge, the mechanisms for delivering mutual aid were organisations such as friendly societies, co-operatives, trade unions, housing societies, social clubs, trustee savings banks and churches (this is not an exhaustive list). Yet, although it is a report that had nowhere near as much influence on the shaping of events as his 1942 report, it nevertheless has more recently been reappraised, with one contemporary biographer of Beveridge arguing that it became a blueprint for what happened after 1948, with the emergence of partnerships between government and the voluntary sector into the

---

16. N. Deakin and J. Davis Smith, 'Labour, Charity and Voluntary Action', in M. Hilton and J. McKay (eds), *The Ages of Voluntarism: How We Got to the Big Society* (Oxford: Oxford University Press, 2011), pp. 69–93.

17. Temple, *Christianity and Social Order*, pp. 70–71.

18. W.H. Beveridge, *Voluntary Action: A Report on Methods of Social Advance* (London: George Allen & Unwin, 1948).

19. W.H. Beveridge and J. Beveridge, *On and Off the Platform* (Wellington, New Zealand: Hicks, Smith & Right, 1949), p. 64.

twenty-first century.[20] Therefore, we shall examine more closely the historical record to gauge whether this was indeed the case, as it would cast doubt on Milbank's interpretation of the history of the Welfare State *vis-à-vis* the voluntary sector.

The Attlee Administration (1945–51) and the Voluntary Sector

We noted in chapter two that Beveridge disagreed strongly with Attlee over the way his administration had weakened the place of the friendly societies, in contravention to his 1942 report which had argued for the preservation of the role they had performed in the administration of state benefits to those who were sick[21] – something that, under Attlee, had been transferred to a government department. Yet, Clement Attlee had stated in 1937: 'I conceive that in the socialist state there will be, besides the democratic framework of the state and of industry, a great variety of voluntary societies controlled by the members, wherein all the time a training in democracy will be taking place.'[22] Moreover, he reconfirmed this thinking in a speech he made in 1947:

> Alongside everything done by the local authority and by the state there are people who want to do a bit more. ... This country will never become a people of an exclusive and omnicompetent State. ... I believe that we shall always have alongside the great range of public services, the voluntary services which humanise our national life and bring it down from the general to the particular. We must keep stretching out to new horizons.[23]

This view was wholly consistent with that held by Herbert Morrison, his Deputy Prime Minister, who, in a speech made to the London Council of Social Service, stated:

[20.] J. Harris, 'Voluntarism, the State and Public-Private Partnerships in Beveridge's Social Thought', pp. 9–20.

[21.] See Oppenheimer and Deakin (eds), *Beveridge and Voluntary Action*, p. 2.

[22.] C.R. Attlee, *The Labour Party in Perspective* (London: Left Book Club, 1937), p. 151.

[23.] Cited in Finlayson, *Citizen, State and Social Welfare in Britain 1830–1990*, p. 281.

> There are certain services, which, because they are or should
> be universal, are the special responsibility of the statutory
> authorities. At the other extreme are what might be called
> the 'unique' activities of associations and concerns. ... In
> between are a great variety of other services where statutory
> and voluntary effort can co-operate effectively.[24]

It is clear, therefore, that, despite taking a different approach to Beveridge
on the friendly societies (i.e. in their view, the societies should not have
a role in the distribution of state benefits), neither Attlee nor Morrison
were ideologically opposed to the voluntary sector playing an important
role in the provision of welfare in tandem with the state sector, and there
is evidence of it doing that during the period of Attlee's time in office.

For example, Aneurin Bevan, Minister for Health in Attlee's
administration, told Parliament in 1947 that the government was
committed to 'extending the field of voluntary work enormously'.[25]
Thus, whilst it was the case that, after 1948, state-run hospitals and
community-based healthcare services in the NHS relied less on voluntary
sector funding for the delivery of patient care, this did not exclude
volunteers from playing an important role in the NHS, or in voluntary
organisations working in the field of health care and well-being, then
or since. There are plenty of examples of this. During the period of the
Attlee administration, the charity MIND (as it is now called) was formed
in 1946 to campaign for the interests of the mentally ill, often working
closely with the NHS in the shaping of thinking in this sphere of health
care. In the same year MENCAP was founded to promote the interests
of children with learning disabilities across the health and education
sectors. In the following year the National Corporation for the Care
of Old People (later renamed as the Centre for Policy on Ageing) was
founded to promote the interests and physical and mental well-being of
old people, including their interface with state sector provision of health
care and social services. Cruse Bereavement Care was established in
1950 and became a leading organisation in Britain in the provision of
counselling support and bereavement advice in the years that followed.
While the newly established NHS took over the former Marie Curie
Cancer Hospital in London, in the years that followed Marie Curie

---

[24.] Cited in Finlayson, *Citizen, State and Social Welfare in Britain 1830–1990*,
p. 281.

[25.] Cited in Deakin and Davis Smith, 'Labour, Charity and Voluntary Action',
p. 82.

Cancer Care grew into a major healthcare support charity for those experiencing cancer, sometimes funding Macmillan nurses who were directly managed by NHS healthcare providers. Charitable trusts such as the Nuffield (founded in 1939) also continued to provide indirect support to the NHS sector from 1948 onwards through a range of developmental projects – a trend that was to continue in the decades since, via voluntary sector organisations such as the British Heart Foundation (1961) and the British Lung Foundation (1985). This was wholly consistent with a 1946 report from the Ministry of Education recommending an expansion of community centres to augment the provision of further education[26] and the National Health Service Act 1946 and the National Assistance Act 1948, which provided the legal framework for the state sector to utilise the voluntary sector to meet some of its statutory obligations.[27]

These are just a few examples of voluntary sector provision of health and well-being services under the Attlee administration, of the state and voluntary sector working in tandem, and in ways that were complementary, in the fields of mental and physical healthcare delivery.[28] Indicative of this trend was a debate that took place in the House of Lords on 22 June 1949, described at the time by the National Council for Social Service as one 'of great significance for voluntary organisations'.[29] It considered Beveridge's report, *Voluntary Action*, and Lord Pakenham, summarising the government's position, stated: 'We consider that the voluntary spirit is the very lifeblood of democracy' and we are 'convinced that voluntary associations have rendered, are rendering, and must be encouraged to continue to render, great and indispensable service to the community'.[30] Also indicative of this trend was that government grants to a variety of voluntary agencies in 1946/47 totalled ten million pounds; a sizeable sum at that time,[31] and this was to increase further in the years that followed.

[26.] See J. Davis Smith, *100 Years of NCVO and Voluntary Action: Idealists and Realists* (London: Palgrave Macmillan, 2019), p. 103.

[27.] Finlayson, *Citizen, State and Social Welfare in Britain 1830–1990*, p. 280.

[28.] M. Hilton, N. Crowson, J.-F. Mouhot and J. McKay, *Historical Guide to NGOs in Britain: Charities, Civil Society and the Voluntary Sector since 1945* (Basingstoke: Palgrave Macmillan, 2012) p. 34.

[29.] National Council of Social Service's Annual Report 1948–49, p. 8, cited in Davis Smith, *100 Years of NCVO and Voluntary Action*, p. 104.

[30.] *Hansard*, HL Deb, (Series 5), 22 June 1949, Vol. 163, col. 119, cited in Davis Smith, *100 Years of NCVO and Voluntary Action*, p. 104.

[31.] Finlayson, *Citizen and Social Welfare in Britain 1830–1990*, p. 280.

The Wilson Administration (1964–70), the Wilson/Callaghan Administration (1974–79) and the Voluntary Sector

Labour's periods in power from 1964 to 1970 and 1974 to 1979 provide evidence of a similar trend. These governments presided over an expansion of the Welfare State, particularly in the areas of health and education. However, they also coincided with the emergence of other influential voluntary sector providers in the field of welfare, as evidenced, for example, by the *Report of the Committee on Local Authority and Allied Personal Social Services* of 1968, which found that '11,000 of the 95,000 elderly people in local authority residential care in 1967 were housed by voluntary organisations working in partnership with local authorities, and that there were approximately 7,000 social clubs for the elderly, mostly being run by voluntary organisations'.[32] Under the Wilson and Wilson/Callaghan administrations, the voluntary sector expanded. Charities such the Child Poverty Action Group (1965), the Disability Income Group (1965), Shelter (1966), the National Association for the Care and Resettlement of Offenders (1966) and Crisis (1967) were founded. Indeed, according to one estimate, by the end of the 1970s 'there were 42 groups in existence which could be defined as belonging to the poverty lobby', which has been perceived as 'those on the political left losing patience with the Labour Party'.[33] This is suggestive of a trend that, according to Rodney Lowe's extensive study, *The Welfare State in Britain since 1945*, had led to a situation where: 'The major national charities had also expanded so fast that by 1976 they were employing a permanent staff which was equivalent in size to one-fifth of that working for the social services departments. It was equally well trained.'[34]

Harold Wilson had argued in 1975 that the role of voluntary organisations was seen by Labour as 'not just a useful adjunct to government services but seen as fundamental and irreplaceable. ... It is a recognition of the distinct, indispensable and socially invaluable role that the voluntary organisations now play in tackling social problems and creating a better society.'[35] Consistent with this had been the creation, in 1974, of the community health councils, with one third of the members being nominated by voluntary organisations. They were

---

[32.] *Report of the Committee on Local Authority and Allied Personal Social Services* (London: HMSO, 1968), pp. 150, 257 and 451.

[33.] Hilton, Crowson, Mouhot and McKay, *Historical Guide to NGOs*, p. 39.

[34.] Cited by Lowe, *The Welfare State in Britain since 1945*, p. 290.

[35.] H. Wilson, *Social Services Quarterly*, Winter 1975. Cited in Deakin and Davis Smith, 'Labour, Charity and Voluntary Action', p. 88.

established to ensure that the voice of patients was being sufficiently heard within health service administration, the aim being to make the NHS more responsive to the community it serves. In 1975, the Wilson government established the Joint Funding Scheme (JFS). The scheme brought in co-funding (of up to 50 per cent) of new initiatives submitted by British charities, particularly those with an international remit and focused on helping the poorest in society.[36] Under the Wilson/Callaghan administration, Merlyn Rees, the Home Secretary between 1976 and 1979, argued in a speech to the Royal Commission on the National Health Service:

> The special role of the voluntary organisations in a democratic society is to complement the statutory services and to adapt and apply them to individual cases: to innovate and experiment; and, in all that is done, to provide an opportunity for self-development and an outlet for that spirit of altruism which is essential to the well-being and happiness of society.[37]

And at the end of the Wilson/Callaghan administration in 1979, the *Report of the Royal Commission on the National Health Service*, provided evidence of 'the unique and varied contribution made by the volunteers to the NHS' and concluded that this was 'of major benefit to the service'.[38] This historical evidence runs counter to a view that the leadership of the Labour Party in the 1970s was hostile to the idea of the voluntary sector playing an important role in the provision of welfare, as an important complementary level of provision to that being provided by the state. On the contrary, the Labour leadership was supportive of the role it was providing in the provision of welfare and recognised the value of the special contribution this sector can provide in the overall welfare mix.

The Welfare State, then, both with respect to its scope and responsibilities, had substantially increased since 1945; but so, too, had the role of the voluntary sector in the provision of welfare and

---

[36.] For more on this, see M. Hilton, N. Crowson, J.-F. Mouhot and J. McKay, *The Politics of Expertise: How NGOs Shaped Modern Britain* (Oxford: Oxford University Press, 2013), p. 204.

[37.] Cited in M. Brenton, *The Voluntary Sector in British Social Services* (London: Longman, 1985), pp. 138–39.

[38.] *Report of the Royal Commission on the National Health Service*, Cmnd 7615 (London: HMSO, 1979), cited by Finlayson, *Citizen, State and Social Welfare in Britain 1830–1990*, p. 307.

related areas of activity, as evidenced by the rise in the number of registered charities in Britain. Their number had increased from c. 56,000 in 1948 to c. 120,000 by 1978, a trend that was to continue, reaching c. 180,000 by 2008;[39] the total income of registered charities had also increased, from £12 billion in 1970 to over £50 billion by 2008, with the total assets held by 'general charities' having tripled from £30 billion in 1980 to around £100 billion by 2008.[40] This recognition of the beneficial effects of the interdependence of government and voluntary sector provision was subsequently and unambiguously acknowledged by the Labour Party in its policy document of 1992, *Building Bridges: Labour and the Voluntary Sector*: 'The inter-dependence of government and the voluntary sector is an established aspect of British society and is warmly welcomed by the Labour Party. ... We do not believe that voluntary activity is either a threat, or a cheap alternative to the provision of statutory services.'[41]

'New Labour' and the Voluntary Sector

Consistent with this thinking, the Labour Party's policy document of 1997, *Building the Future Together*, significantly subtitled, *Labour's Policies for Partnership between Government and the Voluntary Sector*, reinforced this thinking, arguing for a proposed compact (essentially a formal agreement) between the public and voluntary sector.[42] In the introduction to the finalised compact in 1998, Tony Blair explained the government's mission to support voluntary and community organisations: 'They enable individuals to contribute to the development of their communities. By so doing they promote citizenship, help to re-establish a sense of community and make a crucial contribution to our aim of a just and inclusive society.'[43] These compacts were later

---

[39] Cited in Hilton, Crowson, Mouhot & McKay, *Historical Guide to NGOs*, p. 25.

[40] Ibid., p. 31.

[41] Labour Party, *Building Bridges: Labour and the Voluntary Sector* (London: Labour Party, 1992). Cited in Deakin and Davis Smith, 'Labour, Charity and Voluntary Action', p. 91.

[42] Labour Party, *Building the Future Together: Labour's Policies for Partnership between Government and the Voluntary Sector* (London: Labour Party, 1997). Cited in Deakin and Davis Smith, 'Labour, Charity and Voluntary Action', p. 91.

[43] Cited in P. Alcock, *Partnership and Mainstreaming: Voluntary Action under New Labour*, Third Sector Research Centre, 2010, Working Paper 32.

implemented across the majority of local authorities and across the NHS and other national bodies.[44]

This positive view of the role played by voluntary sector organisations in the provision of welfare held by Blair and by Gordon Brown[45] is reflected in other initiatives. For example, the work of the Active Community Unit (later to become the Active Communities Directorate) that was established in 2001 within the Home Office, with a state grant of £300 million to spend over a three-year period,[46] was specifically intended to promote community action that would enhance and embolden state provision of welfare. The result of these kinds of initiatives was reflected in the Home Office citizenship survey of 2003, which reported: '62 per cent of people had volunteered informally (as individuals) at least once in the twelve months before interview. The proportion who had provided help at least once a month was considerably smaller (37%). In numerical terms, these proportions are equivalent to 26.4 and 15.6 million people in England and Wales.'[47]

From these initiatives the Office of the Third Sector was created in 2006, based within the Cabinet Office and with a Minister for the Third Sector. The upshot of these initiatives, according to a National Council for Voluntary Organisations (NCVO) report of 2009, was that income for charities (these only a part of the wider voluntary sector range of providers) over the period from 2000 to 2007, had increased from £24.2 billion to £33.3 billion, with around 31 per cent of this from statutory sources.[48] In 2001 the Blair administration also created the Social Enterprise Unit (SEU) to provide support and co-ordination

---

University of Birmingham. Available as a pdf download at http://epapers .bham.ac.uk/793/ (accessed on 1 January 2022), p.13.

44. See ibid., p. 9.

45. Brown had argued a need for 'Transformation of the Third Sector to rival the market and the state, with a quiet revolution in how voluntary action and charitable work serves the community'. See G. Brown, Speech to the NCVO Annual Conference, February 2004. Cited by Alcock, *Partnership and Mainstreaming*, p. 6.

46. See ibid.

47. U.K. Government, Home Office Citizenship Survey: People, Families and Communities (2003). Published by Home Office Research, Development and Statistics Directorate (2004). Available as a PDF download at https:// dera.ioe.ac.uk//7943/ (accessed 1 January 2022), p. 175.

48. Cited in P. Alcock, 'Voluntary Action, New Labour and the "Third Sector"', in Hilton and McKay (eds), *The Ages of Voluntarism*, p. 173.

for social enterprises – newly emerging non-profit organisations in the voluntary sector with social and environmental purposes. It also established the Futurebuilders Fund in 2005, initially with a state grant of £125 million over three years but later increased in 2008 to £215 million over three years, specifically to provide loans or grants to the voluntary sector to help equip it to bid for public funding.[49] Thus, rather than attempting to diminish the voluntary sector in favour of statist provision, as has been argued by Milbank, we see partnership between state and voluntary sector becoming the term that could be used to describe this approach.[50]

Having briefly examined the post-war Labour administrations' welfare policy towards the voluntary sector up to 2010, it is now necessary similarly to examine the relationship between the post-war Conservative administrations and the voluntary sector.

Welfare Policy and the Voluntary Sector: The Conservative's Approach

Owing to the 'Butskellite' welfare consensus discussed in chapter two, there was little if any significant change in policy direction on the voluntary sector and the Welfare State under the Conservative administrations of Churchill/Eden (1951–55), Eden/Macmillan (1955–59) and Macmillan/Home (1959–64). The voluntary sector continued to expand, most notably with the founding of the Samaritans (1953), the Spastics Society (1953), the British Heart Foundation (1961) and Help the Aged (1961), whilst state welfare provision also increased. Significantly, Madeline Rooff's audit of voluntary sector provision published in 1955 supports this interpretation, concluding that the voluntary sector was well embedded in the fabric of British society in the three areas of policy her review examined: services for the blind, maternity and child welfare, and mental health services. However, she did note that the voluntary services were increasingly reliant on the priorities laid down by public authorities in the shaping of their remit.[51] This trend was later to continue under the administration of Edward Heath (1970–74).

[49.] Cited by Alcock, *Partnership and Mainstreaming*, p. 10.

[50.] For an interesting discussion of this, see Harris, 'Voluntarism, the State and the Public-Private Partnerships'.

[51.] M. Rooff, *Voluntary Societies and Social Policy* (London: Routledge & Kegan Paul, 1957), p. 260.

The Conservative Party Manifesto of 1970 stated: 'We recognise the important contribution to social welfare that volunteers and voluntary organisations are already making, and we believe there is scope for considerable expansion and development.'[52] This was consistent with the wording in a Conservative Party publication of 1970 that stated it was 'convinced that many of the social problems that now scar society can only be solved through a genuine partnership of effort between statutory and voluntary organisations'.[53] The manifesto commitment was followed up in a speech made by the new prime minister in 1971, when he confirmed an increase in state grants to the voluntary social services sector of 'an extra £3.5 million ... over the next four years'.[54] In 1972 Heath established within the Home Office a dedicated body for co-ordinating the voluntary sector contribution to welfare provision called the Voluntary Services Unit (VSU) and government funding for the voluntary sector increased sharply. We shall see below how this approach considerably increased the level of state funding of sections of the voluntary sector, a trend that was continued under the Thatcher and New Labour administrations, with consequences for the relationship between the two.

The Thatcher Administration and the Voluntary Sector
With the election of Margaret Thatcher's government in 1979, however, there was a change of direction. Her administration became committed to encouraging an even greater input from the voluntary sector in areas of welfare, suspicious of the costly, 'socialist' welfare state and its collectivist underpinning, and committed to reducing it, influenced by the New Right ideology discussed in chapter two. Hence, her government was to put greater financial investment into the voluntary sector.[55] Her vision on the merits of volunteering was set out in a speech she made to the WRVS

---

52. The Conservative Party Manifesto of 1970, available at: http://www .conservativemanifesto.com/1970/1970-conservative-manifesto.shtml. Cited by Finlayson, *Citizen, State and Social Welfare in Britain 1830–1990*, p. 307.

53. Conservative Party, *A Better Tomorrow* (London: Conservative Central Office, 1970). Cited in Hilton, Crowson, Mouhot and McKay, *The Politics of Expertise*, p. 192.

54. P. Healy, 'Extra £3.5m in Grants for Voluntary Services over the Next Four Years, *The Times*, 9 December 1971.

55. E. Filby, 'Faith, Charity and Citizenship', in Hilton and McKay (eds), *The Ages of Voluntarism*, p. 146.

in 1981: 'The volunteer movement is at the heart of our social welfare provision.' Her view was that: 'The willingness of men and women to give service is one of freedom's greatest safeguards. It ensures that caring remains free from political control.'[56] In Thatcher's first term there were some cuts to state welfare provision that engendered strong opposition from the churches and elements of the voluntary sector, including the abolition of earnings-related supplements to unemployment and sickness benefits. By the mid-1980s, with over three million unemployed, there was also a shift in direction via a policy introduced in 1986 called Restart, that required those on benefits to work or retrain (something that the New Labour administration under Blair later further developed in the form of the 1997 'New Deal' initiative).[57] Yet, there were examples of novel ways in which the state sector worked with the voluntary sector, one being to help the unemployed find a route back into work.

The Opportunities for Volunteering Programme, for example, administered by the Department of Health and Social Security, enabled the unemployed to undertake short-term unpaid work experience placements with charities and other voluntary providers. Another was the Voluntary Projects Programme administered by the Manpower Services Commission (MSC) that focused on providing opportunities for the long-term unemployed to undertake locally-based community project work. Under this programme there were numerous examples of church/MSC-sponsored initiatives established to try to help the unemployed find work, with government providing participants with a modest living allowance in return for their participation. For example, the MSC-funded Hartlepool Churches Unemployment Programme enabled 70 of the locally unemployed to undertake courses in areas such as car maintenance, photography and computing to help them find work.[58] Another example was in Skelmersdale, Lancashire, called the Liverpool RC Archdiocese

---

56. M. Thatcher, 'Facing the New Challenge'. Speech delivered on 19 January 1981 to the Women's Royal Voluntary Service National Conference. Available at: http://www.margaretthatcher.org/document/104551 (accessed on 18 April 2017).

57. For more on the Restart programme, see D. Price, *Office of Hope: A History of the Public Employment Service in Great Britain, 1910–97* (London: Policy Studies Institute, 2000), pp. 241–57.

58. F. Scuffham, 'foreword', *Action on Unemployment: 100 Projects with Unemployed People* (London: Church Action with the Unemployed, 1984), p. 25. Produced by the National Extension College Trust Ltd., ISBN 0860824705.

Community Services Agency which began in 1982 and had oversight of 25 project areas with c. 500 participant workers. These were involved in environmental work, clearing wasteland and improving gardens for senior citizens, working with the disabled, and also training workers in fields of sewing, clerical skills, retail and distribution, and hairdressing, and many training options for the unemployed to access.[59] A third example was one in Avonmouth called the Bristol Churches Community Programme, which ran courses for over 600 of the unemployed at any one time across 21 different community-based projects, often with an 'outward-bound' emphasis.[60] These are just three examples of over one hundred projects documented in *Action on Unemployment*. The result of these and other such 'Active Citizen' initiatives was that state investment in non-governmental agencies significantly increased; state support to the Urban Programme rose from £18 million to £76 million between 1980 and 1986.[61] Thatcher remained a keen supporter of the voluntary sector throughout her premiership, as evidenced by the White Paper she introduced in 1989, *Charities: A Framework for the Future*, which stated that her government was committed:

> to encouraging a healthy and growing voluntary sector. The impulse to help others in need or distress, or to join with them for some common purpose, is deeply rooted in human nature. Joining in voluntary activity helps to create a sense of belonging and of community, at home, in the workplace or at recreation. For many people engaging in voluntary activity is a most important way for people to make a positive contribution to the community and have an influence on it.[62]

It was a perspective on the value of the voluntary sector in the provision of welfare that her successor was also to embrace.

[59.] Ibid., p. 68.

[60.] Ibid., p. 13.

[61.] Filby, 'Faith, Charity and Citizenship', p. 140. There was, however, some criticism in the churches that the MSC-funded schemes came to a rather abrupt end, as a result of funding streams not being renewed. See, for example, F. Davis, E. Paulhus and A. Bradstock, *Moral, But No Compass: Government, Church and the Future of Welfare* (Chelmsford: Matthew James Publishing, 2008), p. 22.

[62.] *Charities: A Framework for the Future*, Cmnd 694 (London: HMSO, 1989), para. 1.3. Cited in Finlayson, *Church, State and Social Welfare in Britain 1830–1990*, p. 360.

The Major Administration and the Voluntary Sector

The administration led by John Major (1990–97) was also enthusiastic about 'Active Citizenship', reflected in a speech he gave to business organisations involved in charity work: 'People want a more responsible society – a less selfish society. I want you to come with us as partners as we spread the message of social responsibility and responsible capitalism.'[63] In the same speech he reported:

> Volunteers give a range of support in a vast range of areas. In the Health Service 60,000 volunteers have been recruited under the Department of Health opportunity for volunteering scheme; a further 60,000 work on over 2,000 conservation projects across the nation; and there are 2,000 or so volunteers abroad in support of development projects. Thousands more work in social service.

Under John Major's premiership, the Make a Difference initiative was launched in 1994. It was described in a Home Office document as: 'an integrated approach to increasing individual involvement in the community' with a stated aim to 'make it easier for people to volunteer' and to 'involve volunteers in a wider variety of activities which benefit both themselves and their communities'.[64] It had its own dedicated Make a Difference Team that was tasked with devising a strategy for expanding the contribution that volunteers could make to their communities. The result was a series of measures that included the setting up of a telephone line to publicise volunteering, plans to increase volunteering opportunities for young people, and the funding of 70 new locally-based volunteer development agencies (LVDAs), as well as the setting up of a new England-wide body, the Volunteering Partnership, to provide a consultancy/advisory provision to government on volunteering issues.[65] The initiative did not achieve all of its aims, with only limited take-up of the telephone helpline, for example. However, it did lay the groundwork

---

[63.] J. Major, Speech to business leaders involved in charity work in October, 1993. Cited in J. D. Smith, C. Rochester and R. Hedley (eds), *An Introduction to the Voluntary Sector* (London: Routledge, 2005), p. 123.

[64.] Cited in J.D. Smith, 'Volunteers: Making a Difference', in M. Harris and C. Rochester (eds), *Voluntary Organisations and Social Policy in Britain: Perspectives on Change and Choice* (Basingstoke: Palgrave, 2001), p. 187.

[65.] For more on this, see ibid.

for further initiatives that were later pursued by the Blair governments, and which were, in some respects, more successful. Major's support for volunteering was also symbolically reflected in the way he brought about greater recognition for volunteers in the Queen's honours list. Hence, under the Thatcher administration, and later under the administration of Major, the voluntary sector in Britain expanded and often worked in unison with government departments such as the DHSS and the Manpower Services Commission. Far from being a period of decline, the post-war voluntary sector grew and adapted to the increased statutory provision of welfare, seeking opportunities to complement it wherever they could be found.

In Summary

This historical analysis of the Labour and Conservative administrations' welfare policy interface with the voluntary sector from 1945 to 2010 demonstrates that Milbank's negative view of the impact the Welfare State had on that sector is open to challenge. There is compelling historical evidence that none of these administrations was hostile to voluntary sector involvement in the provision of welfare. Indeed, the opposite was the case, with numerous examples of creative interface between the Welfare State and the voluntary sector.[66] Moreover, government statistics relating to the period immediately prior to the launch of the 'Big Society' initiative in the summer of 2010, portray a picture of continued vibrancy in the voluntary sector *per se* (hence not just those confined to welfare provision). The National Citizenship Survey for England 2009–10, reveals that 40 per cent of adults had 'formally' volunteered within the previous twelve months (that is, had taken part in some organised voluntary activity), 25 per cent at least once a month, compared with 27 per cent when the survey was first undertaken in 2001.[67] However, perhaps of even more significance for our analysis is that, using the widest definitions of the non-governmental organisations operating in the sector covering all forms of associational life, the NCVO, in 2010, estimated there to be approximately 900,000 such organisations all over Britain, going from the tiny, local and informal to

---

[66.] For more examples, see J. Davis Smith, C. Rochester and R. Hedley (eds), *An Introduction to the Voluntary Sector* (London: Routledge, 1995).

[67.] P. Thane, 'There has always been a "Big Society"', *History Workshop*, 30 April 2011. Available at: http://www.historyworkshop.org.uk/there-has -always-been-a-big-society (accessed on 10 April 2017).

the huge and highly organised.[68] This is indicative of a high amount of intermediary level activity between the state and the citizen, in contrast to the picture Milbank paints of the British Welfare State being: 'at the expense of intermediary institutions and popular participation' and the cause of 'fragmented mutual organisation'.[69] There is considerable historical evidence, then, to support a view that a 'Big Society' existed in Britain before the launch of the 'Big Society' project by the Cameron administration in 2010.

A 'Big Society' before the 'Big Society' Project

The 'Big Society' that existed in Britain before the launch of the 'Big Society' project was different from what it had been in 1945. The voluntary sector experienced a considerable amount of change in the intervening period, with some sectors experiencing decline and others expansion. Between 1942 and 1979, for example, trade union membership in Britain increased from eight million to over thirteen million,[70] an example of an intermediary level 'grouping' that thrived within an expanding Welfare State. The reasons for the subsequent decline in its membership to c. 6.5 million by 2008 are complex and multifaceted, including the near collapse in coal mining, major contractions in the manufacturing industries and the shrinkage of the steel industry since the 1980s, and increased legal restrictions placed on unions embarking on industrial action. However, the previous period of growth in membership suggests its decline after 1979 is unlikely to be as a consequence of the Welfare State. Likewise, the demutualisation that occurred in the mid-1980s of a large part of the building societies sector (it being one intermediate level 'grouping' in British civil society that was separate from the public and private sectors), with several of the biggest names on the high street converting to banks, was a result of the 'Big Bang' legislation of 1986

[68.] M. Hilton, 'Charities, Voluntary Organisations and Non-Governmental Organisations in Britain since 1945', in A. Ishkanian and S. Szreter (eds), *The Big Society Debate: A New Agenda for Social Welfare* (Cheltenham: Edward Elgar, 2012), p. 82. In 2007 the *Civil Society Almanac*, compiled by the NCVO, had put this figure at 870,000. See Alcock, 'Voluntary Action, New Labour and the "Third Sector"', p. 159.

[69.] Milbank and Pabst, 'Post-liberal Politics and the Alternative', p. 90.

[70.] Cited in Hilton, Crowson, Mouhot and McKay, *A Historical Guide to NGOs*, p. 24.

that allowed building societies to demutualise if they could get sufficient support from their member owners.[71] It had nothing to do with the Welfare State and government policy towards it.

Another key change was the decline in membership of traditional women's organisations as more women entered paid employment. The Mothers' Union membership, for example, dropped from 538,000 in the 1930s to 98,000 by 2009.[72] Nonetheless, at the same time there was a considerable expansion in the number of voluntary sector organisations active in other areas. For example, the membership of environmental organisations (e.g. Friends of the Earth, Greenpeace and the World Wildlife Fund) increased from roughly half a million in 1971 to nearly seven million by 2008.[73] Seen in the round, change rather than decline is the term best able to describe these trends. Certainly, in *relative* terms, between 1945 and 2010, the Welfare State assumed more of the burden of meeting the expanding welfare challenges than did the voluntary sector. However, in *absolute* terms both saw an overall expansion in their activities. This historical evidence does not, therefore, lend support to Milbank's view that the post-war Welfare State 'fragmented mutual organisation' and was 'at the expense of intermediary institutions', at least with respect to their numbers, size and resourcing. Nevertheless, in the post-war period some sections of the voluntary sector changed in character in ways that Milbank dislikes, and which we now address.

'Should the Salt of the Earth Be Managed?'

John Milbank is critical of the way the Welfare State has developed beyond what he thinks was its original purpose:

> To begin with, the British welfare state was understood as a mutual insurance compact against the worst natural and social threats to human survival and flourishing. But in time it has come to be dominated by its other genealogical route, which is the originally Prussian [Hegelian] desire for more efficient and quasi-military management of civilian populations.[74]

[71.] See the Building Societies Act 1986 and the Banking Act 1987.

[72.] Hilton, 'Charities, Voluntary Organisations and Non-Governmental Organisations', p. 81.

[73.] Hilton, Crowson, Mouhot and McKay, *Historical Guide to NGOs*, p. 289.

[74.] Milbank and Pabst, 'Post-Liberal Politics and the Alternative', p. 90.

One aspect of his concern is the way that governments, especially since the early 1970s, have increased the amount of state financing of the voluntary sector, resulting in increased levels of state influence over it. He perceives this as having altered its character in ways he considers are regrettable, diminishing its level of decision-making autonomy and flexibility of response via the incorporation of contract-based commissioning of services from the state sector, that have often been highly prescriptive in character. Influenced by the writings of Ivan Illich,[75] who wrote about what he called the state institutionalisation of charity which turns it into bureaucracy, Milbank sees these developments as an example of the way in which 'Mechanism has displaced the just pursuit of the common good'.[76] Influenced also by the writings of the historian Frank Prochaska, he argues: 'One can fear, with Prochaska, that if much of the money for charities comes from state provision that they will fall under bureaucratic control.'[77]

The establishment of the Voluntary Services Unit (VSU) by Heath's government is often cited as the start of this trend, though there were some signs of it before then.[78] Influenced by the work of the Aves Committee of 1969[79] that examined the role of the volunteer in social services and called for additional support to be made available for the training of volunteers and the co-ordination of these services, Heath was keen for his government to play a part in supporting that aspiration. The VSU was established to enhance the links between government departments and voluntary organisations to maximise the impact the voluntary sector could play in the delivery of welfare services. There was also a significant increase in government grants to voluntary organisations. The Wolfenden Committee Report of 1978 shows that government funding of the voluntary sector increased from £19.2 million in 1974/75 to £35.4 million by 1976/77.[80] Grants distributed by the VSU to

---

[75] Ivan Illich, *Disabling Professions* (1997) (London: Marion Boyars, 2005). See the reference to Illich in Milbank, 'Can the Market Be Moral?', p. 5.

[76] Ibid.

[77] Milbank, 'The Big Society Depends on the Big Parish', p. 4.

[78] See Hilton, Crowson, Mouhot and McKay, *Historical Guide to NGOs*, p. 303.

[79] G.M. Aves, *The Voluntary Worker in the Social Services*, Report of a committee jointly set up by the National Council of Social Service and the National Institute for Social Work Training, under the chairmanship of Geraldine M. Aves (London: Allen & Unwin, 1969).

[80] J. Wolfenden, *The Future of Voluntary Organisations: Report of the Wolfenden Committee* (London: Croom Helm, 1978), p. 255.

the voluntary sector between 1974 and 1986 also reflect this trajectory, increasing from £833,445 for 1974/75 to £17,110,140 in 1984/85; and grants distributed by the Home Office (including through the VSU) increased from c. £1.6 million in 1972 to c. £103 million by 1994.[81] A substantial amount of academic work has been undertaken on the implications that this increased state funding of sections of the voluntary sector in Britain had on their character.[82] A summary of the key findings of these academic studies is as follows:

1. The voluntary sector organisations increased in size and scale of operation.[83]
2. They became more bureaucratic and complex in their structures and contracting arrangements with government, both central and local.[84]
3. They became more result orientated, mindful of the need to meet the contract specifications that came with the state funding.[85]

[81.] Hilton, Crowson, Mouhot and McKay, *Historical Guide to NGOs*, pp. 304, 306.

[82.] See D. Billis and M. Harris, *The Challenge of Change in Local Voluntary Agencies*, Working Paper 11 (London: Centre for Voluntary Organisations, London School of Economics, 1992); R. Butler and D. Wilson, *Managing Voluntary and Non-Profit Organisations: Strategy and Structures* (London: Routledge, 1990); T. Darlington, *Management Learning and Voluntary Organisations* (London: National Council for Voluntary Organisations, 1989); A. David and K. Edwards, *Twelve Charity Contracts: Case Studies of Funding Contracts Between Charities and Local Authorities and Other Bodies* (London: Directory of Social Change, 1990); Hilton, Crowson, Mouhot and McKay, *The Politics of Expertise*; Hilton, Crowson, Mouhot and McKay, *Historical Guide to NGOs*; R.M. Kramer, 'Change and Continuity in British Voluntary Organisations 1976–1988', *Voluntas* 1, no. 2 (1990), pp. 33–59; S. Kuhnle and P. Selle, *Government and Voluntary Organisations: A Relational Perspective* (Aldershot: Avebury, 1992); H. Nathan, *Effectiveness and the Voluntary Sector* (London: National Council for Voluntary Organisations, 1990); M. Taylor, *New Times, New Challenges: Voluntary Organisations Facing 1990* (London: National Council for Voluntary Organisations, 1990).

[83.] Hilton, Crowson, Mouhot and McKay, *Historical Guide to NGOs*, pp. 12–31.

[84.] Kramer, 'Change and Continuity', is particularly strong on this aspect. See also Hilton, Crowson, Mouhot and McKay, *The Politics of Expertise*, pp. 54–79.

[85.] See, for example, Hilton, Crowson, Mouhot and McKay, *The Politics of Expertise*, pp. 80–107.

4. They developed greater concerns with efficiency and effectiveness (these were seen as necessary for demonstrating effective and appropriate use of state-provided funds, often as defined in contracts).[86]
5. They developed more sophisticated criteria and systems for monitoring and evaluating performance, including research-based initiatives.[87]
6. They employed more salaried staff, often in recognition of the need to engage those with the necessary financial and managerial skills to undertake much of the work referred to above (though paid employees still only represented two per cent of the workforce of registered charities in 2006).[88]

Some of these changes also occurred in voluntary sector organisations that did not receive government funding, partly the result of a general trend in the growth in professionalisation of key aspects of work within the wider economy, and partly of more stringent audit requirements of other funding bodies. Some of these developments also relate in part to changes in the Charity Commission's remit in 1960 when it was given wider powers, including compiling a register as a means of ensuring better monitoring and control over charities.[89]

Unsurprisingly, these events have been interpreted by analysts in different ways. Some see them as evidence of what one has called a '"colonisation" by the state (government) sector of the voluntary sector, entailing "domination" – imposing a hierarchy of control – and "appropriation" – redrawing and defining boundaries'.[90] Milbank's interpretation is in line with that way of thinking, seeing this process as

---

[86.] See ibid., and Nathan, *Effectiveness and the Voluntary Sector.*
[87.] See, for example, T. Darlington, *Management Learning and Voluntary Organisations*, and Hilton, Crowson, McKay and Mouhot, *The Politics of Expertise*, pp. 77–78.
[88.] Kuhnle and Selle, *Government and Voluntary Organisations*, p. 98; and see F. Prochaska, 'Voluntary Action – Renaissance or Decline. See also Hilton, Crowson, McKay and Mouhot, *The Politics of Expertise*, pp. 66–67.
[89.] Kuhnle and Selle, *Government and Voluntary Organisations*, p. 103.
[90.] Billis, *Organising Public and Voluntary Agencies*, p. 205. See also D. Wilson and B. Butler, 'Corporatism in the British Voluntary Sector', in W. Streek and P.C. Schmitter (eds), *Private Interest Government: Beyond Market and State* (London: Sage, 1985), pp. 72–86.

an example of increased 'remote bureaucratic control'[91] by the state over intermediary level welfare providers, and state enforcement by contract of a 'universalisation' of provision in that sector.

Neil McIntosh, Shelter's director in 1978, also argued that this increased state funding compromised the ability of the charity sector to be critical of government.[92] This concern is consistent with evidence given by a Barnardo representative to the Wolfenden Committee in 1978: 'It could be said that an organisation with close links to the statutory side must be careful in how far it went in the direction of critic since so much depended on good relationships. Too destructive criticism could well be counter-productive.'[93] Further, a major evidence-based study published in 1989 by two researchers into the impact of increased state funding in the voluntary sector concluded that it had led to 'uniform services' being provided, whereby all users were to be treated alike on the basis of unambiguous criteria of eligibility; a view that chimes with Milbank's criticism that the Welfare State promotes impersonal universalisation and predictability in its service provision and that of the voluntary sector. They also argued, 'as government increasingly penetrates the non-profit sector, it undermines the civic virtues of non-profit organisations such as citizen participation in services development, voluntarism and community definitions of the needy'.[94] This perspective was also reflected in an observation made by the Association of Charitable Foundations, quoted by Iain Duncan Smith in a speech he made on 4 November 2005 at the 'Britain's Most Admired Charities Awards' dinner: 'in a world where funding comes from service contracts, there is a danger that passion is neutralised, in

---

[91.] Milbank and Pabst, 'Post-liberal Politics and the Alternative', p. 91.

[92.] Finlayson, *Citizen, State, and Social Welfare in Britain 1830–1990*, p. 348.

[93.] Oral evidence presented to the Wolfenden Committee. Cited in Finlayson, *Citizen, State, and Social Welfare in Britain 1830–1990*, p. 345. For more on the legal constraints placed on British charities with regard to engaging in political activities, including political campaigning, see Hilton, Crowson, Mouhot and McKay, *The Politics of Expertise*, pp. 195–200.

[94.] S.R. Smith and M. Lipsky, 'Non-Profit Organisations, Government and the Welfare State', *Political Science Quarterly* 104, no. 4 (1989), pp. 625–48. Cited in N. Deakin & J. Kershaw, *Meeting the Challenge of Change: Voluntary Action into the 21st Century: Summary of Evidence and Selected Papers for the Report of the Commission on the Future of the Voluntary Sector* (London: National Council for Voluntary Organisations, 1996), p. 32.

the interest of financial survival. People do what they are paid to do rather than what they care deeply about doing.'[95]

Others, no doubt influenced in part by the Handy Report of 1981 into *Improving Effectiveness in Voluntary Organisations*,[96] which called for more professional management practices to be introduced into that sector, have seen them as a necessary set of changes in the relationship between government and the voluntary sector, that ensured the latter was able to expand the range of its activities in ways that would otherwise not have been possible.[97] Arguments in support of this line of thinking have included the following:

1. Many of these changes can be seen as inevitable and essential if the voluntary sector was to have kept pace with developments in British society and economy that have occurred since the early 1970s. Examples of these have been: increased legal complexities; increased professionalisation and the deployment of modern, scientific management systems of working in organisations such as, *inter alia*, changes to financial and accounting practices and advances in technology and its use; and changes in public expectations as citizens became more aware of their rights to seek legal redress if they felt services they had received had been substandard.

2. There is also evidence that professionalisation of voluntary bodies' management and administrative arrangements delivered increased skills-based training of the volunteers, necessary to be sure they worked in ways that were consistent with meeting the quality standards required in contract specifications.[98]

---

[95] Cited in F. Prochaska, 'The State of Charity: Charity Commission Lecture', September 2014, p. 15. Available at: https://assets.publishing.service.gov .uk/government/uploads/system/uploads/attachment_data/file/356191 /Lecture_-_Dr_Frank_Prochaska.pdf (accessed on 15 December 2021).

[96] See C. Handy, *Improving Effectiveness in Voluntary Organisations: Report of the Charles Handy Working Party* (London: National Council for Voluntary Organisations, 1981).

[97] See C. Landry, *What a Way to Run a Railroad: An Analysis of Radical Failure* (London: Comedia Publishing, 1985).

[98] This was partly the result of increased professionalisation in the voluntary sector that occurred from the early 1970s onwards, including the requirement to pass professional examinations for entry into some posts.

3. Voluntary sector organisations that had not received any state funding often adopted similar practices, not least because other non-state grant providers to the sector often required similar levels of administrative competence, consistency in service provision and financial accountability.

4. State funding streams were often only a part of the wider range of funding sources being accessed by these voluntary sector organisations, amounting to 31 per cent in 2007.[99] Indeed, in 2014 there were approximately 41,000 charities – hence only around 23 per cent of those registered – that were in a contractual relationship with the state.[100]

Therefore, from this perspective there is a danger of exaggerating the extent of governmental 'control' of voluntary sector organisations since the 1970s, when one takes into account that only around a quarter of them were in contractual arrangements with the government to provide welfare. Moreover, all voluntary sector organisations retained their own boards, constitutions, membership, premises and facilities, and the right to access alternative income streams, as well as the decision-making autonomy to provide services that were not state funded. In other words, they could operate in ways that did not need to conform to governmental contract specifications but only to the 'generic' legally enforced regulations in their sector.

In Summary
There is historical evidence, then, that since the 1970s, those voluntary sector organisations that sought and received governmental financial assistance under provider contracts for services, experienced some loss of financial and strategic autonomy as a result, as well as increased state scrutiny of their governance arrangements. They also experienced an increase in the administrative complexity of their operations that impacted on their human resources practices, with more professionally trained salaried employees being taken on to meet these challenges. In addition, owing to the prescriptive nature of state-funded contracts for services, there is some evidence that this diminished their ability to be as flexible and bespoke in the tailoring of their interventions to their client base. However, these developments coincided with an expansion in their

---

[99.] Cited in Alcock, 'Voluntary Action, New Labour and the "Third Sector"', p. 173.

[100.] Cited in Prochaska, 'The State of Charity', p. 16.

activities, made possible by the new funding streams, and hence their ability to contribute to the overall delivery of welfare in British society. The additional state funding also contributed to bringing about the modernisation of their administrative and governance arrangements, which enabled them to keep pace with changing legal and societal expectations. Also, having to meet government contract specifications made them more result orientated and efficient, conscious of the need to be able to show effective use of public money.

Milbank's perspective is therefore consistent with the historical evidence in so far as, since the early 1970s, *some* sections of the voluntary sector have experienced *some* loss of financial and strategic decision-making autonomy to the state, in ways that have reshaped the way they provide welfare services. The question remains, however, whether an alternative approach that entails a disentangling of the state from the voluntary sector and a substantial increase in church provision of welfare (some of it funded by the state) offers a better alternative. Could income streams be developed capable of offsetting the loss of state-provided income that would result? That question will be answered in chapter six when I reach the conclusion to my argument, as it relates in part to the insights that can be gained from the analysis of the 'Big Society' project and its outcome in chapter five.

However, we now need to consider whether the Welfare State was a major cause of the decline in religious affiliation and observance in Britain in the post-war years – a view that underpins much of Milbank's Blue Socialist antipathy towards it, and, as he sees things, the need to reverse that trend if a post-liberal society is to be advanced in England in the twenty-first century.

'Swimming into the Mouth of the Leviathan'

Frank Prochaska's writings, in which he has argued that the Welfare State undermined religious belief and played a significant part in bringing about the decline in religious affiliation and observance in Britain in the post-war period,[101] have received a mixed reception over the years,

---

[101.] F. Prochaska, *Christianity and Social Service in Modern Britain*; *Women and Philanthropy in Nineteenth-Century England* (Oxford: Clarendon Press, 1980); 'The Church of England and the Collapse of Christian Charity', Social Affairs Unit website, 8 November 2004 (http://www.socialaffairsunit .org.uk/blog/archives/000207.php) (accessed 16 December 2021); 'The State

not least from among Anglican Socialists. Kenneth Leech, for example, was sceptical of Prochaska's lines of argument in a critical review of *Christianity and Social Service in Modern Britain*, stating: 'Undoubtedly there has been both an expansion of state activity and a decline in membership of some Churches over the period of time discussed. But, as statisticians would have told the author, close parallelisms or contrasts between curves are notoriously uninformative.'[102] By contrast, Milbank has consistently championed his work, contending: 'Prochaska shows that one reason for the decline of religion in the UK is its perceived "irrelevance" once it has ceased to be involved in the supply of social services and the coordination of economic activity.'[103] As Prochaska's historical writings are consistent with Milbank's own critique of the Welfare State, *vis-à-vis* the voluntary sector, and as Milbank has often adduced his writings in support of his perspective (as has Phillip Blond),[104] a brief interrogation of his key arguments is necessary.

In evidence to the Deakin Commission on the Voluntary Sector in the mid-1990s, Prochaska argued that: 'charities were swimming into the mouth of the Leviathan'.[105] He later attributed the decline in observance and affiliation in the Church of England in the post-war period in significant part to the theology of the state developed by Temple, something he viewed as being: 'more conducive to socialism than to Christianity'.[106] As noted above, Temple had argued that the

---

of Charity'; 'Mrs Thatcher, the Voluntary Sector and Victorian Values', Social Affairs Unit website, 16 February 2005 (http://www.socialaffairsunit. org.uk/blog/archives/000294.php) (accessed 16 December 2021); 'Voluntary Action – Renaissance or Decline?', *History & Policy: Connecting Historians, Policy Makers and the Media*, 2006. http://www.historyandpolicy.org/docs /voluntary_sector.pdf (accessed on 28 August 2017; the article is no longer available at that source. The present writer has a hard copy that can be made available on request.); 'New Labour and the Voluntary Sector', Social Affairs Unit, 15 March 2005 (http://www.socialaffairsunit.org.uk/blog /archives/000324.php) (accessed on 11 June 2019).

[102] K. Leech, 'Christianity and Social Services in Modern Britain: The Disinherited Spirit', *Church Times*, 2 November 2006.

[103] Milbank, 'The Big Society Depends on the Big Parish', p. 4.

[104] P. Blond and J. Noyes, *Holistic Mission: Social Action and the Church of England* (London: ResPublica, July 2013), p. 9.

[105] Prochaska, 'Voluntary Action – Renaissance or Decline?', p. 2.

[106] Prochaska, 'The Church of England and the Collapse of Christian Charity'. For a more extended version of this perspective, see Prochaska, *Christianity*

state was a 'servant and instrument of God for the preservation of Justice and for the promotion of human welfare'.[107] This is a theology of the state that Prochaska thinks is too collectivist – too socialist. He is thus critical of what he interprets as the Church of England's endorsement of it via Resolution 19 passed at the Lambeth Conference of 1948:

> We believe that the State is under the moral law of God, and is intended by Him to be an instrument for human welfare. We therefore welcome the growing concern and care of the modern State for its citizens, and call upon Church members to accept their own political responsibility and to cooperate with the State and its officers in their work.[108]

For Prochaska, views such as these are indicative of the way in which: 'The Anglican hierarchy had turned Jesus into a socialist.'[109] A consequence of this step-change, according to Prochaska, was that it set back parish charity, 'which had been crucial to spiritual life and neighbourliness in the past'.[110] Yet, his article on 'The Church of England and the Collapse of Christian Charity' fails to mention that the same conference passed Resolution 18:

> The Conference affirms it to be the duty of the Church constantly to proclaim the sovereignty of God who is the Father of all and whose law is above all nations; it condemns the concept of the unbridled sovereignty of the nation and such usurpation of power by the state as is opposed to the basic truths of Christianity; further, it denies that the individual exists for the state, but asserts that one of the principal ends of the state is the development of personality, the highest good of the individual.[111]

---

and Social Service in Modern Britain.

[107] Temple, *Citizen and Churchman*, p. 36.

[108] Cited by Prochaska, 'The Church of England and the Collapse of Christian Charity', p. 3.

[109] Ibid.

[110] Ibid., p. 4.

[111] *The Lambeth Conference: Resolutions Archive from 1948.* Available at: http://www.anglicancommunion.org/media/127737/1948.pdf (accessed on 29 December 2017).

The Conference, therefore, recognised there are necessary limits for the state to operate within, not least regarding the sovereignty of God. Moreover, in Resolution 20 it stated: 'In view of a tendency of the state to encroach on the freedom of individuals and voluntary associations, it urges Christians in all lands to guard such freedoms with vigilance.'[112] In 1948 the Anglican Communion was, therefore, in step with the view that Temple, Beveridge and Attlee had held on the Welfare State, of the need for limits to exist in the role the state performs in society, including in areas that voluntary associations had traditionally excelled in, in a way that Prochaska's work understates.

A key line of argument Prochaska develops in support of his perspective relates to the decline in the number of women engaged in some charitable activities in the Church of England after 1945. For example, we have already seen how membership of the Mothers' Union – at the time a predominately Church of England-based charity – had declined by over three quarters in the period between the 1930s and 2009. Prochaska attributes much of this decline to a reduction in Church of England parish societies that occurred after the war, as well as a reduction in parochial visiting, and connects this trend to the Church of England's 'post-war enthusiasm for the welfare state'[113] and, in a sense, its willingness to hand over to the state aspects of welfare provision that had previously been more the preserve of the Church. Thus, he argues: 'It struck a body blow to parish charity' and this 'was particularly true for women, who provided the backbone of church membership and voluntary work'.[114] Yet, whilst there is brief reference made in his work to some of the other possible reasons for why a decline in the number of women involved in the Church of England's charity work occurred in the post-war period, his tendency is to downplay them. For example, the post-war period offered much greater opportunities for women to find paid employment, to participate in expanding recreational opportunities and to engage in more accessible life-long learning activities, which would have happened regardless of the approach the Church of England had adopted towards the Welfare State.[115] An

---

[112] Ibid.

[113] Prochaska, 'The Church of England and the Collapse of Christian Charity', p. 4.

[114] Ibid., p. 3.

[115] For more on this, see C.G. Brown, *The Death of Christian Britain: Understanding Secularisation 1800–2000* (London: Routledge, 2001), pp. 170–191.

alternative perspective on the decline of the Mothers' Union in the post-war period would place more emphasis on the fact that it was a socially conservative organisation, which promoted a traditional version of Christianity centred on motherhood, the home and the family being a woman's priorities. In a post-war age after many women had tasted the fruits of working life during the war and the independence it afforded, it is hardly surprising that some were reluctant to turn the clock back. Additionally, the emergence of the feminist movement in the 1960s and the sexual emancipation that the contraceptive pill afforded women after 1961 challenged the ethos of the Mothers' Union and its traditional outlook on such matters.

Furthermore, as Eliza Filby has argued,[116] it would also be incorrect to assume that the Church of England had vacated the charity sector in the post-war period to the extent that Prochaska's statements might suggest. In the post-war period, the Church Housing Association, for example, established in the 1920s, had, by the 1980s, assumed a major role in the provision of homes for families, the elderly and the homeless.[117] Also, both Church Action on Poverty, a major ecumenical Christian social justice charity founded in 1982 which has focused on campaigning against poverty, and Christians Against Poverty, founded in 1996, which has focused on debt management advice, have a significant Church of England membership. The Church of England's Children's Society also continues to make a significant contribution to the provision of care to children and the disabled, whilst the Church's involvement in the Shaftesbury Project on Christian Involvement in Society that ran from 1973 to 1994 was also considerable, and substantially contributed to the advancement of education of adults and young people in areas such as the interface of Christian faith with the social sciences.[118] As noted earlier, there were numerous Church/MSC-sponsored schemes in the 1980s that focused on reducing unemployment. These are examples of the way in which the post-war state welfare sector and the Church charity sector coexisted, and often worked in tandem and in ways that were complementary.

Another example is the development of the Hospital Chaplaincy Service within the NHS, which, prior to the 1990s, was substantially

---

[116.] Filby, 'Faith, Charity and Citizenship', pp. 135–57. See also E. Filby, *God and Mrs Thatcher*.

[117.] Filby, 'Faith, Charity and Citizenship', p. 137.

[118.] Ibid.; also, see Finlayson, *Citizen, State and Social Welfare in Britain 1830–1990*, ch. 4.

made up of Anglican chaplains because of the close connections between the state and the Church of England.[119] Also, since 1958, the Church of England has retained its influence on the charity sector via its Board for Social Responsibility (renamed in 1999 the Church of England's Mission and Public Affairs Council), which regularly hosts meetings with the NCVO in which it conveys the views of the sector and offers advice and support. It also produces papers on the work of the sector, which have influence within the sector and the wider political landscape. An example was its 2006 *Recent Survey/Mapping Exercises Undertaken across the English Regions to Measure the Contribution of Faith Groups to Social Action and Culture*.[120] This is a significant work that provides, on a region-by-region basis, statistics documenting a vibrant Church of England contribution to social action at a local level, as well as considerable evidence of Christian generosity and social welfare provision. This was consistent with the findings of the *Church Life Profile* of 2001, which found that members of the Church of England contributed 23.2 million hours' voluntary service each month.[121]

Prochaska's work extends beyond the Church of England in its analysis of the retarding impact he argues the Welfare State had on Christian charities in Britain in the post-war period. He argues: 'In the belief that the state was fulfilling "the law of Christ", religious leaders failed to appreciate fully just how much the growth of government welfare would devitalize Christian charity, and, by implication, Christianity itself.'[122] Certainly, there is evidence in the early years of the Welfare State under the Attlee administration that the move towards what came to be called the 'mixed economy of welfare' was not entirely smooth. Some dislocation – indeed confusion – existed in the voluntary and

---

[119.] See Cambridge University Hospitals, *History of Chaplaincy.* Available at: https://www.cuh.nhs.uk/chaplaincy/history-chaplaincy (accessed on 25 August 2017).

[120.] Church of England, *Recent Survey/Mapping Exercises Undertaken across the English Regions to Measure the Contribution of Faith Groups to Social Action and Culture*, 2006. Available at: http://www.ihbc.org.uk/recent_papers/docs /RegionalreportsTable.pdf (accessed on 25 October 2017).

[121.] See N. Spencer, *'Doing God': A Future for Faith in the Public Square* (London: Theos, 2006), p. 44.

[122.] Prochaska, 'The Church of England and the Collapse of Christian Charity', p. 4.

state sectors as to what would be the new demarcation lines in the newly emerging mixed economy of welfare provision.[123] Thus, H.R. Poole, Secretary of the Liverpool Council of Social Service, wrote in 1960 that it could not 'be denied that the few years immediately following the end of the [Second World] war were a period of confusion and uncertainty for many … voluntary organisations'.[124] Undoubtedly, this would have had some impact on the Church providers of welfare, with Prochaska arguing that this was the primary reason for why the 'Church of England consciously "abandoned" regular parochial visiting'[125] in favour of greater state welfare provision in the immediate aftermath of the war, and why he argues that there was a decline in women's participation in these endeavours as a result.[126] However, as he has noted, this line of argument pertains to the context of the aftermath of the Second World War: 'The effect of aerial bombardment, which damaged or destroyed 15,000 ecclesiastical buildings in Britain, dealt a serious blow to religious observance and charitable practice. All the denominations suffered, though Methodists, with strongholds in the targeted industrial cities, suffered more than most.'[127]

With respect to the Church of England, over 1,000 places of worship had been destroyed or badly damaged by Luftwaffe bombing by 1942 (to increase further by 1944),[128] meaning that some fragmentation of parish life and parochial outreach (including proselytization) was inevitable in the immediate post-war period, and not in any way connected with the Welfare State nor the Church of England's embracing of it. Yet, despite this fragmentation, Callum Brown's major study into the decline of Christianity in Britain argues: 'The late 1940s and 1950s witnessed the greatest church growth that Britain had experienced since the

---

[123.] Finlayson, *Citizen, State, and Social Welfare in Britain 1830–1990*, pp. 287–89.

[124.] See H.R. Poole, *The Liverpool Council of Social Service 1909–1959* (Liverpool: The Liverpool Council for Social Service, 1960), pp. 77–78. Cited in Finlayson, *Citizen, State and Social Welfare in Britain 1830–1990*, p. 297.

[125.] Prochaska, 'The Church of England and the Collapse of Christian Charity', p. 4. He cites B. Heeney, *The Women's Movement in the Church of England, 1850–1930* (Oxford: Clarendon Press, 1988), p. 27, as his source for this.

[126.] Prochaska, 'The Church of England and the Collapse of Christian Charity', p. 4.

[127.] Ibid., p. 1.

[128.] Ibid.

mid-nineteenth century.'[129] He offers the following explanation and adduces evidence in support of it:

> Traditional values of family, home and piety were suddenly back on the agenda between the end of the war and 1960. The churches benefited immediately. During the late 1940s and first half of the 1950s, organised Christianity experienced the greatest per annum growth in church membership, Sunday school enrolment, Anglican confirmations and Presbyterian recruitment of its baptised constituency since the eighteenth century … leading to peaks in membership in the 1955–59 period for virtually all British Protestant churches.[130]

His study suggests that the decline in affiliation and observance in the Church of England and in other denominations took off from the beginning of the 1960s; that is, twelve to fifteen years after the rollout of the Welfare State and of the Churches' broad-based support for it – a point that Prochaska's work understates.

There is also evidence that supports a view that Prochaska's work understates the number of Christians who contributed in increasing numbers as volunteers in support of the newly configured state welfare provision. Thus, the 1952 Committee of Enquiry into the Law and Practice Relating to Charitable Trusts (the Nathan Committee) reported that 'so far from voluntary action being dried up by the expansion of the social services, greater and greater demands are being made upon it. Tens of thousands of voluntary workers have been enlisted to operate the statutory services in a manner in which Parliament has laid down that they should be operated'.[131] That report does not, therefore, support a declinist line of argument: that is, that increased state welfare provision led to a decline in volunteering *per se* and by Christians, in particular, and thus a decline in Christian charitable activity, with retarding implications for Christian affiliation and observance. What it does suggest, though, is that volunteers were adapting to the new welfare landscape in the ways they contributed to it, and it can reasonably be

---

[129.] C.G. Brown, *The Death of Christian Britain: Understanding Secularisation 1800-2000* (London: Routledge, 2001), p. 170.

[130.] Ibid., pp. 172–73.

[131.] *Report of the Committee of Enquiry into the Law and Practice Relating to Charitable Trusts* (Nathan Committee), Cmnd 8710 (London: HMSO, 1952), para. 54. Cited in Finlayson, *Citizen, State and Social Welfare in Britain 1830–1990*, p. 288.

assumed that a fair percentage of these would have been Christians given the large percentage of affiliated Christians in the overall population at that time.

A further example of this adaptation was a greater emphasis being placed by Christians on supporting overseas needs. It can be queried how, for example, Prochaska's declinist perspective squares with the rise of Christian charities in the post-war period that have focused on international aid. Take Christian Aid, whose voluntary income increased from c. £30 million in 1970 to over £90 million in 2007;[132] and the Catholic Agency for Overseas Development saw an increase in its voluntary income from c. £3 million in 1973 to c. £41 million by 2000.[133] With respect to religious influence within the wider voluntary sector, an NCVO survey conducted in the 1980s, well after the Welfare State had become an established feature of British life, calculated that over 70 per cent of volunteers considered themselves to be 'religious persons' and over half of these were active adherents.[134] Regarding the non-adherents, one can reasonably surmise that, although some of the Christians who were surveyed may well have stopped attending Church on a regular basis, consistent with the figures showing that from the early 1960s there had been a decline in church attendance of a third and denominational affiliation had decreased by 45 per cent,[135] they were 'believing without belonging'[136] and continued to contribute substantially to the expanding voluntary sector provision of welfare that we have seen occurred in the post-war period.[137]

Of course, this is not to suggest that in the immediate period leading up to the 'Big Society' project everything was optimally aligned between the state and voluntary sector organisations in their delivery of welfare. For example, the Joseph Rowntree Foundation (JRF) report of 2003, *'Faith' in Urban Regeneration?*, drew attention to difficulties that some faith groups encountered with local authorities and their sometimes antagonistic attitudes towards them; and a later JRF report, *Faith as Social Capital*, argued 'local authorities, primary care trusts, police authorities

---

[132] Hilton, Crowson, Mouhot and McKay, *Historical Guide to NGOs*, p. 130.

[133] Ibid., p. 118.

[134] Filby, 'Faith, Charity and Citizenship', p. 137.

[135] Ibid., p.136.

[136] See G. Davie, *Religion in Britain since 1945: Believing Without Belonging* (London: John Wiley & Sons, 1994).

[137] See K.N. Medhurst and G.H. Moyser, *Church and Politics in a Secular Age* (Oxford: Clarendon Press, 1988).

and other agencies have to develop a more sophisticated understanding of faith communities with much closer relationships, if a latent social capital is to be used effectively'.[138] A subsequent study commissioned by Stephen Lowe, Bishop for Urban Life and Faith, reported similar difficulties some faith charity groups had encountered with central government departments and local authorities.[139] It was critical of what it considered to be a lack of understanding of the Church's 'huge moral and civic contribution' by the state, which had resulted in it 'planning without vision or roots'.[140] It also considered there to be a need for it to review its commissioning guidance, in a way that would 'create a level playing field for faith-based agencies seeking to engage in public service reform, contracting and civic action'.[141] It was undoubtedly the case, then, that at the time of the launch of the 'Big Society' project in 2010, there remained scope for further strengthening of the working relationship and strategic interface between the state and voluntary sector providers of welfare, including the faith-based voluntary sector. Yet, between 1945 and 2010 there is much historical evidence of Christians continuing to engage in charitable work on a large scale, often focused on providing welfare within and beyond their churches and often working in tandem with the Welfare State, thereby making a major contribution to a 'Big Society' that existed in Britain before 2010.[142]

This point is further evidenced by research undertaken by the New Philanthropy Capital consultancy in 2014, which found that, of the 188,000 charities registered in the UK, almost 50,000 were faith based and two thirds of these were from the Christian tradition. It also found that, in the preceding ten years, the proportion of Christian charities (38 per cent) that had registered with the Charity Commission was higher

---

[138.] R. Farnell, R. Furbey, S. Shams al-Haqq Hills, M. Macey and G. Smith, *'Faith' in Urban Regeneration? Engaging Faith Communities in Urban Regeneration* (Bristol: Policy Press, 2003), and R. Furbey, A. Dinham, R. Farnell et al., *Faith as Social Capital: Connecting or Dividing?* (Bristol: Policy Press, 2006), ch. 8.

[139.] Davis, Paulhus and Bradstock, *Moral, But No Compass.*

[140.] Ibid., p. 95.

[141.] Ibid., p. 96.

[142.] For example, on the approach taken by New Labour administrations to cultivate religiously motivated community-based voluntary action, see G. Smith, *More than a Little Quiet Care: The Extent of the Churches' Contribution to Community Work in East London in the 1990s* (London: Aston Charities Community Involvement Unit, 1998).

than that of non-faith ones (24 per cent), indicating a level of vitality among Christian organisations in excess of that in non-faith-based ones.[143] The historical evidence cited earlier, moreover, demonstrates how Christians had ample opportunity to engage in such work, suggesting that the decline in Christian religious affiliation and observance since the early 1960s, both within and beyond the Church of England, is more multifaceted and intricate than Prochaska suggests.

In Summary
The reasons for the decline in church affiliation and observance in Britain from the early 1960s onwards, are multifaceted and complex. No doubt they will include *inter alia*: (1) the growing dominance that scientific (positivist) research methods and their epistemological underpinnings have attained in the universities since the 1960s (less so since the 1990s in some subjects owing to the post-modern challenge), which has resulted in what has been described as the triumph of scientific method and reasoning in the academy over faith-based perspectives, at a time when access to higher education has increased exponentially;[144] (2) the sexual 'revolution' of the 1960s and the challenges it posed to traditional Church teaching on sexual matters; and (3) the growing disparity between mainline Church of England teaching on issues such as women's rights and those of LGBTQ citizens with the increasingly liberal views held by large sections of British society on these matters[145] – these being just three of numerous factors that would need to be included in any appraisal of the causes of this complex social phenomenon. Nonetheless, Milbank's and Prochaska's insistence that they were in significant part a result of the Welfare State and the support given to it by the churches is less than consistent with a growing body of historical evidence that indicates otherwise.

[143.] Cited in S. Wells, R. Rook and D. Barclay, *For Good: The Church and the Future of Welfare* (Norwich: Canterbury Press, 2017), p. 29.

[144.] An interesting study that is broadly in support of this trend is D. Skorton and A. Bear (eds), *The Integration of the Humanities and Arts with Sciences, Engineering, and Medicine in Higher Education: Branches from the Same Tree* (Washington, DC: National Academies Press, 2018).

[145.] This is covered in A. Brown and L. Woodhead, *That Was the Church That Was: How the Church of England Lost the English People* (London: Bloomsbury, 2016).

The Church of England's interface with the Welfare State will be considered in the next chapter, when we examine its post-war positions on welfare. Before that, however, our attention turns to Milbank's Blue Socialist vision of an alternative post-liberal polity and society, and the role he argues the Church of England should perform within it, not least with respect to the provision of welfare.

'The Church Is the Site of the True Society'

Central to Milbank's Blue Socialist vision of a post-liberal society in England in the twenty-first century is the substantially enhanced role he sees for the Church of England within it, not least owing to its established status, which he supports: 'The Church of England is indispensable to a new politics of the common good beyond the liberalism of both left and right that underpins the global "market" state.'[146] Milbank and Pabst do not envisage a post-liberal society as requiring an out-and-out supplanting of the state by the Church, for they acknowledge: 'At their best, both Church and State can work together for the dignity of the person, human flourishing and the public common good'; but they want to see the Church of England having significantly more influence over the state in the way it conducts its affairs, by emphasising the need for individual virtue and public honour as paramount for transforming public institutions in a way that better embodies these values, and by: 'transforming the secular emphasis away from individual self-interest and collective power towards the dignity of the person, human flourishing and the common good'.[147] Milbank considers the Temple middle axiom approach towards the state, 'according to which Christianity only contributes vague ideal platitudes and not very specific suggestions about social organisation',[148] as inadequate for this task, being too limiting in the range it affords the Church of England to influence the way the state conducts its affairs. Rather, he wants to see the established Church shaping the new post-liberal politics. It will do this by 'leading the debate and brokering a new settlement that makes gift exchange or reciprocity the ultimate principle

---

[146] Milbank and Pabst, 'The Anglican Polity and the Politics of the Common Good', p. 8.

[147] Ibid., pp. 10–11.

[148] J. Milbank, untitled reply to an analysis of his work by Baker, Atherton and Reader, 'A Case of Ecclesial Over-Optimism', p. 5.

to govern both the economy and politics',[149] in a way that 'restores the state as also the Church'[150] – thus offering a post-liberal alternative to post-war Keynesianism and neoliberalism.

For Milbank and Pabst, this will entail the Church of England *inter alia*: 'promoting just prices, just wages, and a more corporatist political role for guilds and other professional associations',[151] thus redressing some of the injustices they believe have characterised capitalism since the Reformation, not least as a result of the abandonment by Protestant thinkers of the Catholic doctrine of just price in favour of the 'free market' mechanism for determining its level, as discussed in chapter three. The strong implication here is for a *de facto* constitutional realignment in England, shaped by their view that: 'Anglican establishment sustains the idea that the Church is itself a polity and, indeed, the heart of the English polity, since sacramental coronation alone ultimately confers legitimacy upon a political system and a constitution that remains creatively unwritten.'[152]

Hence, though Milbank's writings on his own or with others are less than entirely clear on what this constitutional realignment might mean in practical terms, it is clear it would entail a substantially enhanced

---

[149.] Milbank and Pabst, 'The Anglican Polity and the Politics of the Common Good', p. 4.

[150.] Milbank and Pabst, *The Politics of Virtue*, p. 230. 'Restoring the State as also the Church' connects with Milbank's critique of what he sees as liberal Anglicanism's inclination to see establishment as 'a relic of the past'. By contrast, Milbank sees the need for a strengthening of church establishment as a way of restoring some of the ground it has lost in the political sphere. Thus, he and Pabst argue: 'The political role of the established Church is, therefore, neither to sanctify the state nor to supplant the government' (p. 232). Rather, Milbank sees the established church in a post-liberal context as making an enhanced contribution to shaping the political direction of English society within a new *body politic* that has been shaped by the corporatist thinking that he and Pabst have set down. They describe this as the way in which: 'autonomous and democratic self-governing organisations [the Church being one] … combine in a microcosm the virtuous guidance of "the one" with the assent of "the many" around shared notions of excellence and ethos' (p. 209).

[151.] Milbank and Pabst, 'The Anglican Polity and the Politics of the Common Good', p. 4.

[152.] Milbank and Pabst, *The Politics of Virtue*, p. 230.

role for the Church of England in the decision-making processes that comprise the workings of the state.

Key lines of criticism concerning this vision for the Church of England are likely to be built around the following kinds of questions (this is not an exhaustive list):

1. Does it underestimate the extent of the influence the Church of England has been able to have on the shaping of political affairs in the post-war period via the middle axiom model of engagement?
2. Is being an established church the best route for influencing the political state and holding it to account?
3. For those with a faith commitment, is this vision likely to command the support of an increasingly diverse, multi-faith/multi-denominationally-based society in England in the twenty-first century?
4. Is it likely to command the support of those with no faith?
5. Is it possible, now, for a single nation state to adopt a 'just price' system via a process of corporatist state/church intervention of the kind Milbank advocates, rather than the market, given that the price of goods is often so internationally defined and market embedded?
6. Is it antithetical to the notion of democratic accountability, given that those who wield power and influence in the Church of England are not elected, and thus cannot be removed from these positions of power and influence by the electorate?

As this is a study on welfare and the approach of the Church of England to its provision, this cannot be the place to address all of these questions in the depth they require. However, with respect to the notion of democratic accountability – particularly at a local level – in the event that the Church of England were to secure government contracts for the provision of welfare services that are currently being provided by local government, it is difficult to see how this would not result in an overall diminishing of political accountability given that local government councillors are periodically subjected to ballot box scrutiny in a way that church officials are not. In an increasingly secular society, moreover, there is an unavoidably high probability that such a scenario is unlikely to command the levels of popular support that it would need to succeed.

We now turn to Milbank's vision of the role he sees for the Church of England in the provision of welfare.

John Milbank's Vision for the Church of England's Role in the Provision of Welfare

Milbank (along with Pabst) argues that key to the life of the Church:

> is the social and civic action promoted by the majority of
> churches, above all the Church of England through its unique
> parochial system – whether more social events such as youth
> clubs, dinners for the elderly, mums and toddlers groups and
> coffee mornings or economic and welfare services like food-
> banks, homeless shelters, debt counselling, credit unions and
> health services.[153]

These interventions can legitimately be described as welfare services
as they all contribute to the recipients' mental health and well-being,
and, for some, their physical health and well-being, too. They have been
provided by the Church of England throughout the post-war period,
have been coterminous with the existence of the Welfare State and have
made a significant contribution to civil society and to what is often
referred to as 'the mixed economy of welfare provision'.[154]

In addition to these locally-provided services from within its
buildings, the Church of England has also played a much larger role
in the provision of welfare, often on a national scale. In the field of
education, for example, one in four primary schools and one in six
secondary schools in England are Church of England schools, though
funded by the state, and approximately one million pupils are educated
in more than 4,700 Church of England schools.[155] In the field of housing,
the Church of England has provided (and continues to provide) a
range of properties for rent at modest rates for families living on low
means, as well as provision for those who are homeless in the form
of temporary shelters.[156] In the field of health care, too, it continues
to provide the majority of hospital chaplains to the NHS, as well as
church representatives on NHS ethics committees and on some NHS

---

[153] Milbank and Pabst, 'The Anglican Polity and the Politics of the Common
Good', p. 3.

[154] For example, Eliza Filby documents this well with respect to the 1980s in
'Faith, Charity and Citizenship'.

[155] See the Church of England website: https://www.churchofengland.org/about
-us/facts-stats.aspx (accessed on 26 August 2017).

[156] See ibid.

Trust Boards as non-executive directors.[157] Also, as noted at earlier, the Church has contributed to the retraining of thousands of those without work, often working in tandem with state initiatives. These are just a small selection of examples that demonstrate that throughout the post-war period the Church of England has made, and continues to make, a significant contribution to the provision of welfare. With the exception of the Church's involvement with schools, which is not universally acknowledged as a positive feature in the English education system, there are few (if any) voices of dissent within or outside it saying that this work should not continue.

Milbank's Blue Socialist vision for the role that the Church of England should perform in the provision of welfare, whilst supportive of a continuation of all of the above, goes way beyond this, however. This is clear from his out-and-out endorsement with Pabst of the ResPublica report, produced by Phillip Blond and James Noyes in July 2013, *Holistic Mission: Social Action and the Church of England*.[158] At the time of its launch, Milbank stated: 'If both the Church of England and government implement the recommendations as set out in the ResPublica report, then this could permanently change the way the Church's social action transforms state welfare and other public services.'[159] Hence, a brief summary and interrogation of the key arguments advanced by that report follows.

Holistic Mission: Restoring the Church of England as the Welfare State?

Blond and Noyes argue: that 'the Church is uniquely positioned to create a radical new offer [on welfare provision] on the basis of an ancient institution that can provide universal access and standards combined with local variation and innovation';[160] and that the Church of England should actively engage in 'competition *between* as well as within public

---

[157.] There are currently more than 80 research ethics committees in the NHS. Lay members, i.e., non-medically qualified people, make up one third of the membership. A significant proportion of these have theological training and include some Anglican bishops.

[158.] P. Blond and J. Noyes, *Holistic Mission: Social Action and the Church of England* (London: ResPublica, 2013).

[159.] Milbank and Pabst, 'The Anglican Polity and the Politics of the Common Good', p. 4.

[160.] Blond and Noyes, *Holistic Mission*, p. 3.

service models'[161] in a way that government facilitates by opening 'doors for the Church to enter public service delivery' and thus enable it to 'enter the market for procuring, delivering and grouping public services in holistic provision'.[162] Their report called for the Cabinet Office and their major stakeholders (including the Big Lottery Fund), to support a Big Society Capital fund to assist organisations, including the Church of England, in being able to carry out these welfare interventions, ensuring it had sufficient financial resources at its disposal.[163] It acknowledged this would 'require national, regional and local Church administration to adopt the structures needed to make it possible to deliver services in every locality'.[164] It also acknowledged that the new role for the Church of England in the provision of public services would need to be focused more on locally-based rather than on nationally-based provision, at least in its initial stages, recognising that the Church of England was not yet equipped for providing these services on a national level,[165] though it did not rule out that option in the medium term, arguing: 'the Church should be a national partner (which also partners with others) in health, education, work and training programmes – as well as all the other countless goods that the state quite rightly tries to achieve'.[166]

In a section entitled, 'The Church has to make itself fit for purpose', the authors argue: 'If the Church is to fulfil its purpose and its potential, it has to substantially upgrade its internal and external structures. It has to adapt to the governance demands for accountability and standards by the state whilst at the same time allowing its localities to innovate and create.'[167] Yet, we have seen how 'adapting to the governance demands for accountability and standards by the state' is precisely what those voluntary sector organisations had to accomplish from the early 1970s onwards, when they agreed to take on government-funded contracts for services. It can be queried, therefore, why the concerns expressed by Milbank and others about the limiting effect this had on their decision-making autonomy and ability to provide 'bespoke' welfare solutions, would not equally apply to the Church of England in this commissioning scenario. Likewise, the concerns expressed

---

[161.] Ibid., p. 4.

[162.] Ibid.

[163.] Ibid., p. 5.

[164.] Ibid., p. 4.

[165.] Ibid., p. 32.

[166.] Ibid.

[167.] Ibid., p. 4.

about those voluntary sector organisations being compromised in their ability to criticise the government, owing to the fact that it was increasingly their paymaster. Moreover, this would be occurring when the Christendomists within the Church of England are seeking to move it away from the middle axiom model of engagement with the state, precisely so as to acquire *greater* levels of freedom for exercising a critical voice over its decisions.

Other concerns about this approach relate to capacity and resources. As Atherton, Baker and Reader have queried: 'How much could we [meaning faith groups such as the Church of England] realistically take on, even if it is legitimate to do so?'[168] In one telling exchange between them and Milbank concerning the latter's 2011 article in the *Church Times*,[169] in which he argues for much greater Church engagement in the processes of welfare, medicine, education etc., they counter: 'This analysis is seductive but vague, and out of touch with the real world where many Anglican churches struggle to pay diocesan quotas and recruit church wardens.' Milbank responds by arguing: 'If you don't have this, of course, you won't be able to pay the church warden [not realising that church wardens do not receive payment for their work].' However, it is noticeable that in the article to which the exchange relates, Milbank's arguments are more theoretically based than empirically supported, which may be one reason why Baker, Atherton and Reader consider them to be out of touch with the real world.[170]

A further factor to consider is the extent to which professionalisation of the kinds of welfare services relating to medicine, for example, that the Church of England might seek to compete for in the 'welfare market' described by Blond and Noyes, can be accommodated beyond the small number of examples adduced in their report that focus on mental health. For example, they make reference to the need for more church-based 'health hubs' of the kind that has been established in

---

[168.] J. Atherton, C. Baker and J. Reader, *Christianity and the New Social Order: A Manifesto for a Fairer Future* (London: SPCK, 2011), p. 9.

[169.] J. Milbank, 'The Church Is the Site of the True Society', *Church Times*, 14 December 2011.

[170.] C. Baker, 'A Case of Ecclesial Over-Optimism? A Response to Milbank's Return to Christendom's Social Vision, *Political Theology Network*, 23 February 2012 (article later attributed to C. Baker, J. Atherton and J. Reader). Available at: http://www.politicaltheology.com/blog/a-case-of-ecclesial -over-optimism-a-response-to-milbanks-return-to-christendoms-social -vision/ (accessed on 20 August 2016), pp. 1–3.

a church in Blackburn.[171] This initiative seeks to provide, through talk-based therapy, a more holistic response to meeting the well-being needs of those experiencing mental health difficulties. These hubs may well provide some additional 'holistic' therapeutic support to patients over and above that which a standard ten-minute GP session has been able to achieve, as has been argued by Dr Russ Rook, the founder of the initiative.[172] Yet, they represent a modest contribution to mental healthcare delivery and thus it can be argued do not provide a basis to suppose that other, more ambitious, church-based healthcare interventions could replace those currently being provided by the state sector.

All clinically-based jobs require trained professionals to undertake them, albeit with auxiliary support. This is both a legal requirement and a social expectation, as well as being essential for insurance for these services to be procured. The Church of England would presumably have to employ people with these professional skills and qualifications to undertake the provision of these health care services. However, how likely is it that it would be able to recruit and retain such people, offering commensurate levels of remuneration and pension provision, to that currently provided within the NHS, for example? How likely is it that the levels of technology required for the provision of many of these healthcare services, as well as the need for appropriately designed and maintained buildings in which this work would be undertaken, could ever realistically be provided by the Church of England? Clearly, size matters when it comes to the provision of welfare; a point that Baker, Atherton and Reader make in their exchange with Milbank, stating: 'The British government will spend 40% of its GDP on public expenditure even after proposed cuts, an essential contribution to wellbeing which church and voluntary bodies are incapable of satisfying.'[173] Hence, the scope for more church-based healthcare interventions is likely to remain limited, though not inconsequential.

We begin to see, then, that the Blue Socialist vision that Milbank advocates for the Church of England in the provision of welfare in England is highly problematic: politically, technologically, professionally, financially and practically. It rests on questionable theoretical and historical underpinnings that are clearly open to challenge on several fronts, some of which have been covered in the above evaluation. Yet, it is this vision which impelled Milbank to endorse the 'Big Society'

[171.] Blond and Noyes, *Holistic Mission*, p. 22.

[172.] Ibid.

[173.] Baker, 'A Case of Ecclesial Over-Optimism?'

project in 2010 and to seek to get the backing of the Church of England for it. Part Three will explore the implications this had for the Church of England, and for the wider society in which it exists; before then, a number of conclusions stemming from the analysis in this chapter need to be set down.

Conclusion

There is compelling historical evidence that none of the post-war administrations was hostile to the voluntary sector being involved in the provision of welfare. On the contrary, there were numerous examples of creative engagement between the Welfare State and the voluntary sector. This historical evidence runs contrary to Milbank's view that the Welfare State has grown at the expense of the intermediary level organisations in British civil society.

This historical evidence also supports a view that a 'Big Society' existed in Britain throughout the post-war period; hence, before the launch of the 'Big Society' project in 2010. This has implications for how we are to interpret that project, and the thinking put forward by the Cameron-led administration in support of it, which we will return to in Part Three

There is some historical evidence to support a view that those voluntary sector organisations that entered into government contracts for services since the early 1970s, experienced some loss of financial and strategic autonomy, as well as some diminution of their ability to be as flexible and bespoke in the way they provided welfare interventions to their client base. In this respect, Milbank's concerns over what he perceives as an increasingly statist level of influence over these voluntary sector organisations in a way that has compromised their flexibility of approach are not without some historical evidential support, though there is some evidence indicating that they may be exaggerated. However, these developments were accompanied by an expansion in their activities made possible by the new funding streams, as well as a modernisation of their administrative and governance arrangements.

The perspective put forward by Prochaska, and endorsed by Milbank, that, owing to the existence of the British Welfare State and the support it has received from the churches, charities have been 'swimming into the mouth of the Leviathan', is open to challenge, not least with respect to the historical evidence on which it rests. There are other, arguably more compelling, explanations for the decline in church affiliation and attendance since the early 1960s than Prochaska offers, as well as a growing body of historical evidence that runs counter to his overall thesis.

Throughout the post-war period, the Church of England has provided, and continues to provide, a range of welfare services, sometimes autonomously of the state sector and sometimes in consort with it. With the possible exception of its involvement with schools, there are few dissenting voices who believe it should do otherwise. However, reasons have been given for why it might seek to exercise caution in embracing the vision as set out by Blond and Noyes, in *Holistic Mission* – a vision that Milbank has unequivocally endorsed.

The above provides a historical and theoretical platform for an analysis and appraisal of the response by the Church of England to the 'Big Society' project in Part Three, and the influence Milbank's Blue Socialist perspective on welfare and the Church had on shaping it, as well as the views of others on the 'Big Society' project.

Part Three

John Milbank, the 'Big Society' Project and the Church of England

Chapter Five

The 'Big Society' Project and the Church of England: An Analysis of the Influences that Shaped GS1804

Introduction

According to the National Audit Office, the financial crisis of 2008 resulted in a government-funded bailout to the British banking sector of £850 billion by the end of 2009.[1] It also contributed to an economic recession that officially lasted for six consecutive quarters.[2] Hence, whichever political party assumed office after the May 2010 General Election would face major financial challenges. The election of the Conservative/Liberal Coalition government resulted in an economic programme to reduce the budget deficit and to bring about financial and economic recovery which put a squeeze on public expenditure, including state-provided welfare services. This was coterminous with its launch of the 'Big Society' project, which was, in part, a response to the economic and social challenges the government faced.

How closely did the debates on the 'Big Society' project conducted within the Church of England resemble those that had taken place in the preceding century on the state, the Church and the provision of

---

[1] A. Grice, '£850 Bn: Official Cost of the Bank Bailout', *Independent*, 4 December 2009.

[2] See BBC, 'UK Economy Emerges from Recession', 27 January 2010. Available at: http://news.bbc.co.uk/1/hi/business/8479639.stm (accessed on 4 November 2017).

welfare, between Welfare Statist Anglican Socialists and Christendom Anglican Socialists? More specifically, what part did John Milbank's Blue Socialist thinking play in shaping the Church of England's response to the government's 'Big Society' project? Did its response amount to a paradigm shift in its thinking on the Welfare State and its own role in the provision of welfare, when seen in the light of what had gone before? Chapter five has been structured to enable these questions to be answered.

It will consider:

1. The 'Big Society' project and Phillip Blond's Red Tory influences on shaping it.
2. John Milbank's Blue Socialist thinking on the 'Big Society' project, seen in the context of other perspectives from within Anglican Socialism.
3. The Church of England's post-war positions on welfare for the period 1945 to 2010.
4. The Church of England's response to the 'Big Society' project, with specific reference to the advice it received in General Synod paper 1804 (GS1804) from Malcolm Brown, Director of Mission and Public Affairs, and the influences he cites as key to shaping that advice.
5. The key outcomes of the 'Big Society' project.

The 'Big Society' Project and Phillip Blond's Red Tory Influence on Shaping It

The origins of the 'Big Society' project can, in significant part, be located in Jesse Norman's contributions to the shaping of conservative political thought in the 2000s.[3] In works such as *Compassionate Conservatism* (with Janan Ganesh), *Compassionate Economics* and *Churchill's Legacy* (with Peter Oborne) one finds analyses of what Norman describes as the state-first Fabianism of the modern Labour Party. Norman's

---

[3.] See J. Norman and J. Ganesh, *Compassionate Conservatism: What It Is – Why We Need It* (London: Policy Exchange, 2006); J. Norman, *Compassionate Economics: The Social Foundations of Economic Prosperity* (Buckingham: University of Buckingham Press, 2008); and J. Norman and P. Oborne, *Churchill's Legacy: The Conservative Case for the Human Rights Act* (London: Liberty, 2009).

thinking is nuanced and it would be incorrect to assume that he is ideologically opposed to the state *per se*. However, he is of the view that its ability to meet social needs and to support British society 'ranging from pensions to education, from housing to welfare' has, in the post-war period, been wanting. This has had a detrimental impact on the contributions to social renewal that 'active individuals and linking intuitions' can and should be making, if we are to achieve what he describes as a 'connected society'.[4] Even before the financial crash of 2007/8, under David Cameron's leadership, these views were becoming increasingly influential in the Conservative Party, particularly amongst those from the One Nation wing. It has been argued that Cameron saw compassionate Conservatism as a way of softening the image of the Conservative Party, from what had been described by the then chairman of the party, Theresa May, in her speech to the 2002 Conservative Party Conference, as a party seen by some as 'the nasty party'.[5] This is the context in which, in 2009–10, Phillip Blond's Red Tory thinking on the need for the Conservative Party to adopt a radical new approach to welfare was to gain traction among some thinkers in David Cameron's inner circle and make a significant contribution to what became the 'Big Society' project; hence, it is to these matters that we now turn.

Blond's theoretical contribution to the 'Big Society' project can be located in strands of Conservative and socialist tradition,[6] though it is critical of both when they represent, in the case of Conservatism, *laissez-faire* market individualism and, in the case of socialism, centralist, top-down statism. This is most clearly evident in his book of 2010 aptly called *Red Tory*, which was influential on the shaping of this agenda within Conservative Party circles.[7] As we have seen, Blond is an Anglo-Catholic political theologian and a member of the Radical Orthodoxy grouping.

---

4. See J. Norman, *The Big Society: The Anatomy of the New Politics* (Buckingham: University of Buckingham Press, 2010), pp. 1–12.

5. T. May, 'Full Text: Theresa May's Conference Speech', *The Guardian*, 7 October 2002.

6. See P. Blond, *Red Tory*; J. Norman, *The Big Society*.

7. See Harris, 'Phillip Blond: The Man Who Wrote Cameron's Mood Music'. According to this account, Blond's most fervent fans included the Tory leader's long-standing aide, Steve Hilton (the man who coined the term the 'Big Society'), and Rohan Silva, a member of George Osborne's inner circle. This account also states that Blond's 'thoughts have made it into speeches by David Cameron'. For more on Blond's influence in shaping the 'Big Society' project, see also S. Corbett, 'The Big Society Five Years On', in L. Foster, A.

He holds to a Christendom perspective on history and society, and his views on the Welfare State have been influenced by his wide theological reading, particularly from within the Roman Catholic and Anglo-Catholic traditions, and they are similar to those held by Milbank.

Thus, Blond refers approvingly to Christian Distributionists[8] such as Hilaire Belloc, author of *The Servile State* (1912), which is a trenchant analysis of both capitalism and statist socialism, concluding that both engender master-slave relations as they dispossess the self-sufficient populace of land, ownership and capital.[9] He also refers approvingly to G.K. Chesterton, who, like Belloc, was a member of the Distributionist League, which called for the restoration of property and assets for all. However, Blond is not a Distributionist in a 'purist', anarchistic sense, of the kind that Dorothy Day and Peter Maurin, founders of the Catholic Worker Movement in America in the 1930s, were to become. Rather, he cites approvingly Disraeli's One Nation Conservatism and Lord Randolph Churchill's campaign through the Primrose League for what he terms 'progressive Toryism' in the 1880s, as key sources of inspiration.[10] What these writers have in common is a shared belief that the state can act in ways that are stifling to the rich diversity of social, cultural and economic pluralism necessary for human flourishing.

It should therefore come as no surprise that Blond is also a great admirer of Burke, a thinker who influenced Disraeli a great deal[11] and who has been described by Jesse Norman[12] as 'the founding father of

---

Brunton, C. Deeming and T. Haux (eds), *In Defence of Welfare 2* (Bristol: Policy Press, 2015), pp. 165–67.

[8.] Christian Distributionism is a strand of Roman Catholic theology influenced by Catholic social teaching on the concept of subsidiarity, though its perspective on that is by no means universally held by all Roman Catholics. Distributionists hold to a view that the means of production, distribution and exchange in a given society should be widely owned and not be concentrated in the hands of the few. Also, the role of the state should be minimal in all human affairs. This perspective has elements in common with anarchism (indeed, some Distributionists have called themselves Christian anarchists, such as Dorothy Day).

[9.] H. Belloc, *The Servile State* (1912) (London: Constable and Co., 1950). Also, see Blond, *Red Tory*, p. 29.

[10.] Blond, *Red Tory*, p. 29.

[11.] See C. Hibbert, *Disraeli: A Personal History* (New York: Harper Perennial, 2005).

[12.] See Norman, *The Big Society*.

the "big society"'.[13] For both Norman and Blond, it is Burke who offers a palatable alternative to the way they perceive Hobbes had led to so much that had gone wrong in British politics and society. For it is Burke, they argue, who saw 'man' as a social animal, to be understood within a context of trust, culture and tradition, and thus not capable of being understood independently from society, 'man's natural state being civil society itself'.[14] Norman sums up this thinking:

> We can thus think of the big society as a deliberate, Burkean counterblast to Hobbes, restoring the three elements that Hobbes omits: a focus on human beings not as economic atoms, but as bundles of capability; a focus on intermediate institutions between the individual and the state; and a focus on society and individual rights as such, rather than as mediated by the state.[15]

Indeed, it is this focus on intermediate institutions between the individual and the state, that Blond sees as the way back from what he describes as state-provided 'welfare serfdom', that is, an economic and cultural dependency on the part of many of the recipients of state-provided welfare, that is retarding on an individual and societal level.[16] Thus, he argues:

> The great tragedy of the modern British welfare state has been the corrosion of the long-standing social values held by the working class, and thereby the effective erosion of the mutualism these values enshrined. Norms around community, work, familial obligation and civic and economic participation have been replaced by expectation of, and dependency on, state provision. This tragedy has not been particularly ironic, as welfarist state policies have been designed precisely to shift the primary source of social support from the horizontal social safety nets of civil society to vertically delivered equivalents provided by the state alone.[17]

[13.] Norman, 'The Intellectual Origins of the "Big Society"', *Total Politics*, 18 February 2011. Available at: https://www.totalpolitics.com/articles/interview/intellectual-origins-big-society (accessed on 4 November 2017).

[14.] Ibid.

[15.] Ibid.

[16.] P. Blond, 'Allow Me to Suggest, George', *The Guardian*, 27 September 2008.

[17.] Blond, *Red Tory*, p. 76.

Blond envisaged the 'Big Society' project as, potentially at least, a way of reversing that trend, by placing less reliance on the state as the provider of welfare, and instead rejuvenating horizontal social bonds and the reality of self-regulating communities – as he describes them:[18]

> At its best, the 'big society' is the answer to most of these ills. It is about breaking up the concentration of power in the state and in the economy – it is a distribution and dispersal of capital and capacity throughout our society, so as to create multiple centres of wealth, innovation and ownership.[19]

In this respect, his thinking in *Red Tory* was aimed at doing two key things: on the one hand, encouraging a political direction on welfare that was challenging both to the post-war 'Keynesian re-distributionist' paradigm of the 1945 to the late 1970s, which he argues was characterised by an over-statist approach to welfare provision; and, on the other hand, a political direction that was equally challenging to the *laissez-faire*, market-driven approach of Thatcherism and Blair/Brownism in the years between 1979 and 2010, which, in Blond's words, had led to a situation in which the 'rise of vested interest and the concentration of economic power in the City created an economy based on asset bubbles and debt leverage'.[20] Indeed, it is this thinking that led Blond to state the following about the 'Big Society' project:

> it is about addressing state failure via a revival of our civil society through a radical decentralisation of budgets and power to our localities and communities. Opening up the state to genuine economic participation and co-operative endeavour by citizens through charities, social enterprises and civic groups can create new trust platforms, designing out the audit and compliance bureaucracies that cripple our public services.[21]

This thinking impressed some of David Cameron's inner circle, and there are signs of it in some of his speeches. As noted in chapter three, Cameron defined the 'Big Society' project as embodying three strands:

[18.] Ibid., p. 77.

[19.] P. Blond, 'The Austerity Drive Must Not Derail the Winning "Big Society"', *The Guardian*, 3 October 2010.

[20.] Ibid.

[21.] Ibid.

1. the fostering of voluntarism, philanthropy and social action in support of causes;
2. public service reform; and
3. empowering individuals, communities and voluntary and charitable organisations to take more control over individual and societal affairs.[22]

One way of fostering voluntarism, philanthropy and social action in support of causes was to encourage and support a greater role for churches in the provision of welfare (this aspect will be covered in more detail later in the chapter).[23] 'Empowering individuals, communities and voluntary and charitable organisations to take more control' was also a key objective of 'Big Society' thinking. One way it proposed for achieving this was to initiate a Community Organising Programme, through providing a year's public money to train each of 5,000 (later to increase to 6,422) community organisers to work in their communities to promote more civic-based community initiatives.[24] Another was to establish what it called the world's first social investment bank, Big Society Capital, to be funded initially from dormant bank accounts.[25] A Centre for Social Impact Bonds was also to be created, to encourage private investment in support of social investment initiatives.[26] A Minister for Civil Society was appointed to help to co-ordinate the government's interface with the voluntary sector. The 'Big Society' project also established a National

---

[22.] See Cameron, 'Transcript of a Speech by the Prime Minister on the Big Society, 19 July 2010'.

[23.] See, for example, H. Lambie-Mumford and D. Jarvis, 'The Role of Faith-Based Organisations in the Big Society: Opportunities and Challenges', *Policy Studies* 33, no. 3 (2012), pp. 249–69. Available at: http://www .tandfonline.com/doi/abs/10.1080/01442872.2012.666395?journalCode =cpos20 (accessed on 17 November 2017).

[24.] See Cabinet Office, 'Community Organisers: Inspiring People to Build a Bigger, Stronger Society', Cabinet Office Analysis and Insight Team blog, 11 August 2015. Available at: https://coanalysis.blog.gov.uk/2015/08/11 /community-organisers-inspiring-people-to-build-a-bigger-stronger -society/ (accessed on 17 November 2017).

[25.] For more on this, see its website at: https://www.bigsocietycapital.com/.

[26.] For more on this, see gov.org at: https://www.gov.uk/government/news /centre-for-social-impact-bonds-new-tools-launched (accessed on 17 November 2017).

Citizen Service, where groups of 60 children were to take part in 'outward bound'-style courses in the countryside to learn team-building skills.[27] Large-scale public service reform was to be achieved on a scale not seen since the inception of the Welfare State in the 1940s. It is to this aspect that we now turn.

The 'Big Society' Project and Public Service Reform

In one key respect, the role of the market in the 'Big Society' project was to be enhanced, that is, in the furtherance of public service reform. In this regard, this project can be seen as a continuation of a trend in British politics that can be traced back to Thatcherism, which laid the foundations for the Blairite 'new localism' that followed.[28] This trend was to create, via legislation, the conditions that would enable *competition* in the provision of public services and hence a 'more mixed economy of welfare' to be brought about.[29] We saw in chapter two one example of this trend: the National Health Service and Community Care Act 1990, which established the purchaser/provider split in the NHS that enabled a market to be created for the provision of healthcare services, which had previously been predominantly provided by the state. A more contemporary one was the Academies Act 2010, intended to increase the number of academy trusts whereby schools could opt out of local education authority control.[30] Initiatives such as these were intended to result in a diverse range of providers for what had previously been state-run services, creating more choice and hence less 'Big Government' and more 'Big Society'. Accordingly, the Localism Act 2011 made it easier for services to be outsourced to local providers, with a provision that enabled parish councils, local authority employees and voluntary organisations to exercise a 'right to challenge' local authorities to

---

27. See UK Government, *Take Part: National Citizen Service.* Available at: https://www.gov.uk/government/get-involved/take-part/national-citizen -service (accessed on 17 November 2017).

28. For a summary of 'new localism', see M. Woolf, 'Labour Considers "New Localism" as the Big-Banner Policy for a Third Term', *Independent*, 22 October 2013.

29. J. Edwards (ed.), *Retrieving the Big Society* (Oxford: Wiley-Blackwell, 2012), p. 171.

30. See UK Government, Academies Act 2010. Available at: https://www .legislation.gov.uk/ukpga/2010/32/contents (accessed on 17 November 2017).

contract out services. It also contained the right to bid for their assets of value, from which they could 'deliver exciting new services'.[31] In this way, greater local empowerment would be encouraged. This was consistent with what Prime Minister Cameron said in the prior consultation paper, *Decentralisation and the Localism Bill: An Essential Guide*: 'We will be the first Government in a generation to leave office with much less power in Whitehall than we started with. Why? Because we feel the importance of this in our heads as well as our hearts.'[32] This sense of importance was partly underpinned by a feeling that the state-run model of public services was too bureaucratic and inefficient; on 6 October 2010, speaking in Birmingham, Cameron said: 'So this is what radicalism means, no more top-down, bureaucratic-driven public services. We're putting those services in your hands. The old targets and performance indicators that drove doctors, nurses and police officers mad – they're gone. All that bureaucracy that meant nothing ever happened – we are stripping it away.'[33]

Hence, the 'Big Society' project, partly via the Localism Act 2011, was meant to address criticisms of the way some considered public services in Britain to have become marred by an over-centralised, over-bureaucratic, over-professionalised and under-responsive approach to their delivery. The Act was intended to strengthen more localised, democratic kinds of accountability, by doing the following six things:

1. lifting the burden of bureaucracy – by removing the cost and control of unnecessary red tape and regulation;
2. empowering communities to do things their way – by creating rights for people to get involved with, and direct the development of, their communities;
3. increasing local control of public finance – so that more of the decisions over how public money is spent and raised can be taken within communities;

---

[31] UK Government, *Decentralisation and the Localism Bill: An Essential Guide*, 13 December 2010, pp. 1–12. Available at: https://www.gov.uk/government/publications/decentralisation-and-the-localism-bill-an-essential-guide--2 (accessed on 17 September 2015).

[32] Ibid.

[33] See D. Cameron, 'David Cameron's Speech in Full', BBC News, 6 October 2010. Available at: http://www.bbc.co.uk/news/uk-politics-11485397 (accessed on 23 April 2018).

4. diversifying the supply of public services – by ending public sector monopolies, ensuring a level playing field for all suppliers, giving people more choice and a better standard of service;
5. opening up government to public scrutiny – by releasing government information into the public domain; and
6. strengthening accountability to local people – by giving every citizen the power to change the services provided to them through participation, choice or the ballot box.[34]

The intention was to catapult Britain's public services into a post-bureaucratic age and restore a lost sense of Victorian civic engagement, voluntarism, philanthropic charitableness and social action in the process.

It was a vision that Milbank was to embrace, seeing it as consistent with advancing Radical Orthodoxy's Christendom values and vision. This would be achieved by bringing about a reduced welfare state sector in favour of more community-based, localised, voluntarist forms of welfare provision – a key welfare provider being the Church of England. Indeed, he saw the project as a major underpinning of his 'Blue Socialism with a Burkean tinge' perspective, and its evaluation of Temple's vision for the Welfare State (including its theological underpinning) and the adverse impact he believes it has had on local community cohesion and mutualism, as well as on the Church of England's reduced congregations and increasingly circumscribed role in the provision of welfare in the post-war period. Hence, we examine Milbank's perspective on the 'Big Society' project in relation to other contrasting perspectives.

John Milbank and Other Perspectives on the 'Big Society' Project

The launch of the 'Big Society' project in the summer of 2010 provoked a major debate within the Church of England on how it should respond. Some saw the project as an out-and-out attack on the Welfare State that the Church of England should largely oppose. Others saw it as a project that provided opportunities for the Church of England to re-engage in aspects of welfare provision that it had regrettably relinquished to

---

[34.] UK Government, *Decentralisation and the Localism Bill*, pp. 2–3.

the Welfare State, and hence a project that should be enthusiastically embraced. Yet others sought to develop thinking that in some respects fell between these two perspectives. Illustrative of the one 'extreme' of this debate was the document published in November 2010 by the radical, theological think tank Ekklesia called *Common Wealth: Christians for Economic and Social Justice*,[35] signed by Anglican Socialists such as Steven Shakespeare and Simon Barrow. The opposite 'extreme' was the response to that document by Milbank called 'The Big Society depends on the Big Parish',[36] published in December 2010. Illustrative of an approach that fell between these two perspectives was the book written by John Atherton, Christopher Baker and John Reader, *Christianity and the New Social Order*, published in 2011.[37]

In some ways the *Common Wealth* document can be seen as a qualified (hence not uncritical) defence of the Welfare Statist strand of the Anglican Socialist tradition, though it was signed by some non-Anglicans. The document stated its position as follows:

> As Christians, we are convinced that the actions of the current government are an unjustified attack on the poor. The rhetoric of necessary austerity and virtuous belt-tightening conceals a grim reality: the victimisation of people at the margins of society and the corrosion of community. Meanwhile, the false worship of markets continues unchecked and the immorality of the growing gap between rich and poor goes unquestioned. We call on the churches to resist the cuts and stand in solidarity with those targeted.

With respect to the 'Big Society' project, it stated: 'The Big Society is a Big Lie. It is a smokescreen, another ideological veil. Its pretence of radical change is simply a means of persuading us to live in submission to the great God Capital.' Crucially, it then went on to state what has since been seen by some writers as a central criticism of the Church of England's initially favourable response to the 'Big Society' project:

[35.] See Ekklesia, *Common Wealth: Christians for Economic and Social Justice*, November 2010. Available at: http://www.ekklesia.co.uk/CommonWealth Statement (accessed on 5 November 2017).

[36.] Milbank, 'The Big Society Depends on the Big Parish'.

[37.] Atherton, Baker and Reader, *Christianity and the New Social Order*.

Of course, there are Christians and Christian organisations who see in the Big Society agenda a recognition of what they are already doing in their social activism, and an opportunity to take it further. However, we believe that the craving for relevance is overriding any more searching critique of what is on offer.

Common Wealth thus warned:

> churches who simply seek ways of working with the Big Society agenda risk colluding with forces and principles fundamentally at odds with the gospel. The question is not 'what can advance the cause of the churches and make them look more relevant in today's society?' The question is, 'how can churches bear witness to the radical transformation of society called for by their proclamation of the kingdom of God?'

However, the *Common Wealth* document did not rule out some limited, pragmatic compromises with the 'Big Society' project by churches, drawing on resources being made available by the government, to enable short-term assistance to the poor to be provided at a time of austerity, so long as it was not at the expense of embracing its ideology, stating:

> there may well be overriding pragmatic reasons why churches should compromise, drawing on resources available in the present system in order to make life more tolerable and more humane for those they serve. But the critical, cutting edge of Christian witness must never be lost at such times to an accommodation to Big Society ideology.[38]

The response to the *Common Wealth* document by Milbank was highly critical of most of its key lines of argument and reflected his Christendom kind of Anglican Socialism. It agreed with *Common Wealth* 'about the unnecessary pace and regressive social impact of some of the budget cuts – although [it contended] the scale is being somewhat exaggerated'.[39] Nevertheless, it then described the 'Big Society' project as

---

[38.] Ekklesia, *Common Wealth*.

[39.] Milbank, 'The Big Society Depends on the Big Parish', p. 1.

'a remarkable experiment in seeking to mutualise government services, to give more power in decision-making to front-line operators and to establish a more direct relationship between users and suppliers of various services'.[40] Milbank further pointed out that Ed Miliband, then leader of the Labour Party, was 'cautiously inclined towards his own leftish version of the Big Society' (what became the Blue Labour 'Good Society' model).[41]

Milbank then proceeded to locate the 'Big Society' project as – in part – the result of a welcome recognition of growing awareness in British society of the value that a vibrant 'third sector' could make, and linked this to his assessment of the limitations of representative democracy:

> Central planning cannot assess people's various local and changing needs, while the pursuit of profit leaves many genuine needs and demands totally unmet. In addition, we should welcome the rise of the third sector because it vastly increases the instance of genuine, spontaneous and participatory democracy in operation. By contrast, the overwhelming evidence is that merely representative democracy has reduced the ordinary person's real decision-making power which can only come about through neighbourly collaboration.[42]

His alternative to 'merely representative democracy' is what he calls 'participatory democracy', an essential ingredient of which is the role that churches can play in achieving it:

> Participatory democracy, in the realms both of welfare and of co-operative and stakeholder enterprise, was in the British past (as elsewhere in Europe and the Americas and Australasia) almost entirely tied up with the practice of religion. ... It allowed intimate and collaborative relationships between donors and beneficiaries; it guarded against loneliness; it ensured an holistic union of body and spirit when it came to schooling and nursing; it rendered domestic

---

[40.] Ibid.
[41.] Ibid.
[42.] Ibid., p. 2.

labour communal and collaborative and it encouraged far
more communication across class boundaries than pertains
today.[43]

Milbank saw the 'Big Society' project as a way for churches to enhance
localised, participatory democracy in British society by way of assuming
greater responsibility for the provision of welfare, restoring something
of the role they had undertaken as welfare providers in Victorian
Britain, only to have foolishly ceded it to the Welfare State project after
the Second World War. He lavished praise on the tradition of religious
philanthropy that had developed in Victorian Britain, which he argued
was 'often done by the working class for the working class'; and then
proceeded to appraise the Temple welfare state model of welfare
delivery, stating: 'Ironically, it was the religious tradition of welfare
which itself played a big role, through the influence of William Temple
and others, in erecting the welfare state which quite quickly destroyed
this [religious Victorian philanthropic] tradition and the moral energies
it had nurtured.'[44] For Milbank, 'it is not little short of incredible that
churches should endorse any process of education that neglects the vital
truth about our souls or any process of medicine not concerned with the
soul as well as the body'.[45] He thus argued that: 'the Big Society presents
a huge opportunity for the restoration of "the big parish" in which care
for body and soul go once more hand in hand. It is this opportunity that
Common Wealth crazily wishes to forego.'[46]

By contrast, the Atherton, Baker, Reader perspective was not as hostile
to the 'Big Society' project as the *Common Wealth* document had been,
but neither was it as supportive of its aims as Milbank's writings were. It
was sceptical of the extent to which an increased emphasis on localism
in the provision of welfare, as advocated by Milbank and Blond *et al.*,
could adequately meet the needs of contemporary British society in the
way the Welfare State was resourced and equipped to do, particularly in
the wake of the financial collapse of 2008. However, it argued for a need
to go beyond the approach that, since the Beveridge report of 1942, had
been based on *welfare* (and specifically the slaying of the five giants) to

---

43. Ibid., p. 3.
44. Ibid.
45. Ibid., p. 5.
46. Ibid., p. 4.

one capable of tackling what it described as *well-being*.[47] It concluded with an updated list of middle axioms to those originally established by Temple in his work of 1942. In some respects these broadened the range of areas requiring both state *and* community action to include:

1. The flourishing of every child – with a particular focus on the first three years of a child's life – involving their nurturing in the material and immaterial, including spiritual, experiences of life.

2. The commitment to education as lifelong learning for all through the primary, secondary and tertiary sectors, including embracing initiatives such as the 'universities of the third age'.

3. The fostering of rigorous care for and delight in the environment.

4. The pursuit of greater equality as essential to the pursuit of greater well-being (this already being a key underpinning of state welfare institutions such as the NHS).

5. Developing financial systems to deliver and support greater well-being for all, including ethical economics in collaboration with religious traditions.

6. Recognising the importance of income and work for personal and national well-being (something that the Beveridge report had emphasised in its commitment to full employment).

7. The development of health as personal and communal wholeness for all. Emphasising the need for greater recognition of a spiritual dimension to health and well-being, they argued for: 'curative as well as preventative measures, traditional as well as alternative medicines, private and public health and the growing need to focus on mental health'.[48]

Some of this thinking resonates with Milbank's Blue Socialist insistence on: the need for a greater emphasis to be placed on ethical (including spiritual) precepts in finance and the economy; a more holistic and spiritually informed approach to healthcare provision; the need for

47. Atherton, Baker and Reader, *Christianity and the New Social Order*, pp. 22–74.

48. Ibid., pp. 125–29.

ethically underpinned management of the environment; and a greater focus on the common good in the way British politics is conducted. However, the increased emphasis that Atherton, Baker and Reader place on the need for well-being to be part of the wider welfare remit – including state provision of welfare – could be interpreted by some as fostering an over-encroaching state that could become too intrusive or controlling, thereby undermining the role of the family and civil society – a view that would chime with aspects of Milbank's scepticism of statist approaches to welfare. Yet, this concern may be mitigated by their advocacy of a Temple inspired and informed pragmatism in the way these goals could and should be achieved.

For Atherton, Baker and Reader, as it had been for Temple, state sector measures can and should be a major (though not exclusive) part of the overall provision of welfare (and what they term well-being) where they have been seen to provide, or have the potential to provide, the best route for its delivery, particularly in health and education. However, in line with Temple's thinking, this need not be at the expense of other, more localised options such as community-based initiatives to reduce greenhouse gases or to improve people's mental health via more locally organised recreational activities, which can add to the overall level of well-being. It was for this reason that they saw some potential in the 'Big Society' project for enhancing neighbourliness (and thus well-being) via increased state financial support to the voluntary sector, and, specifically, the faith-based sector, whilst remaining wary of whether this was 'simply a distraction or blind for the real agenda, which is cuts in public services'.[49] Their perspective can thus be located in the Welfare Statist strand, but with an emphasis on broadening and modernising its thinking for the twenty-first century, with a Temple inspired focus on pragmatic as well as ideological underpinning, and his recognition of how community-based welfare initiatives can and should contribute to the overall drive for social improvement.

These three perspectives on the 'Big Society' project, though by no means all-inclusive of opinion within the Church of England on the best ways of responding to it, nevertheless give a sense of the parameters within which the debates were conducted. Much of the thinking then and since can be seen as variations on these perspectives: the extent to which the Church should defend the Welfare Statist legacy or the voluntarist, localist, communitarian evaluation of it – the

---

[49] Ibid., p. 9.

latter offering a more charity-focused, community-based provision of welfare. However, before we analyse the Church of England's response to the 'Big Society' project, we must briefly examine its positions on welfare for the period 1945 to 2010, so that its response can be considered in historical context.

The Church of England and Welfare, 1945–2010

We noted in chapter four that it can be argued the Church positioned itself closer to Temple's theology of the state via the resolutions passed at the 1948 Lambeth Conference, particularly Resolution 19. The result was that the Church of England became a champion of the Welfare State during the period of welfare consensus discussed in chapter two, in effect calling upon its members 'to accept their own political responsibility and to cooperate with the State and its officers in their work'.[50] When that consensus was challenged by the Thatcher administration in the early to mid-1980s during a period of economic turbulence, manufacturing decline, rising unemployment and a squeeze on public sector funding, it responded with an enquiry that produced the *Faith in the City* report in 1985.[51] That report was highly critical of the negative effect it believed the economic and social policies being pursued by the government were having on the poorest members of British society. It embodied much of Temple's and Tawney's thinking in its analysis and mode of presentation; in addition, it drew on a significant number of accounts from recipients of welfare that added to its authenticity. It made 38 recommendations pertaining to the Church of England and 23 to the government and wider society. These latter recommendations included the need:

2. To increase the Rate Support Grant to local government so that it could increase its provision of welfare services. ...
11. To extend state support for the long-term unemployed.
12. To increase Child Benefit. ...
16. To expand the public housing programme.[52]

---

50. Lambeth Conference of 1948, Resolution 19.
51. Church of England, *Faith in the City: A Call for Action by Church and Nation: The Report of the Archbishop of Canterbury's Commission on Urban Priority Areas* (London: Church House Publishing, 1985).
52. *Faith in the City*, pp. 364–66.

As these were all measures that would *increase* the resources required of the Welfare State and the demands placed on it, it can be reliably argued that they amounted to a continuation of Temple's legacy at a time when government spending on welfare was being squeezed (even though it can be argued the report went beyond his thinking on middle axioms). This is a point that was lost on some of the commentators at the time,[53] who focused instead on part of a single chapter influenced by Liberation Theology – with its Marxist overtones – that was theologically unrepresentative of the broad thrust of the report and its recommendations. The report called for a renewed sense of partnership between central and local government and between government and the voluntary sector, to be achieved by providing 'long-term continuity and funding for recognised voluntary bodies working alongside statutory agencies'.[54] This recommendation was fully consistent with Temple's and Beveridge's thinking on voluntary sector provision of welfare, and the positive role it could and should perform in its provision, in tandem with, but not as a substitute for, the Welfare State.

After *Faith in the City*, a working party under the umbrella of the Social Policy Committee of the Church of England, published *Not Just for the Poor: Christian Perspectives on the Welfare State* in 1986.[55] That report was, in large part, written by Ronald Preston, who, as we have seen, was a champion of Temple's thinking on welfare. It provided an analysis of the achievements and shortcomings of the Welfare State, structured around the five giants on which Beveridge had framed his report. It offered a nuanced and balanced assessment of progress since 1945 in slaying them, as well as an analysis of the shortcomings in state-provided welfare. It pointed to:

1. How health care had become far more comprehensive in its coverage.

[53.] For example, it was condemned by one cabinet minister as 'pure Marxist theology'. See J. Bingham, 'Church of England's Pre-election Blast Revives Memories of *Faith in the City*', *Daily Telegraph*, 3 October 2019. For an introduction to liberation theology, see G. Gutiérrez, *A Theology of Liberation* (Maryknoll, NY: Orbis Books, 1973).

[54.] *Faith in the City*, p. 365.

[55.] Church of England, *Not Just for the Poor: Christian Perspectives on the Welfare State: Report of the Social Policy Committee of the Board of Social Responsibility* (London: Church House Publishing, 1986).

2. How educational standards had risen with more children leaving school with qualifications.
3. How social security benefits had improved in real terms since 1945 and ensured that people experiencing hardship had some income.
4. How there had been a massive clearance of slum housing and the development of much high-quality public-sector housing.
5. How the growth in state-provided personal social services had considerably assisted in the provision of day care for children, support to elderly people, the disabled and other vulnerable groups in society.

Yet it also identified shortcomings in state-provided welfare, including:

1. Where means-tested benefits could on occasion trap people in poverty.
2. Where the cost of state-provided health care was proving to be more expensive than had originally been envisaged (resulting, for example, in charges being instituted for glasses and dentures and thus a compromise with the free-at-the-point-of-delivery principle).
3. Where there remained a shortage of social housing provision in a context of an acute shortage of private rented accommodation.
4. Where there were still serious disparities between the achievement of children from professional and managerial families compared to the rest.
5. Where social workers had not been good at communicating to the outside world about what they did, resulting in inflated expectations and some suspicion in the minds of the British public.[56]

The report also analysed voluntary sector provision of welfare since 1945 and concluded:

> Gradually a partnership between the state and the voluntary sector developed. ... It was assumed by some in post-war Britain that the enhanced provision of social security, together

---

[56.] Ibid., pp. 49–72.

with the establishment of the NHS and the implementation of the 1944 Education Act, would render the existence of the voluntary organisations superfluous. This withering of voluntary activity did not occur; some activities were maintained and different forms of action grew in response to changing social needs.[57]

As noted in chapter four, this view is antithetical to the perspective which Milbank was later to advance, that the post-war Welfare State was 'at the expense of intermediary institutions and popular participation' and 'fragmented mutual organisation'.[58] Rather, it is wholly consistent with the thinking of Temple, Attlee and Beveridge, and with much of the historical evidence adduced in chapter four. The 1986 report saw voluntary provision of welfare as complementary to statutory provision by 'providing services which might not otherwise exist',[59] though the report considered these services at times to be rigid and inflexible in their styles of operation.

Not Just for the Poor also examined the voluntarist analyses of state-provided welfare that had been developed since the 1960s by Ivan Illich, Roger Hadley and Stephen Hatch *et al.*,[60] (and which in some respects can be seen as precursors to several of the criticisms that Milbank later advanced). These have included:

1. an alleged over-professionalisation of decisions leading to a 'neglect of people's capacity for self-help';[61]
2. an alleged overly bureaucratic 'top-down' delivery of services; and
3. an alleged insufficient level of focus on the client's perspective when assessing individual needs.[62]

---

[57] Ibid., p. 75.

[58] Milbank, 'The Big Society Depends on the Big Parish', p. 4.

[59] Church of England, *Not Just for the Poor*, p. 77.

[60] Ibid., p. 78.

[61] Ibid., p. 95.

[62] An alternative perspective can be located in the study into professional management in the NHS by P. Hayde, E. Granter, J. Hassard and L. McCann, *Deconstructing the Welfare State: Managing Health Care in the Age of Reform* (London: Routledge, 2016).

Of significance here is that, since the NHS Plan of 2000 and the Wanless Report of 2002, both of which highlighted the need for NHS healthcare professionals to embrace greater patient empowerment and personalisation with patients as partners in care, a considerable amount of work has been done on developing and promoting 'bottom-up', person-centred care in the ethos of the NHS, in the interpersonal approach of its healthcare deliverers and in its systems of healthcare delivery. This is an indication that this line of criticism has been acknowledged by key healthcare professionals as not being without merit.[63] In this respect *Not Just for the Poor* was prescient in its recognition of the reality that: 'We have moved away decisively from being a society which will accept paternalistic services ... today's citizens expect to be able to participate in decisions which affect them'.[64] Yet the introduction of person- or patient-centred care into the NHS in the early 2000s as an alternative model to task- or disease-focused care, which has since received much praise where it has been found to have been consistently applied,[65] suggests that it was a line of criticism that could be addressed, and, to a significant degree, be accommodated, within one arm of the Welfare State (thus setting an example for others). However, due credit must go to writers such as Illich, Hadley and Hatch, who recognised the need for a more person-centred approach to aspects of welfare provision to that being provided at that time by the state sector before many others had.

Yet, *Not Just for the Poor* concluded that, whilst this voluntarist assessment asked 'important questions about power and decision

---

[63.] For an introduction to person-centred care and its incorporation into the NHS, see Health Foundation, *Person-Centred Care Made Simple: What Every Person Should Know about Person-Centred Care* (London: The Health Foundation, 2014). Available at: https://www.health.org.uk/publications /person-centred-care-made-simple (accessed on 20 December 2021). See also Department of Health, *The NHS Plan: A Plan for Investment, a Plan for Reform* (Norwich: HMSO, July 2000), and D. Wanless, *Securing Our Future Health: Taking a Long-Term View* (London: HM Treasury, April 2002).

[64.] *Not Just for the Poor*, p. 123.

[65.] See, for example, A. Kitson, A. Marshall, K. Bassett and K. A. Zeitz, 'What Are the Core Elements of Patient-Centred Care? A Narrative Review and Synthesis of the Literature from Health Policy, Medicine and Nursing', *JAN: Improving Practice and Policy Worldwide Through Research & Scholarship* 69, no. 1 (2013), pp. 4–15.

making', with its emphasis on how 'users of services should have a far greater say in what they are offered', it went on to say:

> But it can be argued that the critique does not take into account the fact that organisations and bureaucracies are crucial for welfare in the twentieth century. They may not work perfectly, but they are vital. Furthermore, the analysis can ... become a new dogma: small is not necessarily beautiful; small can be experienced as oppressive and limiting.[66]

In Summary

Not Just for the Poor was emphatic in its insistence that it was 'not arguing for the status quo'.[67] It acknowledged there were weaknesses in the Welfare State that needed to be addressed – for example, the need for less paternalism and greater participation, with a renewed need for greater flexibility and responsiveness in the delivery of state-provided welfare services. However, it was unambiguous in its overall support for the Welfare State, concluding: 'We thus affirm much of the vision, if not the detail, of the post-war settlement, which was fundamentally sound' and: 'Generous provision by society through the state is essential. But it is not enough on its own to produce the kind of society we wish to see. A mixed economy of welfare, built on co-operation between the public, voluntary and private sectors, is to be welcomed.'[68] Crucial to note here is the word *co-operation*. It did not envisage or advocate a mixed economy of welfare based on *competition* for the provision of welfare services by way of a tendering/commissioning process of the kind the 'Big Society' project was to introduce via the provisions of the Localism Act 2011.

In the period between the publication of *Faith in the City* in 1985 and the launch of the 'Big Society' project in 2010, the Church of England's approach to welfare can be seen as broadly being within the paradigm of thinking that *Faith in the City* and *Not Just for the Poor* had scoped out. *Unemployment and the Future of Work* (1997)[69] – a study undertaken by the Council of Churches for Britain and Ireland (CCBI) but with significant Church of England input – can, in some respects, be seen as a sequel to *Faith in the City* in that it adopted a

---

[66.] *Not Just for the Poor*, p. 96.

[67.] Ibid., p. 134.

[68.] Ibid.

[69.] Council of Churches for Britain and Ireland, *Unemployment and the Future of Work: An Enquiry for the Churches* (London: CCBI Publications, 1997).

similar research methodology, with much evidence being gathered from all over the country by a group of researchers on the plight of the unemployed. It was prescient, for example, in the way it drew attention to the dangers of work capability assessments for the unemployed, forcing people into the labour markets who may struggle to secure suitable employment and arguing against the view that any offers of work 'made to the unemployed should be compulsory'.[70] Subsequent public concern over work capability assessments for the unemployed resulted in the government terminating prematurely the contract of the provider of these assessments (ATOS) in 2014, though they continue to be undertaken by a different provider.[71] *Unemployment and the Future of Work* further argued in favour of in-work benefits, such as family credit and council tax benefit, seeing them as 'an important gain', although it acknowledged that: 'One effect of in work benefits is to reduce the wages offered for relatively unskilled jobs.'[72] This was something that had not been envisaged by Beveridge or Temple and is precisely the kind of extension of the Welfare State's remit and its consequences about which Milbank has been so critical.[73] *Faithful Cities*,[74] a report published in 2006 by the Church's Commission on Urban Life and Faith, focused on inner city life and the need for the Church to focus resources on tackling racism, poverty, social exclusion and the growing divide between the rich and poor in English inner cities. Its research base was more modest than it had been for *Faith in The City* and *Unemployment and the Future of Work* and it had far less impact. As noted in chapter four, the Church of England's Board for Social Responsibility, established in 1958 and replaced in 1999 by the Church of England's Mission and Public Affairs Council, continued to offer advice to successive governments on numerous aspects of welfare. These included how the functioning of the Welfare State could be improved. It also helped to co-ordinate the Church's myriad of voluntary interventions in social welfare. However, it was only with the launch of the 'Big Society' project, that the Church of England was confronted with a radical alternative agenda. Hence, it is its response to that new welfare agenda that we now consider.

---

70. Ibid., p. 132.

71. See 'ATOS Quits £500m Work Capability Assessment Contract Early', *The Guardian*, 27 March 2014.

72. CCBI, *Unemployment and the Future of Work*, p. 139.

73. Milbank and Pabst, 'Post-Liberal Politics and the Alternative', p. 92.

74. Commission for Urban Life and Faith, *Faithful Cities: A Call for Celebration, Vision and Justice* (London: Church House Publishing, 2006).

The Church of England's Response to the 'Big Society' Project

In a speech delivered to charity groups in South London in July 2010, Rowan Williams, Archbishop of Canterbury, gave the 'Big Society' project 'two and a half cheers'; he stopped short of giving it three cheers, stating: 'We need reassuring that the Big Society isn't just an alibi for cuts, and a way back to Government just washing its hands.'[75] At the same time, he said that the project could represent a 'watershed moment' in British politics if it was pursued with imagination. Hence, although his speech was by no means an unqualified endorsement of the 'Big Society' project, it can be seen as broadly supportive of its stated aims. The archbishop, an admirer of Figgis' work, liked the idea that the project saw 'the local as important' and 'somehow built around thickly textured communities'.[76] Milbank's view of the speech was that 'five-sixths support is really quite a lot, and probably gets it about right'.[77]

The Mission and Public Affairs Council of the Church of England then produced an advisory paper in September 2010, written by its director, Malcolm Brown. Brown, in the *Journal of Political Theology*, later described himself as the person who 'was responsible for the Church of England's central responses to the government's "Big Society" proposals'.[78] This key official document was called *'The Big Society' and the Church of England* (GS1804).[79] It stated: 'The Coalition has set out to deliver dramatic cuts to public spending, not least in social welfare. The potential of voluntarism to replace some state welfare provision may

---

[75] Heidi Blake, 'Dr Rowan Williams: Two and a Half Cheers for the Big Society', *Daily Telegraph*, 24 July 2010.

[76] Ibid.

[77] Milbank, 'The Big Society Depends on the Big Parish', p. 1.

[78] M. Brown, 'Red Tory and Blue Labour: More Theology Needed', *Political Theology Journal* 13, no. 3 (2012), p. 348. There is much in the following analysis that lends support to his view and, on reading the final version of the PhD on which this book is partly based, Brown – in email correspondence with the present writer – at no time suggested that I had exaggerated his input into these events or his level of influence on shaping them.

[79] M. Brown, *"The Big Society" and the Church of England*, General Synod Paper GS1804, September 2010. This is available as Appendix One to this book.

make The Big Society financially attractive.'[80] Hence, at that time, Brown was clear in his advice to the Church of England that 'dramatic cuts in public spending, not least in social welfare' was the financial context in which the 'Big Society' project had been shaped, following the financial crash two years earlier. Indeed, in the same document he pointed out: 'David Cameron has indicated that he regards the development of stronger social structures as compensating for a permanent and very large reduction in public spending.'[81] However, Brown also states: 'Yet, despite such caveats, many agree that the ideas behind The Big Society are necessary in a civilised society and that the erosion of community values and the intermediate institutions has gone so far that the basic social structures need rebuilding.'[82] He further argued:

> the churches are not being asked to sign up to, or approve, The Big Society as a single policy programme. However, there is potential for us to use the political narrative of The Big Society to shift the relationships between the state, the individual and intermediate institutions in ways which reflect a Christian understanding of society and reinforce the church's place in a healthy social order.[83]

This quote is revealing in that it suggests that Brown, at that time, believed that the existing relationships between the state, the individual and the intermediate institutions did *not* adequately 'reflect' a Christian understanding of society, or 'reinforce' the Church's place within it. As examined in chapters three and four, this is the essence of Milbank's Blue Socialist critique of Temple's Welfare Statist legacy and, indeed, of Milbank's and Blond's Christendom critique of that whole line of the Anglican Socialist tradition. GS1804 thus proposed a partnership between the Church of England and the new Coalition government on delivering key aspects of the 'Big Society' project, claiming: 'We know of no other current partnership proposals of comparable size and scope.'[84] That partnership was, in part, to take the form of the Near Neighbours initiative, that provided an illustration of what else might be possible.

[80.] Ibid., para. 8.

[81.] Ibid., para. 15.

[82.] Ibid., para. 13.

[83.] Ibid., para. 28.

[84.] Ibid., para. 57.

The Near Neighbours Initiative

The Near Neighbours initiative was a project intended to better promote and improve community relations, particularly in multi-faith areas. It would do this by distributing state funding to parishes for local initiatives to increase the 'intensity of local cross-community relationships. These were to be through small-scale activities generated locally and administered through the local church'.[85] It is for this reason that Brown has since said: 'Near Neighbours was not addressed to welfare issues. Near Neighbours was addressed to interfaith relations.'[86] In a Church of England proposal document of 15 October 2010, the Near Neighbours project was described as an initiative with 'a real potential to connect our existing vocation with the concepts of a Big Society'.[87] Thus, it argued: 'The programme represents a real shift away from governmental programmes to faith community programmes; away from centralised and top-down approaches to locally rooted approaches ... the approach being proposed will open new ways for government and faith communities generally to relate to each other.'[88]

In GS1804 Brown had made it clear that 'significant sums of public money would be involved'.[89] This would be state-provided money received into the Church Urban Fund (an initial grant of £5 million was later provided,[90] with two other grants to follow).[91] Although Brown insisted the Near Neighbours initiative was 'not about the

---

[85] M. Brown, 'Annex', *Near Neighbours: By Faithful Interaction Draft Proposals*, Church of England, 15 October 2010, p. 4.

[86] Brown's reply to question 21 of an interview conducted with the present writer. The interview is reproduced in its entirety as Appendix Four to: Joseph Forde, 'Anglican Socialism and Welfare: John Milbank's 'Blue Socialist' Thinking and the Church of England's Approach to Welfare since 2008' (PhD thesis, University of Manchester, 2020). It is available to access online via an internet search. All of Brown's replies to questions in the references that follow are located in that source. A list of all of the questions the present writer put to Brown is reproduced as Appendix Two of this book.

[87] Brown, 'Annex', p. 8.

[88] Ibid., p. 3.

[89] GS1804, para. 60.

[90] See R. Butt, 'The Church of England Gets £5m for Community Cohesion Project', *The Guardian*, 20 February 2011.

[91] Brown's reply to question 20.

church stepping into the welfare gap left by a retreating state', later in the same document he stated that, if the Near Neighbours initiative proved to be successful, there might be 'further opportunities for similar church/government partnership under The Big Society agenda. Some of these may involve the church in direct service delivery.'[92] When later questioned on this by the present writer, Brown did not give specific examples of the kind of direct service delivery he had been thinking of but, instead, alluded to a number of bishops who had seen the Lutheran churches in Scandinavia and Germany as 'essentially, an arm of the civil service, and they got envious'.[93] He was, then, at least in part, trying to incorporate their expectations into what he had written. He further stated in GS1804: 'the potential of our buildings to be community hubs and accessible to many, could be enhanced if there was less government suspicion about using public money to build shared resources through faith communities'.[94] These ideas resonated with those that were being put forward by Milbank in support of his view that 'the Big Society depends on the big parish', as well as those being put forward by Blond in *Red Tory*.[95] We begin to see, then, how GS1804 was, in part, the catalyst for the Near Neighbours project, as well as for other aspects of the Church's response to the 'Big Society' project, that we now analyse.

GS1804 and the General Synod of November 2010
GS1804 was broadly supportive of the 'Big Society' initiative, fully recognising that it would be rolled out in the context of significant reductions to public expenditure, with implications for the funding of state-provided welfare. The paper concluded by stating: 'The Big Society is, in principle, natural territory for the Church of England. In parishes all over the country, the church is already creating and sustaining a "Big Society". What we now see is a government moving to build social policy around such local commitments.'[96] It continued:

> The Big Society may come to represent a radical and ambitious shift in the way society and government are conceived: one in which the church has more room to be itself. ... Politicians

---

[92.] GS1804, para. 66.

[93.] Brown's reply to question 23.

[94.] GS1804, para. 69.

[95.] Blond, *Red Tory*, pp. 80–81.

[96.] GS1804, para. 76.

who are pursing The Big Society are playing for high stakes.
The church has an interest in seeing the best elements of The
Big Society thinking succeed.[97]

The report was well received by General Synod, as confirmed by the
Report of the Proceedings.[98] In opening remarks, the Rt Revd Timothy
Stevens, Bishop of Leicester, declared: 'We have a responsibility to
stand in critical solidarity with people in power. That remains acutely
important at a time of such dramatic and rapid economic and social
change.'[99] This statement is similar to a point that Brown was later to
make in conversation with the present writer, alluding to the way in
which the vocation of an established church may be: 'to recognise the
intense burden of responsibility that people in authority carry'.[100] This
indicates a perceived need for the established church to be seen to be
in solidarity (albeit not uncritical solidarity) with the government of
the day at a time of crisis, such as in the aftermath of a financial crash.
However, Bishop Stevens went on to state: 'It is, of course, too early to
say what the consequences of the Government's programme will be, but
not too early for us as a Church to be put on warning of our need to be
watchful and attentive, especially to the unintended consequences for
the most vulnerable.'[101] Uncritical solidarity with the people in power
was not, therefore, being advocated.

Bishop Stevens was also keen to point out the limits to state welfare
and the ideological approach underpinning it:

> We need to recognize that there is a great deal more to a
> good society than welfare delivery. The Prime Minister has
> spoken of three strands to this agenda: social action, public
> service reform and community empowerment. All of this
> requires the strengthening of the intermediate institutions
> which enrich human communities without subsuming
> everything into the State. The State can overreach itself
> when it forgets that people find identity and belonging in

[97.] GS1804, para. 79.
[98.] Church of England, *Report of Proceedings 2010: General Synod: November Group of Sessions*, Vol. 41, no. 3.
[99.] Ibid., p. 23.
[100.] Brown's reply to question 30.
[101.] Church of England, *Report of Proceedings 2010*, p. 23.

smaller communities, localities, workplaces, trade unions, educational establishments and churches. If people are to find their full human identity in such communities, the State must know its limits. In that sense, I suggest, the Big Society need not be about the State abandoning its responsibilities but about recognizing that good government requires that there are real limits to its remit, whether in times of austerity or of prosperity.[102]

His opening remarks were, therefore, broadly supportive of the 'Big Society' initiative, seeing it as an opportunity for strengthening the intermediate organisations in British civil society, whilst not wanting the state to abandon its welfare responsibilities, but recognising there are 'limits' to what state welfare provision can achieve. The debate that followed broadly reflected that line of thinking. Archbishop Rowan Williams welcomed GS1804:

I welcome the document before us. I welcome very profoundly the language that is around about the Big Society. In recent weeks, I have occasionally been asked whether I am at all cynical about the Big Society in relation to its contemporaneity with the cost-cutting exercise. The answer is that I am not. What I am is not cynical but opportunistic. Whether or not the Big Society is indeed an absolutely innocent creation of pure political vision or whether it has some elements in it of expediency, never mind: it has given us an extraordinary opportunity for raising in public questions about character and virtue, questions about generosity and justice, and of course a whole set of quite uncomfortable questions addressed to ourselves about our willingness to step up to the plate and respond.[103]

Several other speakers echoed this positive response to GS1804, with the Rt Revd Nicholas Reade, Bishop of Blackburn, saying: 'In a way, it is all win-win: a new culture of volunteerism; opening up public services to new providers like charities, social enterprises and private companies;

[102.] Ibid.

[103.] Ibid., p. 28.

the decentralization agenda – "Nothing is real until it is local" and all that',[104] though he cautioned:

> relationships between Church and State must be bilateral. If partnership is requested, it should be respected. In crude terms, that means Churches not simply being seen as casualty stations for those wounded by political and economic fallout but as reservoirs of carefully developed faith, which condition our hope and help to needy individuals and communities.[105]

There were some other words of caution spoken from the Revd Mark Beach (Coventry): 'What I fear is that, as the tide of central Government funding retreats, many in the community and voluntary sector will be left high and dry on the beach.'[106] Yet, despite these reservations, he was of the view: 'If the Big Society is about enabling local people to fulfil their aspirations, I am all for it. If what is achieved is a real shift of power away from Whitehall, which reduces red tape and allows people to get on with it, then all well and good.'[107]

The debate also contained some historical reflection on the Welfare State and the Church's approach to it, with Mr Gavin Oldham (Oxford) arguing that the position adopted on the Welfare State by the Lambeth Conference of 1948 may have been too unguarded:

> The Church has always risen to the challenge of Christ's call to love our neighbours as ourselves. ... However, the depth of the Church's involvement in community support reduced sharply just after the Second World War, when the welfare state was formed. In contrast to education, where the Church continued to play a major role, we left the welfare field as the Government's provision of social security became deeper and deeper. ... With the benefit of hindsight, we can now see that this provision of State welfare has become more and more secular; a job rather than a vocation. Now, for the first time in 60 years, there is a Government that positively wants voluntary organizations with a vocation to work in partnership with it. It wants this

---

[104.] Ibid., p. 33.
[105.] Ibid., p. 34.
[106.] Ibid., p. 33.
[107.] Ibid.

to be a reality at the local level, and appears to be well-tuned to the risks and challenges of such partnerships, both for the Government and the voluntary organizations themselves.[108]

At the conclusion of the debate, a resolution was passed endorsing GS1804 as a way forward for the Church of England on its handling of the 'Big Society' project.[109]

In Summary
The Synod's support for GS1804 can be seen as a paradigm shift in the way the Church responded to a government that was making major cuts to public expenditure, including welfare expenditure. Whereas *Faith in the City* had been highly critical of government cuts to public expenditure, including welfare, and the impact they were having, GS1804 was broadly in support of the 'Big Society' project, although, as previously noted, it acknowledged that the Coalition government had 'set out to deliver dramatic cuts to public spending, not least in social welfare'.[110] Whereas *Not Just for the Poor* had welcomed the post-war mixed economy of welfare, built on *co-operation* between the public, voluntary and private sectors, GS1804 was broadly supportive of a project that advocated a mixed (market) economy of welfare based around *competition* via the provisions of what became the Localism Act 2011. Indeed, it went so far as to suggest that, by way of this new church/government partnership, the Church of England could become involved more in 'direct service delivery'. This view was wholly consistent with Milbank's support for the 'Big Society' project, not least his insistence that it provided an opportunity for the Church to 'operate as the fulcrum for the growth of civil society'.[111]

Given the importance of GS1804 to the shaping of the Church of England's response to the 'Big Society' project in late 2010, 2011 and early 2012, it is necessary to explore the reasons underpinning Brown's advice to the Church. In what follows I shall draw heavily on the transcript of a recorded interview I conducted with him at Church House, Westminster, on 22 May 2018.

[108.] Ibid., p. 37.
[109.] Ibid., pp. 34–36.
[110.] GS1804, para. 8.
[111.] Milbank, 'The Big Society Depends on the Big Parish', p. 2.

Malcolm Brown's Advice to the Church of England on Its handling of the 'Big Society' Project

A former director of the William Temple Foundation, Brown states: 'Temple's work had been very important in my formation even before I knew his name, because it was the way we were brought up in the 1970s.'[112] However, he later states: 'But my own journey, from being a kind of William Temple, left-leaning Christian Socialist, moved when I started reading MacIntyre in the early 1980s.'[113] Alasdair MacIntyre, a convert to Roman Catholicism, in his work of 1981, *After Virtue*,[114] had been very critical of modernity, particularly the moral structures that had emerged from Renaissance science and the Enlightenment, which he attributed in significant part to its abandonment of Aristotelianism and much of the ancient and medieval (Thomist) teleological understanding of ethics, that focused on an account of good and moral persons based on virtue ethics. *After Virtue* is a critique of modernity and its political offshoot – capitalism, with its liberal ideological underpinning and what MacIntyre sees as its bureaucratic state structures. MacIntyre also advocates more of a localist, communitarian approach to social organisation in preference to a centralist, statist one. Brown said:

> I was trying to take MacIntyre seriously. ... At the same time, I was coming out of a tradition that I didn't want to abandon. So that's why I developed the idea of traditions in dialogue with each other. I was using MacIntyre's idea of epistemological crisis which Maurice Glasman also picks up, on how traditions grow and develop. So, I was trying to get a sort of synthesis of the Temple tradition with MacIntyre. ... I wanted to try and build a bridge. And that was a personal journey.[115]

What Brown means by traditions in dialogue with each other becomes clearer in the following statement he gave in response to being asked whether he had been influenced by the Figgis, Demant, Milbank/ Radical Orthodoxy, Christendom strand of Anglican social thinking:

---

[112] Brown's reply to question 1.

[113] Brown's reply to question 6.

[114] A. MacIntyre, *After Virtue: A Study in Moral Theory* (1981) (Paris: University of Notre Dame Press, 3rd edn, 2007).

[115] Brown's reply to question 8.

> My lineage is Temple, Preston, Atherton … most people had
> gone soft by the end for John [Atherton] because, for him, the
> Demant/Christendom tradition was soft. It was unrealistic,
> it was about a separatist Church. It would lead to Hauerwas
> if you see what I mean. However, my doctorate, *After the
> Market*, was an attempt at holding the two traditions together
> as having something interesting to say, provided one tradition
> is used as a corrective to the other.[116]

Thus, Brown was keen to emphasise that the Temple, Preston, Atherton
tradition can work with the Figgis, Demant, Milbank/Radical
Orthodoxy, Christendom tradition:

> as correctives to each other but not as a synthesising thing.
> That when you are in one tradition you have to look over
> your shoulder and say – maybe they have got something
> here, and so it is not a synthesis. It's what MacIntyre calls an
> epistemological crisis, when you realise that the tradition is
> not up to carrying the questions that are being asked of it –
> what you can get is a new, enlarged tradition.[117]

Brown connected this thinking to his interpretation of what being
Anglican is all about and, indeed, to what is required of him in his role:

> First of all, I am Anglican. The Anglican Church is not a
> synthesis of reformed and catholic – it is the two acting as
> correctives to each other. … My political theology here is
> an Anglican one. … You have to work with them. They are
> not reconcilable. Do bear in mind that's my approach to the
> traditions of Hauerwas, Milbank, and Temple and so on.[118]

It is clear from these quotations that Brown's idea of holding 'traditions in
dialogue with each other' is crucial to an understanding of his thinking
since the mid-1980s and to the shaping of GS1804.[119] A challenge arises
out of this thinking, however. How could Brown accommodate these

---

[116.] Brown's reply to question 12.

[117.] Brown's reply to question 13.

[118.] Brown's reply to question 14.

[119.] He confirms this in his reply to question 14: 'This was certainly behind my
thinking and I am fascinated it comes through in the paper, if it does.'

differing strands of thought in GS1804 in a way that was ideologically and theologically coherent, if, as has been argued in this book, they are antithetical to each other in so many ways? The following quote from him is revealing in this regard:

> I don't think they are as antithetical as all that. There is a beautiful piece in Nicholas Lash in one of his essays on *Theology and Social Theory* – it's about Milbank's pacifism – where he says Milbank calls the Church to exist on the other side of the cross, as it were, to embody the kingdom. What this neglects is that the Church is located on both sides of the cross, including the side of the cross where we have to engage in what Lash calls a kind of politics in the service of a kind of power. In other words, you have to get your hands dirty. Milbank's theology, for Lash, is too ethereal and squeaky clean. It's on the other side of the cross and forgets that the classic Christian vocabulary is now and not yet.[120]

This reveals the full extent of Brown's pragmatic, managerial instincts.[121] We see that Brown is keen for the Church of England to be 'located on both sides of the cross' and 'to get its hands dirty'. Thus, he stated: 'Milbank is quite right that the state is a modern construct, and the Church is where the kingdom of God is, etc. But if we believe in the kingdom of God coming on earth, it must come to some extent in human structures. Not just in "the other side of the cross" structures.'[122] Therefore, for Brown, the Church of England should positively engage, albeit within certain parameters, with Labour, Conservative or Coalition governments in the delivery of their welfare agendas where it can contribute in a way that advances, as he puts it, 'an Anglican ecclesiology, working out as a political theology'.[123] Thus, he argued:

> My thinking on getting behind the Big Society was (a) if they are talking about the Church, we might as well get something out of it, if there is anything to be had, and there wasn't;

[120.] Brown's reply to question 16.

[121.] Later in the meeting he describes his job as being 'a manager – a bureaucrat even'. See Brown's reply to question 32.

[122.] Brown's reply to question 30.

[123.] Brown's reply to question 26.

> (b) here's a chance to align the Church of England in a way that says we do sometimes support the Tories, because the story emerging was that we are a load of pinkos who never support the Conservative governments … if a government is committed to a Big Society in a Figgis intermediate institutions model, then that should be something that governs policy across the board.[124]

It is evident in this quote that Brown, when drafting GS1804, was highly sensitive to the charge that the Church of England never supports Conservative governments. He states: 'My thinking was to move the Church of England from the sterile right/left *Guardian/Daily Mail* argument and try and cut through in the way Rowan Williams used to by framing the question differently.'[125] This can therefore be seen as one reason for his attraction to the Blue Labour/Red Tory political phenomenon. As he puts it: 'the mere titles were about crossover';[126] 'Blue Labour/Red Tory are corrective traditions.'[127] He later confirmed that his drafting of the House of Bishops' Pastoral Letter that was published to coincide with the General Election campaign of 2015 called *Who Is My Neighbour?*, 'was an attempt to move them into that territory'[128] and that it was 'almost pure Blue Labour/Red Tory'.[129] This is consistent with his article in the *Church Times*: 'It was clear that the Bishops' Pastoral Letter reflected the political movements known as Red Tory and Blue Labour. Both drew explicitly, though differently, on Christian conceptions of society, and share explicitly theological antecedents.'[130] This view, of course, accords with the thrust of the current analysis, that Radical Orthodoxy's Christendom perspective has been a significant theoretical underpinning for these political movements.

That Brown saw all this as part of a paradigm shift in the way the Church of England sought to engage with governments on welfare matters is evident in his statement:

---

124. Brown's reply to question 29.

125. Brown's reply to question 25.

126. Ibid.

127. Brown's reply to question 26.

128. Brown's reply to question 25.

129. Brown's reply to question 24.

130. M. Brown, 'Society Needs Us to Be Anglican, not Sectarian', *Church Times*, 11 May 2018.

Thus, we no longer do reports like *Faith in the City*, *Not Just for the Poor* or *Unemployment and the Future of Work* because the message has gone out that they are either embarrassing or they fall flat, and we haven't got the money anyway. There is a shift of method and model between 1997 and 2010. We don't do it anymore like that.[131]

Significantly, this is fully consistent with the view expressed by Milbank and recounted in chapter four, that to maximize its potential as regards welfare provision, the Church of England needs 'a shift in direction away from the Temple legacy of long reports telling the Government what to do … to a more authentic radicalism in which the Church gets involved in all kinds of processes of welfare'.[132] Symptomatic of this paradigm shift was Brown's insistence that the 'Big Society' project 'was, to some extent, describing where the Church was already on this'.[133] Brown thought that it was necessary for the Church of England to move away from its post-war default position of defending the Temple welfare state legacy and, by implication, the Welfare Statist strand of Anglican Socialism out of which it had emerged. It was that strand which, in many ways, had been reflected in reports like *Faith in the City*, *Not Just for the Poor* and *Unemployment and the Future of Work*. As he put it:

What we want and what we need is for all our political parties to be pursing policies that are at least conformable to the Christian ethic. There will be right and left versions of that. … In the Big Society you had the first inkling (that came to very little) of a return to a One Nation Toryism that had a lot in common with the Church of England's understanding of how an organic society works.[134]

Brown was thus keen for the Church of England to embrace the essentials of the 'Big Society' project in late 2010, fully recognising that this was a paradigm shift in its approach to welfare. However, crucially, it was also because Brown thought that the Church's default position of defending the Temple approach was based on an inaccurate understanding of it – one that we now interrogate.

---

[131] Brown's reply to question 6.
[132] Milbank, 'What a Christian View of Society Says about Poverty', p. 5.
[133] Brown's reply to question 17.
[134] Brown's reply to question 29.

Beveridge's Report on 'Voluntary Action' and the Attlee Government

In defending the paradigm shift discussed above, Brown argued that the Church of England's support for the post-war Welfare State settlement insufficiently recognised the difference between the over-statist Attlee delivery vehicle (as he interprets it) and Temple's and Beveridge's recognition of the need for a vibrant intermediate level of welfare delivery in British civil society as complementary to the Welfare State sector: 'You had an essentially state-centralised model of welfare delivery, and the Church of England, until relatively recently, had an instinctive warmth for the Temple/Beveridge legacy without really understanding it: it conflated it with the Attlee and subsequent governments' enactments which isn't the same thing.'[135] The historical accuracy of this assertion is open to challenge.

We noted in chapter four, for example, how the 1948 Lambeth Conference was well aware of the dangers of an over-centralised model of welfare delivery in the resolutions that it passed. Thus, it condemned 'the concept of the unbridled sovereignty of the nation and such usurpation of power by the state as is opposed to the basic truths of Christianity'.[136] It was also critical of a 'tendency of the state to encroach on the freedom of individuals and voluntary associations'.[137] These statements are clear historical evidence of how the bishops in 1948 recognised the dangers of an over-encroaching state. Yet, they balanced that with a recognition of the potential of a state to deliver welfare to the poor and disadvantaged on a scale not seen before. Indeed, it was this recognition that in large part helped produce Resolution 19: 'We therefore welcome the growing concern and care of the modern State for its citizens, and call upon Church members to accept their own political responsibility and to cooperate with the State and its officers in their work.'[138]

We have also seen how *Not Just for the Poor*, which Brown acknowledged 'for a long time, was our position paper on welfare',[139] concluded by stating: 'Generous provision by society through the state is essential. But it is not enough on its own to produce the kind of society we wish

---

[135.] Brown's reply to question 3.

[136.] Lambeth Conference 1948, Resolution 18.

[137.] Ibid., Resolution 20.

[138.] Cited by Prochaska, *The Church of England and the Collapse of Christian Charity*, p. 3.

[139.] Brown's reply to question 5.

to see.'[140] Instead it advocated a mixed economy of welfare, built on *co-operation* between the public, voluntary and private sectors. Brown's interpretation of how, until fairly recently, he considers the Church of England's post-war instinctive warmth for the Temple/Beveridge legacy was 'without really understanding it', conflating it too closely with what he considers to be Attlee's 'over statist' delivery vehicle, is less than consistent with this historical evidence.

Indeed, the same can be argued of his interpretation of the extent of the differences between Beveridge's thinking on welfare provision and the enactment by the Attlee administration of his report of 1942. As Brown argues: 'The Attlee government made it essentially practical politics but lost the element of what you might now call the Big Society or strong intermediate institutions aspect.'[141] Certainly, as discussed in chapter two and chapter four, there were strongly held differences between Beveridge and Attlee on the role the friendly societies might have played in the post-war provision of welfare. Yet, with the exception of the friendly societies, which went into rapid decline after the Welfare State was established, voluntary organisations continued to make valuable contributions to the post-war delivery of welfare, some of which have been documented in chapter four. Moreover, as previously noted, many of them expanded, not least the trade union movement up until 1979 which, in some respects, took over the role of the friendly societies in providing financial support to their members at times of strike action, for example. Others partly took the place of the friendly societies as newly formed welfare charities. Hence, there is a danger of these differences that Brown alludes to between the Attlee government's enactment of the Welfare State and Beveridge's views on voluntarism and, specifically, the demise of the friendly societies, becoming exaggerated in their historical importance in at least three respects: (1) as an interpretation of Beveridge's wider thoughts on welfare *per se*; (2) as an interpretation of his thoughts on Attlee's delivery vehicle for slaying the five giants; and (3) on their historical importance to the shaping of events on the ground at that time and since.

James McKay interprets Beveridge's report of 1948 as a fairly accurate reflection of his thinking in 1948, though not necessarily of his thinking in 1942, which was less developed on voluntarism than it later became. McKay argues: 'it presents an image of voluntary action as socially

---

[140.] Church of England, *Not Just for the Poor*, p. 134.

[141.] Brown's reply to question 5.

pioneering, with its relationship to the state as part-alternative, part-counterweight and part-complement'.[142] This interpretation chimes with Beveridge's statement of 1948:

> Voluntary action is needed to do the things which the State should not do, in the giving of advice, or in organising the use of leisure. It is needed to do the things which the State is most unlikely to do. It is needed to pioneer ahead of the state and make experiments. It is needed to get services rendered which cannot be got by paying for them.[143]

There is nothing in this quote that is suggestive of a need for the state *not* to be doing the things that the Attlee administration had enabled it to do, nor, for that matter, that Temple had thought a welfare state *should* be doing. In *Voluntary Action*, Beveridge did not see voluntary provision of welfare as a substitute for state welfare provision. Rather, he saw it as an essential complement to it. They were both necessary for human happiness:

> Encouragement of Voluntary Action for the improvement of society and use of voluntary agencies by public authorities for public purposes is no less desirable for the future than it has been for the past. The reasons for it have not been diminished and will not be destroyed by the growing activities of the State.[144]

He therefore called for greater *co-operation* between public authorities and voluntary agencies and continuance and extension of public grants to voluntary agencies. However, crucially, in one section of the report he aligned his thinking with that of Beatrice and Sydney Webb,[145] whom

---

142. J. McKay, 'Voluntary Politics: The Sector's Political Function from Beveridge to Deakin', in Oppenheimer and Deakin (eds), *Beveridge and Voluntary Action*, p. 81.

143. Beveridge, *Voluntary Action*, pp. 301–2.

144. Ibid., p. 306.

145. He cites *The Minority Report of the Poor Law Commission of 1906–1909* that was written by Beatrice Webb and George Lansbury. This became a key statement of Fabian thinking on welfare, and the roles the state and the voluntary sectors might perform in the provision of welfare in a democratic socialist society. It was further developed in S. Webb and B. Webb, *The*

he accurately described as 'two of the most effective advocates in history of the extension of the activities of the State',[146] pointing out that they, too, were of the view that 'there was a need for Voluntary Action for public purposes and in urging continued cooperation between public authorities and voluntary agencies':[147]

> The special point which they make, that voluntary agencies should not undertake the distribution of relief, is in accord with all that has happened since these words were written. Voluntary agencies have in fact largely ceased to be concerned with meeting basic needs for food, clothing or fuel and will be concerned with such things even less in the future, through the extension of social security. In accord with the argument of the Webbs, they will be needed even more than in the past, for exploring as specialists the new avenues for social service which will open when want is abolished.[148]

Thus, Beveridge did not see the Welfare State as a vehicle for diminishing the need for voluntary agencies, or voluntary agencies as a vehicle for diminishing the need for the Welfare State; rather, the Welfare State was a way of opening up new avenues for voluntary agencies, when, via the Welfare State, want is abolished.

This sentiment is accurately reflected in the wording contained in *Not Just for the Poor*: 'Generous provision of services by society through the state is essential. But it is not enough', calling for a mixed economy of welfare 'built on co-operation between public, voluntary and private sectors'.[149] Moreover, when one considers the wide range of examples of voluntary welfare provision that the Church of England has engaged in since 1945, some of which are set out in chapter four, it is hard to square this with Brown's view that the Church had 'forgotten a bit of the tradition that had once won them over. That is, the richness of Beveridge's vision in *Voluntary Action*.'[150]

Prevention of Destitution (London: Longman, 1912). This thinking is what, in significant part, shaped the approach taken on welfare by the leadership of the Labour Party in the post-war years.

[146] Beveridge, *Voluntary Action*, p. 308.

[147] Ibid.

[148] Ibid..

[149] Church of England, *Not Just for the Poor*, p.134.

[150] Brown's reply to question 5.

However, Brown's thinking on Beveridge has been influenced by Milbank and Blond, and that influence now needs to be analysed.

Milbank's and Blond's Views on the Need for a Minimalist State

It can credibly be argued that Milbank's and Blond's perspectives on the Welfare State have more in common with (though are not identical to) the *minimalist* perspective on the state that Temple and Beveridge rejected in favour of a Welfare State, and that has since been described by Brown as follows:

> Looking at the late 1920s and early 1930s when Temple was doing a lot of his work with the Oxford Conference and things like that, you are looking at a hugely *laissez-faire* Conservative approach which led to the depression, countered by totalitarianisms in Spain, Germany, Russia, Italy and so on. So, for Temple, these were two models: the minimalist state, as we now call it, and the power state of Mussolini and Hitler, for which the Christian couldn't give any allegiance to at all.[151]

Milbank and Blond, whilst rejecting a *laissez-faire* (neoliberal) approach to economics as discussed in chapter three, nevertheless embrace much of what can be described as a minimalist perspective on the state.[152] This cannot yet be said of Brown's, though the following statement by him about his intellectual journey is strongly suggestive that this is the path on which he is headed:

> So, if we believe the state has a role, that the state is justified by seeking to maximise the welfare of the citizen, it doesn't follow that the Beveridge settlement is the only mechanism by which you can do that. Maximising the wellbeing of the citizen might be done by devolving powers into the smallest units, you know, the villages, the towns, the streets. This might be a totally different way of saying how you deal with

---

[151.] Brown's reply to question 1.

[152.] This accords with Milbank's liking of Ivan Illich's radical perspective on the state's deficiencies (as he sees them) in areas such as education and health, and the need for these to be devolved to a lower level of delivery and accountability (see chapter four).

welfare because ... Beveridge looked at the five giants' evils and, well, they are still around.[153]

This indicates why Brown framed GS1804 in the way he did. Clearly, Brown acknowledges that the state has a role to play in the provision of welfare in the way Temple and Beveridge had advocated; yet, he was attracted by a level of devolved welfare delivery that has much in common with the Christendom strand of Anglican Socialism, and thus to the perspective on welfare held by Milbank. Brown explained to me that:

> for over forty years now [that is, since Thatcherism], we have had governments with a very different understanding of the role of the state, and so we have had to trim ours to some extent. I think this has on the whole been good, and the trimming has been largely away from the centralised state model of delivering welfare that the Beveridge report of 1942 embodied.[154]

Brown thus thought that, since Thatcherism, 'the rationale for the state as the Welfare State has cut little ice. We have to work with the reality on the ground. And this is the Church's classic dilemma: between what it thinks as being theologically sound and what it has to do to make a difference on the ground.'[155]

In Summary
With the collapse of the welfare state consensus and the rise of Thatcherism, Brown thought that the Church of England, though initially inclined to resist that trend (e.g. in reports such as *Faith in the City* and *Not Just for the Poor*), had since moved to a point where it had adapted its thinking on welfare to accommodate it. The Church had felt a need to remain politically relevant in what was seen by some supporters of Blue Labour/Red Tory politics, as an acknowledgment of the extent to which the collapse of the welfare state consensus has taken hold in modern British society. Thus, with the election in 2010 of the Coalition administration in the context of a major financial crisis,

---

[153.] Brown's reply to question 30.
[154.] Brown's reply to question 3.
[155.] Ibid.

Brown's advice in GS1804 was, in part, shaped by a desire for the Church to be willing to work (and, indeed, to be seen to be willing to work) with and not against the grain of the Coalition government's welfare agenda: that is, as Brown put it, to 'find a language that engaged with them, so that we were not simply the opposition in waiting'. The 'Big Society' project spoke that language; hence Brown's view was that 'we have got something we can build on here'.[156]

Crucially, the 'Big Society' project was also something that could be aligned theologically with the Church of England's journey away from what Brown described as 'the Christian realism of Niebuhr and Temple' to something incorporating aspects of what he describes as the 'starry-eyed romanticism' of Milbank's theological contributions; as Brown put it: 'what you have got, actually, are two things – they are both necessary'.[157] When pushed to elaborate further on this point, Brown's response was as follows:

> You have to work with the reality of what can be done on the ground as well as what is theologically sound. Milbank has also gone on this journey. He has taken that challenge on board and all credit to him. He is now actually trying to deal in something that is do-able and not just highfalutin' romanticism, and he is doing a pretty good job of that.[158]

Brown took a similar view of Blond who was also:

> a fellow traveller in some respects because Phillip crystalised in *Red Tory* the sort of ideas we were working on here. For us, and I say this in the plural as I am working in a team here with a tradition which is moving on from Temple but we are still drawing on Christian realism to some extent, we are trying to get out of the situation that whatever we do as the Church of England is immediately forced into either 'it's a *Daily Mail* idea or a *Guardian* idea': that is, that it is either right or left. We are trying to say that the Church of England's interventions in politics are not partisan. They are based on

---

[156.] Brown's reply to question 6.
[157.] Brown's reply to question 9.
[158.] Brown's reply to question 10.

a sound political theology that is not the same as a partisan political philosophy.[159]

Yet, he was unimpressed by the report produced by Blond and Noyes in 2013, *Holistic Mission*: 'It is an example of how communitarians risk retreating into nostalgic utopianism when direct experience of the institutions they discuss is deficient.'[160] Consequently, Brown ensured he 'forgot all about *Holistic Mission*'.[161]

Yet Brown, as well as the wider leadership within the Church of England, came to hold a different opinion on the Big Society project and its apparent merits.

The 'Big Society' Project in Retrospect

In a paper published by Brown in 2014, his assessment of the 'Big Society' project had become far less favourable:

> Three years on, we have seen very little of the Big Society. Instead, the voluntary sector is facing a pincer-like squeeze between declining income from giving (normal during a prolonged recession) and considerable cuts to government funding. There is very little to show for the Church's strong support for a new settlement between the state and local voluntary action.[162]

Brown's critical assessment of the outcomes of the project had been preceded in June 2012 by Rowan Williams' assertion that the 'Big Society' comes across as 'aspirational waffle' and that it was 'designed to conceal a deeply damaging withdrawal of the state from its responsibilities to the most vulnerable'.[163] Brown's critical assessment of its outcomes made a similar point:

[159.] Brown's reply to question 11.

[160.] M. Brown, 'Civil Society, Welfare and the State', *Modern Believing* 56, no. 1 (2015), pp. 11–21.

[161.] Brown's reply to question 28.

[162.] M. Brown, 'The Church of England and Welfare Today', in Spencer (ed.), *The Future of Welfare*, p. 55.

[163.] T. Helm and J. Coman, 'Rowan Williams Pours Scorn on David Cameron's 'Big Society'', *The Guardian*, 24 June 2012.

A Church Urban Fund survey of around 900 churches at the end of 2011 found that more than one in four had a food bank. ... The contribution of Christians to hundreds of social action projects which alleviate poverty in many ways is considerable. ... It is clear that without action by churches, the plight of many people would be insupportable. This action, part of our witness to the love of Christ and the pursuit of the common good of all, is generously given – but those most involved know that it is not filling the gap left by the cuts to welfare provision.[164]

Brown was clear that the voluntary sector, though capable of mitigating and alleviating aspects of the contraction in state-provided welfare, was nevertheless incapable of 'filling the gap left by the cuts to welfare provision'. His assessment of the impact the 'Big Society' project had on the charities and voluntary sector was equally damning:

Other funding cuts are severely hampering the work of numerous charities and volunteer schemes. Programmes of social care are under immense pressure as a result of local authority cuts. The gap between need 'on the ground' and the capacity of voluntary action to respond is considerable – and widening.

Brown concluded by reasserting the Church of England's support for the Welfare State:

But the Church's commitment to a welfare state is not mere nostalgia. It is a theological judgement about what the state should be and should do for its citizens. Where the poor and vulnerable carry a disproportionate share of the burden created by the financial crisis, something is wrong.[165]

This is in line with the perspective on the Welfare State that *Faith in the City* and *Not Just for the Poor*, had held. What had brought about this change in Brown's perspective on the 'Big Society' project? Clearly,

---

[164] Brown, 'The Church of England and Welfare Today', pp. 58–59.
[165] Ibid., p. 59.

some of it relates to the outcomes he describes above. Hence, we shall now focus on some of the project's key performance indicators and, secondly, on the impact the project had on the Church of England.

The Key Outcomes of the 'Big Society' Project

By far and away the most comprehensive audit of the 'Big Society' project was published in January 2015 by Civil Exchange, a think tank that defines its purpose as strengthening civil society's connection to government. It was the last of three such audits it had carried out on the 'Big Society' initiative.[166] Working in conjunction with DHA, a policy and communications agency specialising in social change, the Joseph Rowntree Charitable Trust and the Barrow Cadbury Trust, *Whose Society? The Final Big Society Audit* was the result of a comprehensive information-gathering exercise and an opinion survey. Its overall conclusion was:

> despite some genuinely positive initiatives, the Big Society has failed to deliver against its original goals. Attempts to create more social action, to empower communities and to open up public services, with some positive exceptions, have not worked. The Big Society has not reached those who need it most. We are more divided than before.[167]

Key findings were reported under four headings as summarised below:[168]

1. Community Empowerment
There had been a significant decline in (a) the number of people who felt they could influence decisions about their local area, (b) in people's sense of belonging and (c) in neighbourliness. There had also been an increase in racial intolerance. Far from being strengthened, key parts of the voluntary sector were struggling, with reduced income to meet demand

---

[166] See C. Slocock (ed.), *Whose Society? The Final Big Society Audit* (London: Civil Exchange in Partnership with DHA Communications, 2015), p. 6. Available at: http://www.civilexchange.org.uk/wp-content/uploads/2015/01/Whose-Society?_The-Final-Big-Society-Audit_final.pdf (accessed on 15 December 2017).

[167] Ibid., p. 4.

[168] Ibid., pp. 8–12.

and threats to the independent voluntary sector having increased. It did, however, find that more information was available, and the number of police and crime commissioners was steadily expanding. However, trust and faith in the political system remained low.

2. Opening up Public Services

The voluntary sector had lost £1.3 billion in state funding in real terms in 2011–12 compared to the previous year, with smaller organisations and services to disadvantaged people primarily affected. Public services had become less, not more accountable, especially as a result of increasing contracting out. The voluntary sector's sense of partnership with government had weakened. There had been a failure to mobilise the private sector for the common good. Social investment remained in its infancy and levels of corporate giving had not increased to replace shrinking state funding for the voluntary sector. Choice in public services had opened up under successive governments but was still limited and was working less well for disadvantaged groups. Despite government commitments to co-design, consultation with the sector had become truncated, with the policy and campaigning voice of the sector under attack.

3. Social Action

There were more young people volunteering but the overall trend for volunteering was broadly flat. Individual giving had increased over the previous year, though it was not back to pre-recession levels. Payroll giving and text donation were up. Numbers of community organisers were increasing, but there remained doubts about the effectiveness of the initiative. The number of looked-after children rose steadily in the period since 2010.

4. The Big Society Gap

Rural and southern areas had more voluntary activity than those in the north. For the least affluent, cuts in public services had impacted the most. Disabled people had been particularly hard hit by cuts in public services and welfare payments, and had experienced problems with contracted-out public services. They were also affected by the loss of income to voluntary sector groups in the field of social services and employment. The young were worryingly disengaged politically, but were socially engaged. Volunteering rates amongst the young had increased dramatically; however, services to both younger and older people had been reduced as a result of cuts.

Overall, the findings of this comprehensive audit of the 'Big Society' project against its stated performance indicators were negative and broadly correspond with other work that has been produced.[169] The consequences for the Church of England were considerable.

The Outcomes of the 'Big Society' Project for the Church of England

In 2014 a biennial national church and social action survey reported that 114.8 million volunteer hours were spent on church social action, an increase of 54.4 per cent from 2010.[170] Consistent with this trend, the Blond and Noyes report of 2013 found that: 'levels of social action are considerably higher amongst Church attendees than the general public'.[171] In 2014 a Church Urban Fund survey reported a 45 per cent increase, since 2011, in the number of clergy in the Church of England who considered: 'engaging with the poor and marginalised in the local area to be a vital activity for a healthy church'.[172] It also reported that one third of Church of England churches were involved in food banks in 2011, with the number increasing to two thirds by 2014.[173] Hence, there is evidence that indicates there was a sizeable increase in the levels of Church of England participation in social action/poverty alleviation activities in the

---

[169] See, for example, C. Elliott, *Whatever Happened to the Big Society?*, Centre for Policy Development Occasional Paper 25, February 2013. Available at: https://cpd.org.au/2013/02/whatever-happened-to-the-big-society/ (accessed on 20 December 2021).

[170] See National Church and Social Action Survey 2014. This statistic is cited in G. Knott, Jubilee +Social Action and Church Growth report, 2015. It is available as a pdf download at: https://glasgowchurches.org.uk/connecting-church-based-social-action-and-church-growth/ (accessed on 31 December 2021)

[171] Blond and Noyes, *Holistic Mission*.

[172] Cited in Wells, Rook and Barclay, *For Good*, p. 28.

[173] The increase in the number of food banks was not a stated objective of the 'Big Society' project. There is some evidence that it related in part to benefit sanctions changes brought in by the Coalition government in 2010, however. The *Guardian*'s social policy editor reported that: 'The Trussell Trust figures show the biggest proportion, 44%, of food bank referrals last year – marginally lower than the previous year – were triggered by people pitched into crisis because their benefit payments had been delayed, or stopped altogether as a result of the strict Job Centre sanctions regime.' P. Butler, 'Food Bank Use Tops Million Mark over the Last Year', *The Guardian*, 22 April 2015. Cited in Wells, Rook and Barclay, *For Good*, p. 28.

period since the launch of the 'Big Society' project. Yet, this was at a time when decreases occurred in Christian affiliation in the UK, as evidenced by a study that found that Anglican Church membership in the UK declined by eight per cent between 2010 and 2015.[174] This trend, though constituting historical evidence relating to a period of only five years and hence requiring caution when interpreting its significance for the long term, nevertheless runs contrary to the argument advanced by Milbank (see chapter four) that increased levels of social action activities within the Church of England would lead to increased levels of Church affiliation.

Of course, the possibility that the decline may have been steeper had it not been for this increase in social action activities cannot be ruled out. A report published in November 2020 by the Theos think tank working in partnership with the Church Urban Fund, *Growing Good: The Future of the Church?*,[175] lends some support to that view. Based on interviews conducted with 350 people in 66 parish communities, it provides some evidence that in churches where consistent efforts have been made to enhance their social engagement with local communities by way of providing food banks, toddler groups, lunch clubs and night shelters, there has been growth, spiritually and numerically, through their engagement in social action. However, the research base on which this study rests was too limited in scope to be sure of the significance of the conclusions it reaches.

Some of this increased social action related to the rollout of the Near Neighbours initiative, as previously discussed. Since April 2011, the initiative has provided a range of community-based projects, particularly in the Midlands and northern English towns, which have contributed to the delivery of its two main goals: (1) to develop positive relationships in multi-faith areas; and (2) 'to encourage people of different faiths or no faith to come together for initiatives that improve their local neighbourhood'.[176] According to its *Impact Report*,[177] Near Neighbours has funded 1,433 projects across England, disbursing over

---

[174.] See Faith Survey, 'Introduction: UK Christianity 2005–2015', *Church Statistics* (no author cited). Available at: https://faithsurvey.co.uk/download/csintro.pdf, p. 2 (accessed on 23 April 2018).

[175.] See H. Rich, *Growing Good: The Future of the Church?* (London: Theos, 2020).

[176.] See the Near Neighbours' website, https://www.near-neighbours.org.uk, for more on this.

[177.] See Near Neighbours, *Near Neighbours Impact Report: April 2011-March 2017.* Available at: https://static1.squarespace.com/static/5a68889a90bade540

£4,724,000. Over one million people are estimated to have benefited from its small grants. Eighty-nine per cent of projects have brought people together from at least three faith groups or those of no faith. Ninety-eight per cent of project leaders have agreed that participants felt more connected in their local community and 95 per cent of project leaders have agreed that there is a greater sense of togetherness or community spirit. Over 430 young people have taken part in the Catalyst leadership programme, which equips them with the skills and confidence to take on leadership roles, develop local social action and transform their own communities. Impressively, National Partners (a group of charities specialising in training volunteers to build capacity in community groups/networks and partly funded by the Near Neighbours initiative) have also organised over 650 events in local areas, which have brought together over 37,000 people.

Based on this impact assessment, the state financial support provided to the Near Neighbours initiative, and the contribution it has since made to enhancing interfaith community engagement and neighbourliness in England, demonstrate that it has brought about a significant set of social achievements. Yet, seen in the context of the negative outcomes the Civil Exchange's audit found on the Big Society's impact on British society, not least on the voluntary sector, there is a question that the Church of England must now confront. On the back of its desire to be 'politically relevant' and also to acquire financial support for the Near Neighbours initiative as part of its overall response to the 'Big Society' project, was the qualified support given to it in 2010, 2011 and the early part of 2012 a theo-political misjudgement when taking into account the outcomes of the 'Big Society' project?

The Church of England's Response to the 'Big Society' Project

Brown does not think it was a theo-political misjudgement and offers a defence of the initial support the Church of England gave to the 'Big Society' project:

---

b4da177/t/5b239001aa4a99a4bb1ac216/1529057287026/Near+Neighbours +Impact+Report.pdf (accessed on 20 December 2021).

At best it was a project that fell into the ground. Yet, whilst it was live, we had the chance to say we could be part of redefining the Tory party. … In the Big Society you had the first inkling (that came to very little) of a return to a One Nation Toryism that had a lot in common with the Church of England's understanding of how an organic society works. So, if we could have leveraged the Big Society issue into a complete rebranding of the Tory Party, what an achievement that would have been. If it had been a serious government proposition, we would have gone on working with it. Not just in order to deliver things at ground level, but to, first of all, assert in public discourse that those small acts of neighbourliness that go on in communities are valuable and not just invisible and overlooked. This is about us. It's about a development in government that could have been quite a significant win-win for Christian ethics, and, actually, the future of the Conservative party.[178]

Yet how realistic was it that the Church of England could have been involved in redefining the Conservative Party in the way that Brown describes? The evidence that was available to him at the time casts doubt on the feasibility of such an aspiration. For we have already seen that Brown was clear in GS1804 that: 'The Coalition has set out to deliver dramatic cuts to public spending, not least in social welfare.'[179] One way it was going to achieve that goal was to reduce its financial support to local government, and a significant proportion of the £1.3 billion of state disinvestment in voluntary services that occurred in 2011/12 to that of the previous year, stemmed from this.[180] Why was this not foreseeable to Brown in the way it was for those who signed the *Common Wealth* document in 2010, for example? Was it because, as they argued 'we believe that the craving for relevance is overriding any more searching critique of what is on offer'?[181] That is putting it too strongly; nevertheless, the following statement from Brown is pertinent in this regard:

[178.] Brown's reply to question 29.

[179.] GS1804, para. 8.

[180.] See the Joseph Rowntree Foundation, *The Cost of the Cuts: The Impact on Local Government and Poorer Communities* (York: Joseph Rowntree Foundation, 2015). Available at: https://www.jrf.org.uk/sites/default/files /jrf/migrated/files/Summary-Final.pdf (accessed on 19 July 2018).

[181.] Ekklesia, *Common Wealth*.

Whereas in the *Faith in the City* years, we were broadly seen as being the unofficial opposition to Thatcherism. ... Now, thirty years on, we have got far less legitimacy. What we were looking for, and this was not theology or political theory but *realpolitik*, was what can we say that shows that Conservatives were not the enemy of the Church of England – that there were some policies on which the Church of England and the Conservative government can align themselves. Along comes the Big Society.[182]

Brown's advice in GS1804 can, in part, thus be attributed to 'the craving for relevance' to which the authors of *Common Wealth* allude, that is, a pragmatic desire for the Church of England to demonstrate that the 'Conservatives were not the enemy of the Church' at a time when the Church had 'far less legitimacy'. However, it would be erroneous to suppose that this pragmatic imperative is the only explanation, or even the overriding one, for his advice at that time. At least as important was Brown's own intellectual journey away from what had once been a staunch defence of the Temple Welfare Statist legacy – a defence that had in part been nurtured by John Atherton, his PhD supervisor – to what had become a belief in the virtue of holding intellectual traditions in dialogue, as correctives to one another when shaping church policy on welfare.

In this respect, as we have seen, MacIntyre's *After Virtue* was important in shaping Brown's change of direction. It laid the intellectual foundations for being able to engage with Radical Orthodoxy thinkers, including Milbank, Blond and Pabst, as their relevance within the Church of England and wider political circles gathered pace in the period since the publication of Milbank's *Theology and Social Theory* in 1990, which had set things in motion. This was particularly so for the period encompassing the financial crash of 2008 and the subsequent rise of the Blue Labour/Red Tory political phenomenon. As Brown put it in an essay on Anglican Social Theology published in 2017:

Many years ago I dismissed Milbank and Radical Orthodoxy for having nothing to say about the economic realities which drove contemporary politics. I was wrong – both in falling for the old line that 'it's the economy, stupid' and for missing the potential of Radical Orthodoxy, which I dismissed as 'mere'

[182.] Brown's reply to question 6.

romanticism, for making romanticism a catalyst for changing the way things are perceived. The Red Tory/Blue Labour movements are probably the closest that AST [Anglican Social Theology] (in partnership with Catholic Social Teaching) has got to influencing political ideologies for many decades. And the House of Bishops, through commissioning and endorsing the Pastoral Letter of 2015 [which, as we have seen, was, in large part, written by Brown], have placed themselves in a pole position to help shape those movements by making the theological and ecclesiological connections explicit.[183]

This is indicative of the extent to which the Christendom revival launched by Milbank in 1990, has since permeated sections of the Church of England to a point where major policy formulation on welfare is increasingly being influenced by its advocates.

An example of this trend is a shift in the Church of England's position on the theology of the state. The following two quotations from Brown are relevant in this regard: 'There is no official theology of the state. Temple's views were never the official line of the Church of England, but a lot of Anglicans, after his death in particular, sought inspiration from them.' Brown elaborates on this:

Could there ever be one coherent theology of the state in the Church of England given that we are a coalition church – a coalition of parties who have very different theological foundations? … I am saying, as Anglicans, we don't look for a final settlement in these things. What we look for is – something that works for now. But we recognise its provisionality. There is always the authenticity of another theology over the horizon just saying, when we think we have got it right, by definition, we have got it wrong. And so that is part of the Anglican settlement since the Reformation, and certainly since the Civil War. … So, I think the idea of an Anglican theology of the state is not coherent. What you will have is at any one time there will be a dominant model, and it will be provisional.[184]

---

[183] M. Brown, 'Anglican Social Theology: Today and Tomorrow', in Spencer (ed.), *Theology Reforming Society*, p. 139.

[184] Brown's reply to question 30.

Brown was, then, of the view that the different theological perspectives on the state held by those in the Church of England, given that it is a 'coalition of parties', can never provide 'one coherent theology of the state'. Yet, he also thought that a 'dominant' theological model of thinking on the state will exist in the Church 'at any one time', though it will be 'provisional'. His view was that that Temple's theological perspective on the state occupied that position in the period before Thatcherism, and this is partly reflected in Resolution 19 passed at the Lambeth Conference of 1948, which he thinks 'reflected the mood of the times'.[185] Crucially, it is also reflected in the theo-political responses that the Church of England made in defence of the Welfare State when it came under challenge by Thatcher's administration in the 1980s, at a time of major financial pressure for that government, as evidenced by official reports such as *Faith in the City* and *Not Just for the Poor*, both heavily indebted to the Temple/Tawney approach.

This research suggests, however, that since 2010 – as evidenced by the Church's handling of the 'Big Society' project – the dominant model in the Church of England has shifted closer to the Christendom model advocated by Milbank *et al.* Building on themes in the House of Bishops' Pastoral Letter of 2015, Brown's document of May 2016, *Thinking Afresh about Welfare: The Enemy Isolation*,[186] is a case in point. In it he argues for the need for an additional sixth giant to be slayed, this being 'The Enemy Isolation', which he defines as loneliness, estrangement and friendlessness – in some ways resembling the thrust of the Atherton, Baker and Reader manifesto of 2011.[187] Crucially, Brown goes on to argue for: 'Openness to renegotiating the state/voluntary boundary – and willingness to step up to the plate where the virtues of voluntary action are clear',[188] this being the essence of Milbank's and Blond's critique of what they perceive as the Church's previous over-adherence by default to Temple's theology of the state and the post-war Temple/Beveridge welfare state settlement that was, in part, indebted to it.

[185.] Brown's reply to question 2.

[186.] M. Brown, *Thinking Afresh about Welfare: The Enemy Isolation*, Internal Policy Document, Church of England Publications, 2016. Available at: https://www.churchofengland.org/sites/default/files/2017-11/The%20 Enemy%20Isolation.pdf (accessed on 16 December 2018).

[187.] Atherton, Baker and Reader, *Christianity and the New Social Order*.

[188.] Brown, *Thinking Afresh about Welfare*, p. 16.

However, before we reach conclusions to the chapter, I will briefly consider the extent to which the evangelical voice on welfare influenced Brown's advice on the 'Big Society' project and also two other voices – neither of whom are evangelical but both of whom merit a mention.

Evangelical and Other Voices

As this is a study in Anglican Socialism and welfare, with a particular focus on the influences that shaped GS1804, the evangelical voice has not featured. It is noticeable, from the interview with Brown, that he does not refer to the evangelical tradition as being a key influence on the shaping of his advice in GS1804, though he does make reference to Lord Wei, an evangelical peer who proposed the Big Society Bank and who served as government adviser (unpaid) for the 'Big Society' project between 2010 and 2011.[189] Certainly, in the post-war period there have been evangelical contributions to debates on welfare in the Church of England that have influenced its approach; the input from David Sheppard in the 1980s – not least his contribution to the drafting of *Faith in the City* – comes to mind.[190] In the interview Brown also mentions Stanley Hauerwas, an American theologian sometimes cited as a member of the evangelical left, though it is a description of his thinking that he might not accept as accurate. Brown is cautious of Hauerwas' thinking on welfare, which he describes as an approach 'which is to diss everybody who disagrees with him'.[191] Though far more sympathetic to capitalism than Milbank is, Hauerwas shares his sense that charitable provision by the churches has been, and must remain, a key priority for them in contemporary capitalist contexts, in preference to an overly statist approach.[192] Yet, there is much truth in Jonathan Chaplin's view (himself an evangelical writer) that: 'Evangelicals have, to put it mildly, a much stronger history of social activism than of social theology.'[193] By social theology he means:

---

[189] GS1804, para. 25.

[190] See also, D. Sheppard, *Bias to the Poor* (London: Hodder & Stoughton, 1983).

[191] Brown's reply to question 12.

[192] S. Hauerwas, *The Peaceable Kingdom* (Paris: University of Notre Dame Press, 1984). See also S. Hauerwas, 'How to Remember the Poor'. Available at: https://togetherforthecommongood.co.uk/leading-thinkers/how-to-remember-the-poor (accessed on 20 December 2021).

[193] J. Chaplin, 'Evangelical Contributions to the Future of Anglican Social Theology', in Brown (ed.), *Anglican Social Theology*, p. 102.

'a coherent and enduring body of theological reflection that goes beyond occasional or ad hoc justifications for particular stances or practices and offers a larger, integrated theological vision of a flourishing social order'.[194] This contrasts with the contributions to debates on welfare and the Church that have come out of the Anglican Socialist tradition, and may partly reflect what Chaplin describes as a tendency in the evangelical movement 'towards anti-intellectualism'.[195] However, Brown notes that Blond's thinking was partly shaped by his connections with evangelical circles: 'this idea of taking over the Welfare State was big in evangelical circles, the HTB [Holy Trinity Brompton]-style empire-building churches'.[196]

It may be that the evangelical voice on welfare and the Church will become louder and, arguably, more coherent, in the years to come. Certainly, since the appointment of Justin Welby as Archbishop of Canterbury in March 2013 – himself a former congregant of Holy Trinity Brompton – the HTB movement has been on the rise in the Church of England. Evidence of this is how it has increasingly facilitated church planting and the rejuvenation of so called 'failing' churches, with its emphasis on charismatic worship and the use of contemporary music in its services.[197] It is likely to be a grouping that will have more influence on shaping the Church's strategic interface with the state in the future.

In GS1804 Brown also refers to the American-based thinker, Luke Bretherton, describing his perspective as 'in line with the judgement that there is much potential in The Big Society for the Church to work with, but that a residual element of scepticism remains in order'.[198] Bretherton is a theologian who does not label himself as evangelical, Anglo-Catholic or broad church, but does see himself as someone who is sympathetic to the English political pluralist perspective advanced by Figgis and his later followers.[199] It is for this reason that he saw potential in the 'Big Society' project for advancing that vision.

---

[194] Ibid., p. 104.

[195] Ibid., p. 111.

[196] Brown's reply to question 27.

[197] See M. Davies, 'Southampton Church Will Change Its Spots to Attract a Student Congregation', *Church Times*, 18 May 2018.

[198] GS1804, para. 47. See L. Bretherton, *Christ and the Common Life* (Grand Rapids, MI: William B. Eerdmans Pub. Co., 2019), and 'Big Society and the Church', *The Guardian*, 7 October 2010.

[199] He confirmed this to the present writer in an email dated 5 May 2021.

Samuel Wells, a broad-church Anglican and former junior colleague of Hauerwas who is currently vicar of St Martin-in-the-Fields, has also focused increasingly on welfare and the Church in his writings.[200] He has done much to popularise the Asset Based Community Development (ABCD) approach. This seeks to take a 'bottom-up' approach to welfare provision, prioritising community assets and emphasising the strengths of community-based interventions, though recognising that the state must retain a vital role in the provision of welfare. Although he sees the role of the Church as being: 'To hold the state to account in addressing the five great evils since the state is undoubtedly best placed to address them', at the same time, he thinks the Church has a vital role in creating 'cross-generational community' and cherishing 'people for what they are, not what they are not'.[201] In some respects his thinking can be seen as a bridge between Milbank's out-and-out statist scepticism and Archbishop John Sentamu's unequivocal evangelical defence of Temple's Welfare Statist legacy.[202] Writers such as Bretherton and Wells are also likely to continue to have some influence on the shaping of the Church of England's approach to welfare in the years to come.

Conclusion

Much of the thinking on welfare in the Church of England since the financial crash of 2008 can be located in the themes and perspectives on the Church, state and welfare that have been developed by writers from within two strands of the Anglican Socialist tradition: namely, the Welfare Statist strand and the Christendom strand. A case in point was its handling of the 'Big Society' project.

I have shown that the Church of England's post-war positioning on welfare underwent a paradigm shift in 2010, from what had previously been a default tendency to operate within and defend the Temple Welfare Statist approach, to one more receptive to the communitarian analysis of it. This had been spearheaded in significant part by writers from within the Radical Orthodoxy grouping, particularly Milbank (Blue Labour) and his intellectual protégé, Blond (Red Tory).

[200.] See, for example, Wells, Rook and Barclay, *For Good*.

[201.] Ibid., p. 12.

[202.] J. Sentamu, 'Hope Today for a Brighter Future', in J. Sentamu (ed.), *On Rock or Sand* (London: SPCK, 2015), pp. 1–26.

This paradigm shift – as expressed in official policy – can, in significant part, be attributed to the official advice the Church received on the handling of the 'Big Society' project from Malcolm Brown, and his attempt to hold corrective traditions in dialogue. Brown's thinking has been assessed as inconsistent with the historical record with respect to the Church of England's engagement with the Temple Welfare Statist legacy and Beveridge's report *Voluntary Action*.

In addition, it has been suggested that the key outcomes of the 'Big Society' project, not least the contraction in state support for the voluntary sector that occurred via George Osborne's budget of June 2010, were foreseeable to Brown and, via GS1804, to the Church of England, based *inter alia* on things that David Cameron had made explicit at or around that time. Evidence of this is in GS1804: 'The Coalition has set out to deliver dramatic cuts to public spending, not least in social welfare.'[203] This *had* been foreseeable to those who had signed the *Common Wealth* document and some of the explanation for the Church of England's response can be explained by their view that: 'the craving for relevance was overriding any more searching critique of what was on offer'. However, Brown's advice can also be explained in significant part by his growing affinity with Blue Labour/Red Tory thinking.

Finally, I have noted that the rise in the levels of social action in the Church that were witnessed between 2010 and 2015 did not lead to a corresponding increase in affiliation in the Church of England, contrary to Milbank's argumentation, though any extrapolation of this historical outcome to suggest a likely long-term trend must be treated with due caution.

[203.] GS1804, para. 8.

Chapter Six

John Milbank and the Church of England's Future Approach to Welfare

Introduction

There is much in this book that supports a view that the Anglican Socialist tradition is a useful lens to look through when examining the Church of England's approach to welfare. We have seen how Temple and Tawney had considerable influence on shaping the British post-war welfare state settlement, as well as post-war thinking within the Church of England on welfare. Moreover, since the late 1960s via the works of 'non statist' Anglican Socialists such as Nicholls and, since 1990, the works of Milbank, we have seen that there has been a resurgence of interest in the Christendom strand of Anglican Socialism. This is particularly so with respect to its evaluation of the Temple Welfare Statist legacy, both from within the Church of England and further afield. The Blue Labour/Red Tory political phenomenon partly reflects this, as does the rise of the Radical Orthodoxy grouping as one key strand of theological underpinning for it.

The Anglican Socialist tradition is likely to remain relevant, not just for the shaping of the Church of England's approach to welfare in the future, but to wider British society. The influence its thinkers have had – and continue to have – on shaping debates on welfare and related topics in the Labour Party, for example, bears this out. We have seen how Anglican Socialists such as Temple and Tawney were important figures in shaping Labour's post-war thinking on welfare and the role the state can play in its delivery in a parliamentary democracy. Tawney's writings on equality were pivotal to the intellectual development of several Labour Party thinkers who came after – not least Roy Hattersley, whose influential book of 1987, *Choose Freedom: The Future for Democratic Socialism*, was, in many respects, a defence of Tawney's thinking.[1] The book remains a central plank in the intellectual armoury of those in the Labour Party who continue to argue for a social democratic approach to welfare provision.[2] Tony Blair's contribution to 'Third Way' thinking in the mid-to-late 1990s was also, in part, shaped by his Anglican Socialist roots, as he has since acknowledged.[3] This strand of thinking was later influential on shaping the Purple Labour perspective that emerged in the party in 2011 and that was, in some respects, a form of 'Blairist revivalism', although it did contain some Blue Socialist influences.[4] Therefore, at a time when the Church of England is seeking to enhance its perceived relevance in English society, politics and the public square generally, this book shows that the Anglican Socialist tradition offers it an intellectual resource of considerable depth on which to call. Yet, it is a diverse and complex tradition, and, as we have seen, this is reflected in the way the Welfare Statist strand and the Christendom strand have contrasting theologies of the state that have helped to shape their advocates' thinking on welfare, and to which we now return.

Differing Theologies of the State

We have seen that, whereas for Temple the state had a 'spiritual function' and was a 'servant and instrument of God', for exponents of Christendom theology, such as Milbank, it is more often seen as a secular product of the modernist challenge to Christendom that the Protestant Reformation represented – thus it is the Church, not the state, that is 'the kingdom of God in embryo', and hence the place where spiritual functionality resides. These may well be irreconcilable theologies of the

---

[1] Hattersley, *Choose Freedom*.

[2] For a selection of writers who hold that opinion, see R. Hattersley and K. Hickson (eds), *The Socialist Way: Social Democracy in Contemporary Britain* (London: I.B. Tauris, 2013).

[3] For more on Tony Blair's Christian faith and how it has shaped his politics, see G. Hinsliff, 'Blair's Christianity', *The Guardian*, 8 April 2007.

[4] See R. Philpot (ed.), *The Purple Book: A Progressive Future for Labour* (London: Biteback Publishers, 2011).

state, as argued by Malcolm Brown, and therefore incapable of being synthesised into a coherent whole. As Brown puts it: 'Could there ever be one coherent theology of the state in the Church of England given that we are a coalition church?'[5] This concern connects to a point Brown made in an article in 2015 – that there is no consensus within the Church, at present, 'about where the proper boundary lies between public, private and voluntary provision in the shared task of building up the common good'.[6] It may not be possible (nor even desirable) to achieve such a consensus in the Anglican Church, but, as Brown argued with respect to the theology of the state, at any one time 'there will be a dominant model, and it will be provisional'.[7] Clarity from the Church of England on the model by which it is *currently* operating by would be helpful in shaping its future approach to welfare. Also, when reflecting on the Church's handling of the 'Big Society' project and the lessons to be learned, it would be of assistance to know what that 'dominant' *future* model of thinking is likely to be, at least in the short to medium-term, as it will no doubt help to shape the Church's remodelling of its approach to welfare.

Crucially, the Church's leadership should bear the following in mind when deliberating on this: Milbank's (and Radical Orthodoxy's) Christendom theology *vis-à-vis* the state is a minority perspective both within Anglo-Catholicism and Roman Catholicism. With respect to the latter, for example, it can be argued that Christendom theology is unrepresentative of Catholic social teaching on Church and state, which, in the post-war period, the leadership of the Roman Catholic Church has seen as compatible with the emergence of welfare states in countries such as those in Western Europe and elsewhere. It has, nevertheless, acknowledged that an over-statist approach can have dangers with respect to encroachment on individuals' human rights and freedoms, which need to be avoided. Consequently, it has seen the doctrine of subsidiarity[8] as necessary for putting limits on government encroachment into people's lives, whilst being wholly supportive of the need for government to act when local communities cannot solve problems on their own. Milbank's interpretation of the Roman Catholic doctrine of subsidiarity is thus open to challenge when he states: 'the

---

5. Brown's reply to question 30.
6. Brown, 'The Church of England and the Common Good', p. 132.
7. Brown's reply to question 30.
8. See Pius X1, *Quadragesimo Anno*.

doctrine of subsidiarity remains corporatist, since it seeks to devolve central sovereign powers to groups that are economically vocational and voluntary, as well as to local political formations'.[9]

Certainly, in John Paul II's *Centesimus Annus*,[10] a document often adduced by those who seek to interpret Catholic social teaching in a way that appears to be antithetical to welfare states, the Pope cautioned against the excesses of a 'social assistance state' and was critical of aspects of welfare state provision when 'they are dominated more by bureaucratic ways of thinking than by concern for serving their clients'. However, in the same encyclical the Pope described the need for the state to defend the weakest and ensure in every case the 'necessary minimum support for the unemployed worker' as one example of how this should be achieved. Mainstream Roman Catholic thinking on welfare does not hold that the doctrine of subsidiarity is inherently antithetical to either the concept or actuality of a welfare state. However, it considers it is necessary to ensure that an over-statist approach to welfare provision is avoided, thus welcoming the contribution that non-state organisations can and should make to the provision of welfare, often by working co-operatively and in partnership with state welfare providers.

Crucially, Catholic social thinking on subsidiarity is, of course, only one pillar of Catholic social teaching – solidarity being another. Solidarity relates to a need for people to have a keen sense of the common good; that is, the things that bind us together and enable friendships and fraternity to flourish and which, from a Catholic perspective, is a guiding principle that should shape everything that we do. Consistent with this, in his encyclical *Caritas in Veritate*, Pope Benedict XVI wrote, '*The principle of subsidiarity must remain closely linked to the principle of solidarity and vice versa*, since the former without the latter gives way to social privatism, while the latter without the former gives way to paternalist social assistance that is demeaning to those in need [emphasis in original].'[11] There has, therefore, from a Roman Catholic perspective, to be a balance struck between these two pillars of Catholic social teaching when it comes to the provision of welfare, which, in

---

9.   Milbank and Pabst, *The Politics of Virtue*, p. 87.

10. John Paul II, *Centesimus Annus: Encyclical Letter on the Hundredth Anniversary of Rerum Novarum*. Available at: http://w2.vatican.va/content /john-paul-ii/en/encyclicals/documents/hf_jp-ii_enc_01051991_centesimus -annus.html (accessed on 29 October 2018).

11. Benedict XVI, *Caritas in Veritate: Encyclical Letter on Integral Human Development in Charity and Truth* (London: Catholic Truth Society, 2009).

some ways will reflect a need for a balance to be struck between state and non-statist contributions to the provision of welfare in a democratic society – indeed, a recognition of the desirability for state, charity-based and private sector contributions to the delivery of welfare to be working co-operatively and in tandem in ways that maximise their respective attributes. When considering Milbank's Christendom thinking on the Church, state and welfare, the leadership of the Church of England should be mindful that it is often seen by mainstream Roman Catholics (and Anglo-Catholics) as being romantically medievalist, both in its theology of the state and in its 'restorationist' theo-political aspirations, and should therefore be treated with the caution that merits.[12]

The Importance of Historical Analysis

Much of the research in this book is historically based and evidenced. This reflects my epistemological bias as to the merits of this research methodology when analysing political and theo-political events. From this standpoint, it is crucial that any rethinking on the Church of England's approach to welfare is underpinned by sound historical analysis of the events that have precipitated such a rethink. In this book we have seen in the reports and academic works adduced in chapter four – works that were in the public domain and thus available to the Church of England – how there is compelling historical evidence that there was a 'Big Society' in Britain before the 'Big Society' project was launched in the summer of 2010. This casts doubt on claims to the contrary by the Coalition government and its 'Big Society' advocates such as Milbank and Blond. Rather, this lends some support to the perspective advanced at the time by the signatories to the *Common Wealth* document: that the 'Big Society' project was a 'Big Lie', 'a smokescreen', 'another ideological veil' and a front for making major cuts to state-provided welfare at a

---

[12.] For a liberal Anglo-Catholic critique, see C. Insole, *The Politics of Human Frailty: A Theological Defence of Political Liberalism* (London: SCM Press, 2012). For a Roman Catholic critique, see M. Doak, 'The Politics of Radical Orthodoxy: A Catholic Critique', *Theological Studies* 68, no. 2 (2007), pp. 368–93. Available at: https://journals.sagepub.com/doi /abs/10.1177/004056390706800207 (accessed on 1 July 2019). She argues: 'we must conclude that Milbank's remnant Christendom ecclesiology is inconsistent with a religious freedom that is more than bare tolerance and non-coercion of those who do not adhere to the Christian faith'.

time of severe pressure on the public finances. In any case, the historical evidence should have been sufficient to have enabled greater foresight in the Church of England's handling of the 'Big Society' project at the time the events unfolded.

Decreasing Levels of Church Affiliation

As the Church of England is rightly concerned about decreasing levels of affiliation, it is understandably keen to enhance its relevance in wider society. Yet, as noted in chapter five, between 2010 and 2015 it experienced an increase in its social activity levels at a time when Anglican Church membership in the United Kingdom decreased by eight per cent. This is an indication that the reasons for the decline in membership are complex and multifaceted, as was argued in chapter four. So, any remodelling of its approach to welfare needs to bear this in mind. This shall be especially apposite when assessing the viability and desirability of church-based initiatives that seek to replace state-provided welfare services. These should be assessed on the likely impact they will have for the recipients of welfare, rather than the impact they may have on church affiliation.

As levels of church affiliation and attendance in the Church of England continue to decrease, this will have a negative impact on its human capacity to deliver welfare. As a result, there is a need for a realistic human resources assessment of the Church's capacity to deliver welfare: one that is based on accurate information and informed prioritisation criteria. Therefore, when remodelling its approach to welfare, and paying due regard to lessons that it can learn from its handling of the 'Big Society' project, a key aspect the Church of England will need to revisit are its priorities for welfare in the wider theo-political context. Prioritisation is vital as it relates to the finite availability of resources. This pertains not just to the capacity to do things but also the capacity to understand and comment – and to do that with authority despite diminished numbers. Brown was correct in his assessment of how wildly over-optimistic and unrealistic Blond's and Noyes' vision for the Church of England's role in the provision of welfare was in their report *Holistic Mission* (discussed in chapter four). However, it reinforces the need for the Church of England to be realistic about what its capacity to deliver welfare is likely to be, before making any commitments. A dynamic, ongoing capacity assessment of its financial, physical and human resources is necessary, so that a realistic sense of its ability to deliver welfare provision in the short to medium term can be gauged and prioritised, as well as the scale and specificity of its interventions and any risks associated with their delivery.

The Failure of the 'Big Society' Project

No doubt the failure of the 'Big Society' project to deliver on most of its *stated* objectives, and the reality that it compounded several of them, relates in part to its implementation. Recognising the demise of the 'Big Society' project in the autumn of 2012, Blond wrote in an article in the *Guardian*: 'The PM has given up something for nothing, ceding all his strategic and visionary thinking to George Osborne's tactical and failing approach to the deficit. A new conservatism has been strangled at birth; a failure to rethink the party's economic offer means that old economics have killed new politics.'[13]

He can thus argue that the project was never given a fair wind, and hence its failure cannot be seen as undermining the credibility of the project's theoretical underpinning. However, regardless of whether one agrees or disagrees with that assessment, it does not remove its supporters from taking some responsibility for that failure, including those from within the Church of England. For the reality was that Milbank's and Blond's influence on Brown's thinking, for example, and hence on the Church of England's handling of the project, meant that the Church's ability to evaluate and challenge the cuts of £1.3 billion in state provision to the voluntary sector in 2011/12 was significantly compromised, largely because of its stated support for the project at that time.

The Viability of Disentangling the State from the Voluntary Sector

I argued in chapter four that Milbank's Blue Socialist perspective is consistent with the historical evidence in so far as, since the 1970s, *some* sections of the voluntary sector have experienced *some* loss of financial and strategic decision-making autonomy to the state, in ways that have reshaped the way they provide welfare services. The question remains,

---

13. See P. Blond, 'David Cameron Has Lost His Chance to Redefine the Tories', *The Guardian*, 3 October 2012.

however, whether an alternative approach that entails a disentangling of the state from the voluntary sector and a substantial increase in Church provision of welfare (some of it funded by the state), as advocated by Milbank and Blond, offers a better alternative, including income streams sufficiently capable of offsetting the loss of state provided income that would result. Relevant to answering that question are the findings of *Whose Society? The Final Big Society Audit* discussed in chapter five, which reveal that levels of corporate giving had not increased to replace shrinking state funding for the voluntary sector and that, although individual giving had increased, it was not back to pre-recession levels. The result was that many voluntary organisations were facing closure, not being able to find alternative sources of income.

This had been predicted by Patrick Butler, the *Guardian*'s editor for society, health and education in July 2010, when he wrote 'thousands of small community-based charities expected to help deliver David Cameron's "big society" idea are facing potentially devastating cuts, leaving some under threat of closure, and putting services to some of Britain's poorest and most vulnerable people at risk'.[14] It occurred at a time when changes to welfare benefits, particularly to the unemployed, including the imposition of a harsher system of benefit sanctions, were introduced. These changes were not a stated policy objective of the 'Big Society' project and came from a different government department. Nevertheless, they compounded the effects that cuts in the voluntary sector providers of welfare were having on the most vulnerable in society. This outcome was partly ameliorated by the increase in social action and welfare provision in the churches, including the increase in church-based food banks. Thus, as noted in chapter five, Brown, three years into the 'Big Society' project, had concluded that action by the churches had been crucial in responding to the plight many people were in, but 'those most involved know that it is not filling the gap left by the cuts to welfare provision'.[15]

It is for reasons such as these that the effects of the cuts to state provision for voluntary services, evidenced in *Whose Society? The Final Big Society Audit* as being a direct result of the rollout of the 'Big Society' project, should not be underestimated; nor should the significant but inadequate level of alleviation of their consequences by the Church of England be overestimated. Size matters when it comes to welfare

---

14. See P. Butler, 'Local Charity Cuts Jeopardise David Cameron's "Big Society"', *The Guardian*, 23 July 2010.
15. Brown, 'The Church of England and Welfare Today', p. 59.

provision, as Baker, Atherton and Reader recognised in their riposte to Milbank, recounted in chapter four, when they pointed out that the British government will spend '40% of its GDP on public expenditure even after proposed cuts', an essential contribution to well-being, 'which the church and voluntary bodies are incapable of satisfying'.[16] It is difficult to envisage this situation substantially changing in the future, not least based on historical trend analysis embracing the period of the rollout of the 'Big Society' project. Even with further additional state funding, the Church of England's *capacity* to deliver welfare on a scale anywhere remotely close to that provided by the state sector is unrealistic, as well as highly problematical for the reasons discussed in chapter four. In some respects, but not all, the same can be said of the wider voluntary sector providers of welfare.

Prior to the setting up of the Welfare State, one can point to numerous historical examples of how voluntary-based or charity provision of welfare, not least that provided by the Church sector, played a vital part in alleviating the plight of the poor and disadvantaged. Prochaska's works are strong on this aspect of British social history. Yet, it was only with the coming of the Welfare State in the 1940s that the *scale* of welfare that was necessary to tackle the five giants identified by Beveridge was made possible. Brown may well be right in his view that, in a sense, 'they are still around'.[17] To suppose that they will ever be entirely 'slayed' would stretch the imagination beyond what is sensible. Nevertheless, in comparison to the scale of welfare deficiency prior to the coming of the Welfare State, massive progress has since been made towards slaying them. This is particularly apparent in the fields of education and health, and on a scale that has broadly been commensurate to the task. By 1952, this trend was already evident to Tawney, who was able to include in his epilogue to *Equality* a list of major improvements across a range of performance indicators that were directly attributable to the Welfare State. Advocates of a more localist, voluntarist, communitarian-based model of welfare delivery, such as Milbank and Blond, promoting *competition* with state sector providers with a view to diminishing their size and resources, rather than based on working in *co-operation* with them, have yet to make out a convincing, evidence-based case that this alternative model can deliver welfare on a scale commensurate to the task in hand.

[16.] Baker, 'A Case of Ecclesial Over-Optimism?', p. 1.

[17.] Brown's reply to question 30.

This is not, of course, in any way to suggest that the Welfare State should be immune from a need for dynamic and sometimes substantial changes to the way it defines and delivers welfare, so as to try to keep pace with society's constantly changing welfare needs and expectations. It is also not to suggest that the voluntary sector should not continue to play a vital and integral contribution to the delivery of welfare provision in Britain, working in co-operation with the state and private sector providers as envisaged by Temple, Beveridge and the authors of *Not Just for the Poor*. However, it is to suggest they cannot become substitutes for state welfare providers, unless there are sound, professionally informed and publically accountable justifications for that, reached on a case-by-case analysis and not on market-driven imperatives.

Temple always envisaged a need for the state and intermediate sectors to coexist and mutually thrive within a welfare state, as has been argued and shown in chapter one. There is compelling historical evidence to support a view that they did coexist and mutually thrive in the period from 1945 until the financial crash of 2008. In the post-war period it has been Christendom writers such as Demant, Reckitt and Milbank who have sought to paint a different picture, often based more on sophisticated ideological and theological argumentation than on sound historical analysis.[18] The rise of the Radical Orthodoxy grouping – providing a key theological underpinning for the Blue Labour/Red Tory political phenomenon – has lent weight to their cause. We have seen in the evidence provided by Brown in chapter five, the extent to which

---

[18.] This cannot be said of David Nicholls with respect to historical analysis, as he was skilled in that field. That said, he had a tendency to interpret the past in ways which reflected his understanding of what had come after, not unlike Milbank. This is why his interpretation of Rousseau, for example, as being a 'totalitarian' writer (not a term or, arguably, a concept that Rousseau would have been familiar with and antithetical to much of his thinking in any event) is open to challenge. The totalitarian regimes that have since emerged have hardly embraced a commitment to direct democracy of the kind Rousseau championed. An alternative and much more credible interpretation of Rousseau's concept of the 'General Will', for example, would be a Christian understanding of the concept of 'the common good' – something that could only be realised via political engagement and the collective action of citizens participating in their own self-government, admittedly, in Rousseau's thinking, via direct and not representative democracy and thus with all of the impracticality that goes with that. See Nicholls, *Deity and Domination*, p. 27.

Milbank and Radical Orthodoxy can now exercise influence on the Church of England's position on welfare, as one corrective tradition to the Temple Welfare Statist legacy.

Milbank's Approach to the Writing of History

When one looks closely at the historical evidence relevant to much of Milbank's theo-political outlook, whether it be *inter alia* in respect of the early modern period and the reasons for the rise of capitalism, or nineteenth-century British labour history, both of which were considered in chapter three, we begin to see how open to challenge his perspectives on history are. We saw in chapter three how Milbank's perspective on historical source criticism stems from his openly acknowledged affinity with romantic thinking, as evidenced by his statement: 'a romantic view of history is more realistic than a cynical one'.[19] This *a priori* commitment to writing history from a romantic perspective Milbank sees as a necessary corrective to what he argues are the distortions inherent in liberalism and its 'cynical' accounts of history. These have been derived in significant part from the application of positivist research methods that place a primacy on *a posteriori* reasoning. It is Milbank's post-modernist scepticism of positivist research methods and their epistemological underpinnings which partly accounts for his unorthodox attitude to the conventions of historical source criticism that have been developed over the last 185 years or so. Thus, he argues:

> The positivism which defines religion at, beyond, or across the boundaries of the 'social fact' is always subverted by a more radical positivism which recognizes the peculiarity and specificity of religious practice and logic, and, in consequence, the impossibility of any serious attempt at either scientific explanation or humanist interpretation.[20]

This outlook has resulted in a problematic and questionable approach to the writing of history from Milbank; an approach that overemphasises ideas as being the shaper of historical events and that is often based on the use of novel categorisations that fit with his theological and theo-political presuppositions – theology, for Milbank, being 'the queen of

---

[19.] Milbank, 'Blue Labour, One Nation', p. 6.
[20.] Milbank, *Theology and Social Theory*, p. 144.

the sciences'[21] – and, as we have seen in chapter three, these are open to considerable challenge when tested against the historical evidence.

It is one reason why historical source criticism has been used throughout this book as an approach to addressing the issues it raises. It is also why the Church of England should be cautious when seeking

---

21. See ibid., p. 382. A key strand of Milbank's thought is that Christian theology must regain its medieval status as being 'queen of the sciences', as his outlook is singularly ontologically theological and Catholically Christocentric. His work *Theology and Social Theory*, in some respects, can be seen as an attempt to achieve this within the academy. It is a trenchant, critical analysis of modernist, positivist research methods of enquiry that social scientists and others have often used, and the epistemological claims to truth that have been made on the back of their use. The body of thought that is commonly referred to as historical source criticism has been heavily influenced by positivist thinking, not least by the emphasis it places on primary sources (empiricism) as the basis for historical criticism via the primacy it places on *a posteriori* knowledge. L. Rank's seminal work *The Theory and Practice of History* (1836) (London: Routledge, 2010) exemplifies this approach, and can be seen as the starting point in the development of modern historical source criticism. G.J. Garraghan's highly influential book *A Guide to Historical Method* (New York: Declan X. McMullan, 1946) is also heavily indebted to positivist theory. Although there are some contemporary historians who have been influenced by post-modernist assessments of positivist historical method, and thus are more sceptical of some of the epistemological claims to historical truth that have been made by their advocates (see, for example, M. Bentley, 'History, Truth and Changing Perspectives', *The Social Affairs Unit*, August 2006, available at: http://www.socialaffairsunit.org.uk/blog/archives/001046.php [accessed on 18 July 2018]), they nevertheless continue to adhere to what are essentially positivist (empiricist) methods in their evidencing of what they write about history. Milbank's post-modernist scepticism of positivist research methods is more incredulous, however, and is reflected in his words: 'the impossibility of any serious attempt at either scientific explanation or humanist interpretation' of what he describes as 'religious practice and logic'. It is one reason why his thinking on 'Socialism of the Gift', for example, as an interpretation of commodity exchange in Catholic medieval society is highly theoretically based and this is reflected in the sources it draws upon which often tend to be more theoretically than empirically supported – see his article, 'Socialism of the Gift: Socialism by Grace'.

to engage with – let alone accommodate – Milbank's views on history, not least those on the British Welfare State *vis-à-vis* the voluntary sector providers of welfare that were analysed and evaluated in chapter four.

Getting the Church's Voice Heard on Welfare

However, Milbank is right to draw attention to weaknesses in the Welfare State that need to be remedied. Thus, we noted in chapter five the Council of Churches' *Unemployment and the Future of Work* was broadly in support of in-work state benefits,[22] which fails to reflect a concern voiced by some, that such benefits can supplement inadequate and possibly unjust remuneration practices by low-paying employers at the expense of the taxpayer. This was something not envisaged by either Beveridge or Temple as a function of the Welfare State and is precisely the kind of extension of its remit that Gordon Brown's New Labour administration did much to advance, and of which Milbank has rightly been so critical.[23] So, in any rethink of its approach to welfare, the Church of England should ensure that it continues to have a strong voice in areas where it feels the state may be getting things wrong, as well as on options for how it might better get them right. Milbank's and Pabst's ambitious but problematic vision for how this could be achieved merits rigorous, critical examination by the Church of England. This could be part of a wider review of its strategic interface with the state, taking into account the lessons that it can learn from its handling of the 'Big Society' project and the need for clarification on its theology of the state.

The Church of England will also need to consider what is likely to be the optimal way for it to get its voice heard on welfare, at least in the short to medium term. Malcolm Brown's statement that the Church of England does not do reports like *Faith in the City* anymore is relevant to answering that question.[24] The danger with this 'shift of method and model', however, is that the Church of England could become too reactive (hence insufficiently proactive) in shaping the welfare agenda. To avoid this, it needs to reassess the extent to which it needs to engage in research projects and initiatives on welfare provision. It may be that reports in the style of *Faith in the City* are no longer optimal or even affordable. If this is the case, other opportunities need to be identified

---

[22.] CCBI, *Unemployment and the Future of Work*, p. 139.

[23.] Milbank and Pabst, 'Post-Liberal Politics and the Alternative', p. 92.

[24.] Brown's reply to question 6.

for the Church of England to influence the analytical, academic and political debates concerning welfare provision, perhaps working in concert with other churches, charities, think tanks and university departments currently engaged in research on welfare on the best ways of delivering it. Encouragingly, the Archbishops' Commission on Housing, Church and Community that reported in February 2021, may be an example of this approach being put into practice.[25] The report reflects the desire of the Church of England to make a significant contribution to remedying the housing crisis in England, such as freeing up land that it owns for affordable housing developments, whilst also recognising the positive role that government must play in shaping the housing agenda, including making short-term reforms to the benefits system to meet the shortfall between housing support and the true cost of housing. Another example, may be the support that the Archbishops of Canterbury and York gave to the report produced by the National Churches Trust in October 2020, *The House of Good*, that makes out a convincing, evidence-based case for why church buildings are so essential to the ongoing provision of social welfare, and which calls for greater levels of state funding for their repair and upkeep, arguing that government funding would be more than recompensed.[26]

The Church of England should also reconsider how best it can communicate its purpose with regard to welfare provision, making best use of social media resources, but also shaping more and reacting less to perceived stereotypes such as the Church of England 'is a load of "pink" communist types'.[27] *Faith in the City,* for example, was, in some respects, flawed, being, as Brown described it in 2017: 'theologically deficient, flirting, as many of us did, with Liberation Theology with insufficient appreciation that urban England and its people were more than a little

---

[25.] For more on this, see Church of England, the Archbishops' Commission on Housing, Church and Community, *Coming Home: Tackling the Housing Crisis Together*, April 2019. Available at: https://www.churchofengland.org /ABChousing (accessed on 10 June 2019). See also G. Tomlin and M. Brown, *Coming Home: Christian Perspectives on Housing* (London: Church House Publishing, 2020).

[26.] C. Walker and L. March, *The House of Good* (London: National Churches Trust, 2020). Available at: https://www.houseofgood.nationalchurchestrust .org/wp-content/uploads/2020/10/House-of-Good-AW-digital-small.pdf (accessed on 20 December 2020).

[27.] Brown's reply to question 21.

different from El Salvadorian base communities'.[28] Nevertheless, it was a heavyweight analytical challenge to the Conservative government's handling of the welfare agenda at that time, which resonated with many in the United Kingdom and certainly did not go unnoticed in high political circles. The recommendations were supported by a considerable amount of evidence-based research, which had been amassed by the authors talking to people 'on the ground' and which was well presented and communicated via a skillful handling by the Church of the media at that time. Contrast that approach with the statement that Brown offered about the Church's initial handling of the 'Big Society' project: 'What we were looking for, and this was not theology or political theory but *realpolitik*, was what we can say that shows that Conservatives were not the enemy of the Church of England.' The danger is that tactical considerations – the perceived need for political acceptance and ongoing legitimacy, admittedly as part of a wider theoretical reconsideration of its post-war position on welfare – might now be becoming too prominent a theo-political imperative, and may on occasion be taking precedence over theologically underpinned proactive analysis in the Church of England in its handling of its interface with government on welfare matters.

Reprioritising Equality as a Christian Goal

As considered in chapters two and three, since the publication of Tawney's seminal work on the subject, equality has been a key intellectual feature of the Welfare Statist strand of Anglican Socialist thought, though it has to be balanced with a need for liberty and fraternity which will place limits on the extent to which it can be realised. An example of its application in the Welfare State is that access to health services provided by the NHS to British nationals is based singly on clinical need. Yet, equality is antithetical to the thinking of Burke, who, as noted in chapter three, is a key intellectual influence on Milbank's Blue Socialist thinking. It is also noticeable that equality does not feature much in Blue Labour thinking, and Milbank does not appear to place much importance on equality as a theo-political aspiration. Yet, for many Christians, equality, albeit constrained in its achievability, is an important imperative relating to the concept of the common good (and certainly to a Catholic sense of it). It raises the question how far a society based on a notion of the common

---

28. Brown, 'Anglican Social Theology: Today and Tomorrow', p. 128.

good can accommodate levels of inequality in the levels of access to the political, economic, social, educational, intellectual and cultural aspects of life that are necessary for human flourishing. Enhancing equality in society should therefore be a goal for the Church of England in its handling of welfare, however difficult it is to put into effect.

The Church of England's Future Approach to Welfare

It is for reasons such as these, as well as the research findings in this book relating to them, that the answer to the question posed in chapter one – namely, should the Church of England's approach to welfare be one characterised primarily as shaped around a defence of the Welfare State and consistent with the thinking of Temple (as, by and large, it had been up to 2010) or should it be one characterised by a move towards a more localist, community-based, voluntarist, Christendom model of delivery, with the Church of England playing a greater role in the provision of welfare and a smaller Welfare State as argued by Milbank? – is that it should be *much more of the former than the latter.*

Conclusion

Back to the Future

There can be little doubt, as this book has demonstrated, that the Church of England needs to keep reflecting theologically and practically on its role *vis-à-vis* the state and the provision of welfare. Consequently, it needs to take into account policy developments on welfare in the Labour Party that emerge in the aftermath of its electoral defeat in December 2019, as well as those brought forward by the Boris Johnson Conservative administration.

Blue Labour thinking on welfare remains an intellectual force in the Labour Party, though the term is less often used to describe it. An example of its ongoing influence is *The Dignity of Labour*, published in 2021 by Jon Cruddas.[1] Cruddas argues that elements on the left – including within the Labour Party – have completely lost touch with the day-to-day needs and expectations of working-class folk in Dagenham (his constituency) and elsewhere. These go beyond their material needs, for which he argues that the imperative for distributive justice via welfare and other redistributive state interventions has tended to dominate the radical and social democratic lefts' purpose in the post-war period, and that 'an over reliance on distributive issues can appear indifferent to the wider emotional well-being of citizens and the lives they wish to live'.[2] We saw in chapter five how this chimes with the increased emphasis that Atherton, Baker and Reader's book of 2011 had placed on the need for a greater focus on emotional well-being, and not just welfare, in the contribution that churches (and other voluntary groups) can make to enhancing the lives of those who

---

[1] J. Cruddas, *The Dignity of Labour* (Cambridge: Polity Press, 2021).

[2] Ibid., p. 159.

access their charitable services – something that was also reflected in the document written by Malcolm Brown in 2016, *Thinking Afresh about Welfare: The Enemy Isolation*. Yet, there is a danger of seeing well-being and welfare as an either/or choice when *both* are essential to human flourishing. It may well be that greater emphasis will need to be placed on enhancing well-being by the Church of England (and other voluntary bodies) in the years to come, and it has much to offer in this regard. However, it would be a mistake if it were at the expense of the provision of adequate welfare services, either by the Church of England or by the state.

Red Tory thinking on welfare in the Conservative Party is less evident than it once was. The thrust of this study, based on the evidence examined, is that the Church of England should reassess its connections with the Blue Labour/Red Tory political phenomenon and return to a position of defending the Temple Welfare Statist legacy. However, in doing that it must remain cognisant of the need for ongoing modernisation of that legacy to meet the ever-changing welfare *and* well-being needs and expectations of twenty-first century English society. This book shows why the continuing legacy of Welfare Statist Anglican Socialism should remain a key theological component in any debates it has with other perspectives in the years ahead, as well as a formative intellectual and historical resource to draw on when formulating its strategic thinking and theo-political praxis on welfare and its future delivery. It is on that basis that the following eight action points are put forward as suggestions for the Church of England to consider, when formulating its future approach to welfare:

1. To revisit the historical record of the Welfare State *vis-à-vis* the voluntary sector, and to learn lessons from its handling of the 'Big Society' project.
2. To shape its approach to welfare around a defence of the Welfare State, consistent with the emphasis Temple and Tawney placed on equality as a value underpinning the Welfare State, whilst retaining the freedom to be critical of it where evidence suggests such criticism is merited.
3. To continue to play a vital and integral contribution to the delivery of welfare *and* emotional well-being provision in Britain, working in cooperation with the state and private sector providers as envisaged by Temple, Beveridge and the authors of *Not Just for the Poor*.

4. To identify and clarify the *current* dominant model of its theology of the state and what any *future* model is likely to be because of its relevance to shaping its approach to welfare. It should therefore undertake a review of its theological and practical interface with the state, including a rigorous, critical examination of Milbank's and Pabst's vision for it.

5. To undertake, on a dynamic basis, a realistic and prioritised assessment of its capacity to deliver welfare – one that is based on accurate information and informed prioritisation criteria.

6. To ensure it continues to have a strong voice in areas where it feels the Welfare State may be getting things wrong, as well as on options for how it might better get them right.

7. To reassess the extent to which it should engage in research projects and initiatives on welfare provision with others, and how best it can communicate its purpose.

8. To exercise caution when seeking to engage with – let alone accommodate – Milbank's views on history, and, specifically, on the history of the Welfare State *vis-à-vis* voluntarism, and to be more sceptical of the broad thrust of his Blue Socialist vision for its role in the provision of welfare, as well as his views on the role the Welfare State should perform in British society in the coming years.

It is not suggested that these eight action points are an all-inclusive list of what needs to be done by the Church of England. No doubt other aspects will also need to be considered that have not fallen within the remit of this analysis or have been inadequately covered by it. However, it is suggested that they offer a way forward that is reflective of the lessons that the Church can learn from its handling of the 'Big Society' project.

Epilogue

The Covid-19 Pandemic

Most of the research for this book was completed in early 2020; hence, just before the onset of the Covid-19 pandemic that took hold in Britain in March of that year. This epilogue is being written in winter 2021; a time of growing optimism that the major vaccination rollout will bring an end to the pandemic. The full extent of the ramifications stemming from the pandemic are unknown and will be for some time to come, not least the impact they may have on the funding of welfare provision in the United Kingdom going forwards. Nevertheless, it is evident that the financial costs of managing the crisis have been huge. According to a research briefing for the House of Common's library by Matthew Keep and Philip Brien published in December 2021, current estimates of the cost of Government measures announced so far in response to the pandemic, range from about £315 to £410 billion.[1] Consequently, pressure on the public purse will be intense for many years to come as measures are put in place to try to repay this debt. However, it is unlikely that the extent of government borrowing stemming from the pandemic will reach the level that the Attlee government had inherited after the Second World War.[2] Despite that level of borrowing, it had felt able to implement the key recommendations of the Beveridge Report on the

---

[1] M. Keep and P. Brian, *Public Spending During the Covid 19 Pandemic* (London: House of Commons Library, December, 2021). Available at: https:// commonslibrary.parliament.uk/research-briefings/cbp-9309/ (accessed on 31 December 2021).

[2] See D. Milliken, 'Factbox: UK on Course for Highest Borrowing since World War Two', Reuters, 25 November 2020. Available at: https://www .reuters.com/article/us-health-coronavirus-britain-borrowing/factbox-uk

setting up of the Welfare State; this is a point we should not lose sight of as we move out of the current crisis.

The pandemic has brought to the fore the extent to which the British people value the NHS (perhaps the most ambitious component of the post-war Welfare State settlement), symbolically reflected week after week in the clapping of its workforce by millions of people in streets across the country, as its staff grappled with meeting the healthcare needs of those struck down with Covid-19. Although under-resourced to meet the full extent of the challenge, the overall performance of the NHS has been commendable on many levels. It is why, for many, the blurb on the dust jacket of a book that was published in 2020 as a tribute to its staff for their skillful handling of the crisis is not an exaggeration when it states: 'The NHS is our single greatest achievement as a country. No matter who you are, no matter your health needs and no matter how much money you have, the NHS is there for you.'[3] This is not a view that is commonly held by British people concerning the provision of social services that, in the post-war period, has been more market based and localist in its organisation, and which is seen by politicians across the political divide as deficient and in need of a major overhaul.[4]

Yet, if the Welfare State is to continue to be the primary deliverer of welfare provision in the United Kingdom in the twenty-first century, it has to be adequately resourced to meet that challenge. This can be problematic in a world that has become increasingly global and transnational in its economic modes of production, distribution and exchange, despite the recent populist reaction against this trend in some countries. The result has been that the level at which a UK government elects to levy corporation tax, for example, needs to be carefully calibrated if it is to avoid the risk of 'seeing jobs shipped overseas'.[5] In other words it has to take account of international comparators, many of whom will not have welfare states, or, if they do, they will not be on anything like the size of the British Welfare State and so will not require resourcing to that level.

-on-course-for-highest-borrowing-since-world-war-two-idUSKBN28500D (accessed on 12 January 2021).

[3.] A. Kay (ed.), *Dear NHS: 100 Stories to Say Thank You* (London: Trapeze, 2020).

[4.] See A. Hill, 'Matt Hancock Asks MPs and Peers for Views on Adult Social Care Reform', *The Guardian*, 6 March 2020.

[5.] This was a view most notably held by President Barack Obama, who often used this phrase.

The trend towards more online shopping and the impact this is having on traditional 'bricks and mortar' outlets, is also adversely impacting the Exchequer's revenue streams, as high street shops find it increasingly difficult to compete with their online competitors, partly owing to the fact that there is not a level playing field between the high street and the online business sector when it comes to tax levying. The Covid-19 pandemic has exacerbated this trend as people have been encouraged to 'stay at home' or at least limit the number of journeys they make.

The upshot of these trends is that there is a growing awareness in British society of a need for a rethink on how taxes are best levied, and the level at which they are levied, if the government is to be able to meet its ongoing commitments to welfare provision in the medium to long term, not least the funding of the Welfare State. The Church of England's contribution to that rethink will matter, not least to those who see welfare provision as a vital component of Christian discipleship and appreciate the contribution the Church of England has made – and continues to make – to shaping and delivering on the welfare agenda in England.

We would do well to end by reflecting on the words of the current Labour Party leader, Sir Keir Starmer, writing in the *Church Times*, when he said of the Covid-19 pandemic: 'For all the loss and difficulty, we should not let this year be defined by pain. Throughout this pandemic, we have also seen the best of humanity.' He went on to state that, during the pandemic: 'religious institutions and local communities have banded together for the common good, showing us the very best of Britain'.[6] Evidence of this has been the high levels of support for food banks at a time of increased demand stemming from the economic dislocation resulting from lockdown. We have also seen numerous examples of people delivering food to neighbours and contacting by phone those who have been experiencing self-isolation. Destructive individualism has given way to a renewed sense of community and a recognition of how important social interaction is to people's mental well-being. Support for the NHS has soared and will need to remain high as it faces the immense challenges that the post-pandemic context will bring, not least the need to reduce waiting times for elective treatments that have had to take a back seat during the pandemic. This all bodes well for those who believe that collective action on welfare provision is vital for a civilised society to be civilised, and who consider the state in a democratic society to be an effective way of delivering welfare on a large scale, whilst also recognising the value that voluntary and private

---

[6.] See E. Thornton, 'Keir Starmer: Best of British Values Are the Best of Christian Values', *Church Times*, 18 December 2020.

sector contributions make to the overall welfare mix. This sentiment is reflected in the report commissioned by the All Party Parliamentary Group for Faith and Society and published in November 2020: *Keeping the Faith: Partnership Between Faith Groups and Local Authorities*. The report makes out a case for further strengthening the relationships between Local Authorities and local faith groups in the provision of welfare in a post-pandemic context, and provides some evidence of this already happening.[7]

There is a growing awareness in some of Britain's political circles of the relevance of a Keynesian approach to handling the post-pandemic economic challenges necessary for bringing about a recovery; an approach that is long-term in its planning and execution. In this regard, in a keynote speech in February 2021, Tony Danker, the leader of the Confederation of British Industry, argued a need for government, business and trade unions to work together on a fightback plan: 'I believe we must, and we will, come together to forge a better decade. More 1945 than 2008.' Referring to the creation of the Welfare State and the birth of the NHS after the war as a moment when 'real shifts for the better' had taken place, Danker added:

> Let's be clear. The scale of the shocks we're facing today – Brexit, Covid, and the climate imperative – demand a similarly dramatic moment of unity and foresight. So, what will we take from this crisis? Where, in our darkest times, have we made real shifts for the better? Most notably, of course, in the aftermath of the Second World War, when post-war reconstruction gave birth to the NHS and creation of the welfare state.[8]

When planning for the post-pandemic future, politicians, economists, business leaders, trade unionists, academics and the clergy would do well to remember that.

---

7. C. Baker (lead author) *Keeping the Faith: Partnership Between Faith Groups and Local Authorities, November, 2020.* Available for downloading at: https://www.faithandsociety.org/wp-content/uploads/APPG_CovidReport_Full_V4.pdf (accessed on 31 December 2021).
8. See R.J. Partington, 'UK Should Respond to Economic Crisis with 1945-style Reboot, Says CBI Chief', *The Guardian*, 3 February 2021.

Appendix One

GS1804:
'The Big Society' and the
Church of England[1]

The Big Society – Background

1. 'The Big Society' emerged as a theme in Conservative Party thinking prior to the General Election. It implied a clear renunciation of the statement that 'there is no such thing as society' and was seen as part of the project to reposition the party as more compassionate and aware of human needs and desires. It was not universally welcomed within the party, nor, apparently, did campaigners find that it resonated amongst voters on the doorstep.

2. During the campaign, David Cameron explained that he believed that there is such a thing as society: but it is not the same as the State. The Big Society was seen as a foundation for policies which reduced the extent – and the cost – of direct state involvement in social and welfare activities.

[1.] In a preliminary discussion with Malcolm Brown prior to the recorded interview commencing, he pointed out that GS1804 was not an academic document. Its status was an official, advisory document intended to provide focus for the discussion to be held on the 'Big Society' project at the General Synod in November 2010. This Appendix provides the full document debated by General Synod.

3. The Conservative/Liberal Democrat coalition is now putting considerable energy into developing The Big Society in policy terms and there have been a number of major speeches, not least by the Prime Minister, which are starting to give content to the general theme.

4. In a speech on 19 July 2010, the Prime Minister set out three main strands of The Big Society agenda:

   • Social Action – the government will foster and support a new culture of voluntarism and philanthropy;
   • Public service reform – getting rid of the centralised bureaucracy and in its place giving professionals much more freedom, opening up public services to new providers like charities, social enterprises and private companies so we get more innovation, diversity and responsiveness to public need;
   • Community empowerment – creating communities with neighbourhoods who are in charge of their own destiny, who feel if they club together and get involved they can shape the world around them.[1]

5. Within modern Conservatism, the intellectual and conceptual energy behind The Big Society has come from thinkers such as Jesse Norman (now MP for Hereford) and the Director of the ResPublica think tank, Phillip Blond, himself a theologian of the Radical Orthodoxy school.[2] A number of ministers have been drawing on ideas like these since well before the General Election.

6. Although The Big Society clearly taps into a particular strand of Conservative thinking, it is not intrinsically alien to certain traditions within the Labour Party or Liberalism. Labour can trace an important part of its history in working-class self-help movements, co-operatives and local action. Ed Miliband has already spoken of his aspiration to build 'The Good Society'. He appears to be drawing on a similar tradition of the civic virtues whilst avoiding the overtly anti-state rhetoric of the Conservatives.[3]

7. Historically, the Liberal Party has also given a strong emphasis to localism. Potentially, the principles of The Big Society are capable of being 'owned' across a wide political spectrum, although their adoption as the policy of the coalition government may, in

practice, limit their cross-party appeal. If Blond's arguments are accepted, The Big Society may also have demonstrable roots in Christian theology.

The Big Society and the Economic Crisis

8. Whichever party or parties had won the election this year, the agenda would have been dominated by the economic crisis. The Coalition has set out to deliver dramatic cuts to public spending, not least in social welfare. The potential of voluntarism to replace some state welfare provision may make The Big Society financially attractive.

9. For a number of Coalition members, the intrinsic goods of The Big Society are fundamental, regardless of the state of the economy. Nevertheless, the economic crisis may constrain and confuse its implementation. A clear articulation of how The Big Society can be realized in a time of austerity has yet to emerge.

10. There is a widespread fear, especially within the voluntary sector and those working with the most vulnerable people, that The Big Society is an attempt to shift responsibility for welfare and social cohesion from the State to the voluntary and charitable sectors. Whilst there are many who contend that existing welfare provision has fostered too much dependency, it remains that simply withdrawing welfare does not tackle the dependency problem without other, potentially expensive, measures to address behavioural patterns and economic opportunities.

11. Some fear that, whatever the relationship between The Big Society agenda and budgetary austerity, the programme of cuts will prevent the voluntary sector from responding adequately whilst simultaneously creating greater social need and distress.

12. The Comprehensive Spending Review of October 2010 has been described by the Institute of Fiscal Studies as, overall, regressive in that poorer people will be hit more sharply by public spending cuts than richer groups (with the exception of the very richest). Communities, especially northern cities, whose post-industrial regeneration depended heavily on public spending, are likely suffer more than areas with more mixed economies. Overall, poverty, unemployment and social exclusion seem likely to increase rapidly. There are many doubts whether the hoped-for resurgence in private sector activity will be sufficient to offset the

impact of public expenditure cuts. The rather tentative concept of The Big Society faces an immense, and growing, challenge.

13. Yet, despite such caveats, many agree that the ideas behind The Big Society are necessary in a civilized society and that the erosion of community values and intermediate institutions has gone so far that basic social structures need rebuilding. Such structures are essential partners to the state in any political economy. Some blame the depredations of an inadequately regulated market economy for the breakdown of social bonds: others blame liberalism's disregard for authority and tradition. This is another sign that The Big Society themes may have the potential to attract those of different political persuasions.

The Government's Evolving Agenda

14. The Big Society currently appears to be a work in progress. The Prime Minister has staked a good deal of his personal capital on its success. The appointment of Lord Wei as a working peer with responsibilities for coordinating The Big Society agenda across government departments is another sign of the importance the government is placing on the matter.

15. Nevertheless, some contributions by ministers to the debate suggest that The Big Society is not understood in the same way by all. David Cameron has indicated that he regards the development of stronger social structures as compensating for a permanent and very large reduction in public spending. Lord Wei emphasises the release of local potential rather than making budget savings.

16. Some policies announced in the Comprehensive Spending Review, for example, the proposal to end lifetime tenure for council house tenants and the cuts in housing benefit which will push claimants out of some high-cost areas – are hard to square with the idea of building stable communities. In education, the new government's plans for academies leave little room for local communities to be involved in their governance.

17. Some of these diverse viewpoints may be compatible, but not all are obviously so. Although every government department is being asked to look at the implications of The Big Society for their work, not all are as securely 'on board' as others.

18. Concrete policies to deliver aspects of The Big Society are only slowly emerging and many will be dependent on the detailed outcomes of the Comprehensive Spending Review. Some are

small ventures in partnership with others (the Near Neighbours programme, outlined below, is in the vanguard here). Lord Wei is proposing a Big Society Bank which will be funded in part from dormant bank accounts, and which will help provide working capital for community ventures. Four 'pilot areas' identified in July 2010 are likely to be the first recipients of funding from the Big Society Bank.[4]

19. In March, the Prime Minister launched the Big Society Network as a 'campaign for social change'. The Network is conceived as independent of government (although the extent of its independence is disputed within the charitable sector) and aims to mobilise existing organisations to push forward the Big Society agenda. Its 'flagship' project is called 'Your Square Mile', designed to encourage people to engage with issues in their immediate geographical locality.

20. The substantive content of these initiatives is still emerging. Overall, the rhetoric shows real commitment to change the terms of the debate about society and government – but policy detail seems thin at present.

The Bishop of Leicester's Debate

21. On 16 June 2010, the Bishop of Leicester initiated a debate in the House of Lords focussing on The Big Society thinking. During the debate, Lord Wei made his maiden speech and Bs. Warsi summed up for the government. Her speech referred to a wide variety of social policy options, and gave the impression that The Big Society may be seen as a kind of 'brand' under which disparate policies could be brought together.[5] This confirms the impression that the government is trying to generate a 'narrative' about the nature of society in order to underpin specific policies which, themselves, may or may not conform to a single political or social model. This has been borne out by later conversations and encounters.

Bs. Warsi and Lord Wei at the College of Bishops

22. On 15 September 2010, both Bs. Warsi and Lord Wei addressed the College of Bishops on the subject of The Big Society.[6] Some early policy directions emerged, but it was also interesting to compare the rather different social models which informed the two presentations.

23. Bs. Warsi stressed the role of religion as a force for good in society. Her aim is to restore religious life to an honoured place in the life of the nation and the thinking of government. She was alert to the ways in which the Church of England understands itself to be embedded in English life.

24. Lord Wei looked more to a kind of post-modern social model in which local communities are empowered through the new opportunities offered by technology. He envisaged the internet as a democratising force in which myriad ideas competed for attention and in which the best ideas would always triumph. This is not a universally-held analysis of the impact of IT on political and democratic life.

25. Lord Wei's social model is strongly shaped by American thinking, including the work of Saul Alinsky which has influenced Barack Obama.[7] His understanding of religion in society also appears to reflect American, rather than European models. This is not to suggest that Britain cannot learn from America, only that religious life in the two contexts is manifested very differently and that social policy does not always translate directly if underlying social institutions differ radically.[8]

26. Neither speaker made any connection between the strength of social bonds and the workings of the wider economy. The impact of aggressive competitiveness in business and the workplace, the impact of growing material inequality, and the crushing effects of large-scale unemployment do not figure, as yet, in the public depiction of The Big Society.

Preliminary Assessments

27. If the impressions given by these encounters are correct, two things follow. First, there may be tensions ahead within the coalition (and within the Conservative Party) – first, between those who see The Big Society as an article of political faith and those for whom it is merely expedient in the current economic climate and, secondly, between those committed to localism but whose social models differ considerably.

28. Secondly, the churches are not being asked to sign up to, or approve, The Big Society as a single policy programme. However, there is potential for us to use the political narrative of The Big Society to shift the relationships between the state, the individual and intermediate institutions in ways which reflect a Christian

understanding of society and reinforce the Church's place in a healthy social order. Aspects of the Government's agenda, epitomised in Bs. Warsi's speeches, appear to be moving in this direction, but the overall trajectory is less clear.

29. Whilst some government ministers have expressed strong support for the Church of England's social role, one test of their seriousness about localism is whether they promote the flourishing of communities and bodies which may disagree with, or actively oppose, some aspects of central policy. For example, do mutual organisations like trade unions have a place in The Big Society? The jury is still out: but some such understanding of plurality is necessary if the Church is to be true to its prophetic calling as well as serving the common good.[9]

30. Many have observed that the rhetoric of devolving power to regions and local communities, deployed by governments of different political persuasions, has almost always foundered on an overwhelming trend towards greater centralisation. If The Big Society can turn around this trend, it will have succeeded indeed – but the historical odds are against it.

The Big Society – Shifting the Social Model

31. There are a number of practical opportunities, opened up by The Big Society agenda, which may involve or benefit the churches. At least as important, however, is the way that some aspects of Big Society thinking have the potential to shift perceptions of the relationship between the state, communities, and the individual.

32. To illustrate this, it is worth reflecting on some aspects of social legislation under the previous administration and, at times, evident in the policies of successive governments since 1979.

33. In a number of instances, social legislation was conceived in ways which:

   • failed to take into account the way in which understandings of society, and of difference, are often grounded in historic traditions (not least the Christian faith) and that there are more ways than one of conceiving plurality;
   • devalued the importance of conscience in favour of a single, governmental, interpretation of how social relationships should be understood;

- were grounded, not in actual people's lives so much as in an abstract conception of 'the individual', understood to exist outside tradition or community, and thus attempted to legislate against hypothetical problems rather than actual mischief.

34. In short, governments have often assumed an atomised society in which it is the state's job to mediate between competing individuals from a position of assumed neutrality. This view pays insufficient attention to the way in which persons are formed in communities, starting with the family and including schools, local settlements, churches and religious communities, and a plethora of voluntary associations. If communities and institutions are to help form moral individuals, they themselves need building up.

35. Moreover, the legacy of terrorist attacks by militant Islamist groups was too often met by an attitude which problematised all religion. Language was used in ways which suggested that all faiths were conceived as essentially the same kind of phenomenon; all were regarded as sub-rational, and the task of government was to contain, and mediate between, religious groups whose place in the public sphere was not generally conceded. Whilst this attitude was, to an extent, moderated by a more positive stance towards (e.g.) 'faith schools', the general thrust of policy and rhetoric was not 'religiously literate'.

36. A historic fear, dating back to the 16th- and 17th-century wars of religion, was stirred by 9/11 and 7/7 in ways which excited classic liberalism's self-image as the only defender of reason and civility against superstition. Critiques of classic liberalism, commonplace among political philosophers for over thirty years, had not yet entered the lexicon of government. This was exacerbated by a widespread inability (ideological or political) to separate aspects of militant Islam, which did indeed constitute a threat to liberal ideals, from Islam itself. Some of the rhetoric around the 'Prevent' programme illustrated this quite starkly.

Key questions

37. The question now arises: Does The Big Society represent a break with this entrenched politico-social model in ways which are closer to the church's social vision and in ways which might reflect religious bodies' own sense of their place in a vibrant and diverse society?

38. The evidence so far is mixed. On the one hand, we have supportive statements such as that by Eric Pickles who has said that, 'Religion is often seen as part of the problem. The new government sees it as part of the solution; the days of the state trying to suppress Christianity and other faiths are over.'[10] On the other, the mainstream view among LibDems (and perhaps among some Tories) continues to reflect the social model characterised above which is suspicious of religion in the public square.

39. A third position, present in all parties, values the churches – but only in social roles which may or may not reflect Christian theological priorities, and sees religion as a means to achieve political ends rather than an end in itself.

40. As noted below, staff of MPA [Mission and Public Affairs], with the backing of the Archbishops, have been in discussion with ministers about practical partnerships for building social cohesion. This is an opportunity to strengthen the aspects of The Big Society narrative which will enable the church's ministry and mission to flourish in the long term.

41. The Big Society agenda has not yet secured these advances, but there is much to play for and the Church of England should continue to press its case on many fronts.

The Big Society as a Theological Motif

42. The theologian Luke Bretherton suggests, 'It seems that what policymakers dream of when they dream of an active citizenry cannot be separated in practice from what religious groups do.'[11] There is a natural congruence between the impulses behind The Big Society and the way the churches understand themselves and their discipleship.

43. Phillip Blond identifies an established strand of Christian social thought within which his own work on Big Society themes is located. It runs backwards from John Milbank and Radical Orthodoxy, through V.A. Demant and the Christendom movement, to J.N. Figgis and others.[12] Like Figgis, Jesse Norman takes up the theme of the iniquities of a Hobbesian 'Leviathan state' and proposes instead a model of the state as the 'community of communities'.

44. Bretherton argues that there are three 'ideal types' which can be appealed to in the debate about citizenship. The first sees the citizen as **voter**. Here, citizenship is a matter of individuals

aggregating their preferences through the ballot box. The pursuit of shared goods in community barely features.

45. The second type sees the citizen as **volunteer**. This model lies behind many initiatives to strengthen social bonds whilst reducing the scale of state action – including much of the rhetoric around The Big Society. But, Bretherton argues, the focus on volunteering tends to separate the virtues of community from the world of paid work and ignores the contradictory imperatives of the market economy which demands flexible, footloose, workers, uncommitted to anything but economic gain.

46. Finally, Bretherton makes the case for the citizen as **vow-keeper** – focussing on the priority of relationships and faithful commitment to others. He shows how this understanding is not only grounded in Christian theology but is reflected in many grass roots movements, especially those which have 'a symbiotic relationship with popular religion'.[13]

47. Bretherton's conclusion is that 'people of faith need to avoid co-option into being either voting blocks or service providers and be true to their own best insights by upholding a vision of the citizen as vow-keeper'. This is in line with the judgement that there is much potential in The Big Society for the Church to work with, but that a residual element of scepticism remains in order. As the Archbishop of Canterbury put it, 'Two and a half cheers for the Big Society'.[14]

48. The strength of The Big Society idea for the church lies in the extent to which it reflects a Christian understanding of being human. A Christian anthropology locates each person within a rich network of relationships and recognises the perpetual tension between our dependency on others and our autonomy. This reflects the nature of God's relationship with human beings who remain dependent upon His grace for all good things whilst retaining the freedom to reject His love. As in so many of Jesus' parables, God makes Himself known to us in the person of the other – and it is when we ourselves recognise our dependence on others that we understand a little of God's love for us.

49. This kind of recognition needs strong social bonds which help ensure that those around us become neighbours and not merely others. It stresses the importance of doing things which serve the good of all rather than relating to structures, institutions and services merely as an autonomous consumer interested

only in personal benefit. Neighbourliness is the first condition for treating others (and being treated ourselves) as ends and not means.

50. The Church is, in many ways, a paradigm community, holding fast to the virtues of neighbourliness and fellowship because these reflect the relational nature of God as Trinity and the Kingdom in which all relationships are modelled on God's unconditional love. But the empirical church in the world will often struggle to embody the virtues of community if the surrounding culture belittles and marginalises such virtues. The Church not only models community to the world but needs there to be strong communal bonds in the wider society so that Christians have the chance to extend discipleship into the whole of their lives.

51. A Christian vision of the good society aims to generate the kind of strong social bonds that also appear among the objectives of The Big Society project. It will be important for us to stress that, for Christians, such bonds are the prerequisite of any viable human society and are not to be valued merely for economic, expedient or utilitarian reasons.

Practical Partnerships between Church and State within The Big Society

52. Prior to the General Election, staff from MPA spent time getting to know key Shadow Cabinet members and prominent thinkers in the Conservative and LibDem parties. CUF [the Church Urban Fund] also built up numerous political contacts and relationships, and is well-established within the wider voluntary sector.

53. These discussions considered the potential for creative church/state partnerships, not only for delivering social welfare programmes but as a way of enabling a richer and more cohesive society to develop. Central to any such project was the move from treating all religion as essentially problematic and illegitimate within the public sphere, to a view of religion as an important motivation for good citizens and strong social bonds.

54. In particular, we stressed the ways in which the popular image of 'faith communities' fails to reflect the realities of the Church of England. We emphasised the Church of England's foundational

commitment to the common good of all the people, expressed through our presence in every parish of the land and manifested in the way we use our buildings, our schools and our ministry to serve the people as a whole. We highlighted the work of the Presence and Engagement [P&E] programme as an example of extensive commitment to the work of neighbourliness and the Church's prominent role in inter-religious dialogue.

55. Following the election, the desire to work in partnership with the Church of England has been taken up strongly by the Secretary of State for Communities and Local Government (Eric Pickles) along with his Minister for Decentralisation, Greg Clark and Under Secretary, Andrew Stunnell (LibDem) and with enthusiastic support from Bs. Warsi.

56. Our response to The Big Society policies has been to try to embody what the Bishop of London, in his speech during the debate on 15 June, called the Church's 'Big Offer'. Because we believe the Church of England to hold great potential for building cohesive communities, especially in areas of social stress, we sought ways to give concrete expression to that conviction, working with the grain of the coalition's thinking but staying firmly within the Church's understanding of its vocational, existing structures and partnerships. On these grounds, we proposed a substantial development of many aspects of existing work.

57. This proposal appears to be one of the first-fruits of the government's Big Society initiative. We know of no other current partnership proposals of comparable size and scope. In this, the Church of England is in the vanguard. However, the proposal does not exhaust the potential of The Big Society in relation to the Church of England by any means.

Near Neighbours – Faithful Interaction

58. The proposition under discussion is for DCLG to fund a significant expansion of the Church's existing set of activities based on the Presence and Engagement and related programmes, learning from, and extending, the kind of work that P&E has piloted in the past five years to encourage new initiatives. The provisional title for the project is Near Neighbours – Faithful Interaction. An outline description, reflecting the current state of discussions, is attached as an Annexe to this report.

59. The intention is to direct funding into four main areas – eastern London, the 'M62 corridor' urban areas, Leicester and east Birmingham and to work through a range of existing Christian, or Christian and other faith, partnerships. These areas correspond to the focal work of the Presence and Engagement programme.

60. As significant sums of public money would be involved, a proper system of accountable and focussed management is required. The proposals envisage that the funding will be received by the Church Urban Fund to make clear its separation from any internal Church of England finances and to provide the confidence that CUF's track record brings. A subsidiary charitable company of CUF with trustees appointed by CUF and the Archbishops' Council, will be responsible for implementation.

61. The premise of the project, shared on both sides of the table, is that (as Eric Pickles has intimated) it is mistaken to see religion as a prime source of community divisions and a problem for government to solve: on the contrary, faith communities and religious groups have potential to promote community cohesion at the level of personal human relationships. In particular, the Church of England, present in every community and committed to the good of all, is uniquely placed to promote positive relationships, particularly but not only among those of different religions, and to lead on shared ventures in pursuit of the common good.

62. The aim of Near Neighbours, in colloquial terms, is to 'enable "Mr and Mrs Smith, Mr and Mrs Patel and Mr and Mrs Hussain", living in the same local neighbourhood, to relate more positively to each other and to release energies for the benefit of the wider local community'. It is predicated on the idea that good relationships between people of different faiths cannot be brokered from a position of assumed neutrality – one must be 'religiously literate' and this literacy stems from commitment.

63. Near Neighbours is a chance for the church to do more of what it alone can do. It is not about the church stepping into the welfare gaps left by a retreating state.

64. A brief statement about the Near Neighbours proposals, agreed with the Department of Communities and Local Government and including a quotation from the Secretary of State, was placed on the Church of England (MPA) and CUF websites at the beginning of August.[15]

65. The proposals went forward as part of DCLG's bid to the Treasury in the government's Comprehensive Spending Review. The Spending Review reported on 20 October 2010 and DCLG is now examining the implications for its budget and programmes. We expect to hear during November whether Near Neighbours can go ahead. This report had to be prepared for Synod before the outcome was known.

Further Potential in The Big Society

66. If Near Neighbours proves to be successful in its delivery and impact, there may be further opportunities for similar church/government partnerships under The Big Society agenda. Some of these may involve the church in direct service delivery; others may be opportunities to strengthen community bonds in different ways. Bretherton's distinction between 'the citizen as volunteer' and 'the citizen as vow-keeper' may be worth holding in mind as an indicator of how far a partnership proposal mirrors the Church's sense of its proper calling.

Schools and Education

67. The unique commitment of the Church of England to education through church schools is an obvious example of how The Big Society may enable our work to develop for the common good. Recent years have seen public ambivalence towards 'faith schools'. On the one hand, parents seem to want their children to experience the kind of ethically committed education which our schools embody. On the other, the suspicion of religion in the public square, already mentioned, has been manifest in the misrepresentation of church schools as divisive and sectarian in nature.

68. The Big Society offers a good opportunity to emphasise that Church of England schools are part of our commitment to serve the Common Good and not a smokescreen for sectarianism. The Big Society suggests that the government recognises that a flourishing society needs moral citizens formed in local communities and institutions, and needs its children to be educated in communities which embody virtues specific to particular traditions and not constrained by ideological relativism. Church schools, then, are clearly part of the solution and not the problem.

Church Buildings

69. Similarly, the potential of our buildings to be community hubs and accessible to many, could be enhanced if there was less government suspicion about using public money to build shared resources through faith communities. The many examples of church buildings taking on important social functions, including rural post office facilities and community meeting places, show the way forward. There is much unlocked potential in church buildings (including, but not confined to, places of worship) which could be released with relatively small expenditure on upgraded facilities etc. once the reluctance to see religious groups as anything but exclusive sectarian associations has been overcome.

Widening the Big Society Debate

70. The government's outreach to churches is not restricted to the Church of England. Overtures by the Conservative Party to the independent evangelical and Pentecostal sectors (including the black-led churches), and to non-denominational Christian social action projects, have been very effective and many such groups are enthusiastic about The Big Society. This is further evidence of the trend towards new alliances among Christians, based on 'horizontal' distinctions around issues and beliefs rather than the established 'vertical' divisions between denominations. It may also indicate a more American-style understanding of religion in society and scepticism about the potential of established churches.

71. Many government departments and related bodies are exploring what The Big Society may mean for them. For example, MPA recently responded to a consultation set up at short notice by the Commission for Rural Communities on The Big Society and rural areas. Our submission emphasised the major, often unique, contribution of the Church of England to rural life. Further such consultations may be expected.

72. We should expect approaches to the Church on Big Society themes to come from many directions and at different levels – national, regional and local. Work may be needed to help parishes and dioceses to access the right levels of support and good practice to enable them to respond effectively and creatively to overtures which seek to involve the Church in building strong communities and institutions.

The Church's Prophetic Voice

73. There is always a tension between Christian engagement with others in work for the common good and the Christian calling to hold up the mirror of God's demands to the powerful in critical solidarity. At a time when the government's austerity measures are sure to have an impact on the most hard-pressed communities and on vulnerable people, it is vital that the Church should not be co-opted into such close partnerships with government that its ability to speak truth to power is compromised.

74. Against that legitimate fear, it can be argued that some of the Church's most effective critiques of government policies down the years have stemmed from congregations and clergy who have taken action – often in partnership with others, including government agencies – to address social ills and pursue the common good. Their critique of policies has been grounded in practical experience and they have earned a right to be heard. The 'prophetic voice' need not always be that of the strident outsider.

75. Nonetheless, the line between working together and being co-opted is a fine one requiring constant vigilance. In the case of The Big Society, it will be important to ask, of any proposal: How far does this enable the Church to be authentically itself, witnessing to Christ and pursuing the good of all?

Some Conclusions

76. The Big Society is, in principle, natural territory for the Church of England. In parishes all over the country, the Church is already creating and sustaining a 'Big Society'. What we now see is a government moving to build social policy around such local commitments. However, it is not yet clear exactly how the government will embody the theme across its policies.

77. In Near Neighbours, we have made an 'earnest of intent' to work with the government in the pursuit of social cohesion. It will be up to us to ensure that the reasons for our participation, the terms of our involvement and the sticking points beyond which cooperation is impossible, are clear and help to inform any future relationships under the banner of The Big Society.

78. In other areas of church life, including the developing use and maintenance of our buildings and our unique investment in education through church schools, The Big Society offers real potential for 'shifting the dominant narrative' of people,

community and society in ways which will enable the Church to live out its vocation more openly and constructively. There will also be many opportunities at local level for the Church to engage with statutory and other bodies to develop new programmes and initiatives which enhance the common good and sustain local communities. The Church needs to be prepared, at diocesan and parish level, as well as nationally, to respond constructively but wisely to a new phase in the relationship between government, Church and community.

79. The Big Society may come to represent a radical and ambitious shift in the way society and government are conceived: one in which the Church has more room to be itself. Whether this shift away from individualism is achievable, given the power of wider economic and cultural factors, is another question, but this does not invalidate the aspiration. Politicians who are pursuing The Big Society are playing for high stakes. The Church has an interest in seeing the best elements of The Big Society thinking succeed.

Revd Dr Malcolm Brown
Director, Mission and Public Affairs
September 2010

Notes

1. From the Conservative Party webpage, accessed 5 August 2010, http:// www.conservatives.com/News/News_stories/2010/07/Our_Big_Society _Agend a.aspx.
2. Norman's thinking can be found in his book, *Compassionate Conservatism* which can be downloaded from his website (Accessed 5 August 2010), http://www.jessenorman.com/downloads/Compassionate _Conservatism.pdf. Blond is best known for his book, *Red Tory*. ResPublica's contribution to the debate may be found here: http://www .respublica.org.uk/blog/2010/07/what-does-big-society-value.
3. See: http://www.guardian.co.uk/politics/2010/sep/28/ed-miliband speech-maurice-glasman. See also the chapter by John Cruddas and Jonathan Rutherford in, Rowan Williams and Larry Elliott, *Crisis and Recovery*, Palgrave Macmillan, 2010.
4. The four pilot areas are: Liverpool, the Eden Valley (Cumbria), Sutton, and Windsor and Maidenhead.
5. The full text of the debate, including speeches from the Archbishop of Canterbury, the Bishop of London and the Bishops of Leicester, Chester and Salisbury, can be found at: http://www.publications.parliament.uk /pa/ld201011/ldhansrd/text/1006160004.htm#10061677000453.

6. The text of Bs. Warsi's speech can be found here: http://www
    .conservatives.com/News/News_stories/2010/09/Warsi_speaks_about
    _the_importance_of_faith.a spx.
7. See: Saul Alinsky, *Rules for Radicals*, Random House, 1971.
8. See: Grace Davie, *Europe: The Exceptional Case*, London: DLT, 2002.
9. Some in the Conservative Party may be mindful of the period in the
    1980s when the Church of England was sometimes perceived as the
    most effective critic of the then Conservative government's social
    policies. (See: Henry Clark, *The Church Under Thatcher*, London: SPCK,
    1993). It is possible that the present government, also committed to large
    reductions in public spending and welfare provision, is keen to get the
    church on board before the social consequences become intolerable.
    This analysis may have some validity, but our engagement with
    ministers to date suggests that their view of the Church is more a matter
    of political commitment than an expedient alliance. We shall see.
10. Letter from the Rt Hon. Eric Pickles in *The New Statesman*, 2
    August 2010.
11. Luke Bretherton, 'Votes, Vows and Volunteers' in *The Tablet*, 10
    July 2010.
12. See: J.N. Figgis, *Churches in the Modern State*, London: Longmans,
    Green, 1914.
13. Bretherton means the awkward but alliterative term 'vow-keeper' to
    emphasise how commitment to others and to strong social bonds means
    doing things which are time-consuming and not necessarily personally
    gainful (such as attending lengthy committee meetings, or even
    corporate worship) because they are beneficial to the common good
    rather than delivering one's own wants.
14. The Archbishop of Canterbury, speaking at an event at the Oasis Centre
    in London on 23 July 2010.
15. http://www.cofe.anglican.org/info/socialpublic/neighbourlyproposals/.

Appendix Two

Questions put to Revd Dr Malcolm Brown in a semi-structured interview held on 22 May 2018 at Church House, Westminster, London

Question 1

Would you like to set out some of the background to your advice to the Church of England on its handling of the Big Society project?

Question 2

Do you think the Resolution 19 passed at the 1948 Lambeth Conference that stated: 'We believe that the State is under the moral law of God and is intended by Him to be an instrument for human welfare,' is evidence that it had embraced William Temple's theology of the state, as set out in his work of 1941, *Citizen and Churchman*?

Question 3

Has it since been replaced by a better theology of the state?

Question 4

Do you think William Temple's thinking on the state embraced a full enough understanding of the need for a strong intermediate level in society?

Question 5

Do you, then, draw a clear distinction between the Beveridge/Temple perspective on the Welfare State and the Attlee delivery model?

Question 6

Do you think there was a paradigm shift in the Church's response to the 'Big Society' project 2010, to that of its position in *Not just for The Poor*, in that the latter emphasised a need for *cooperation* between the state, voluntary and private providers of welfare, whereas the former emphasised a need for greater *competition* between them via the Localism Act of 2011?

Question 7

So MacIntyre and Plant were key influences on your theoretical development?

Question 8

Where did you go from there?

Question 9

Where, if at all, does Radical Orthodoxy fit into this development in your thinking?

Question 10

So you think you have to have something of the Temple/Niebuhr realism but also something of the romantic challenge to it?

Question 11

Has Phillip Blond's thinking been an influence on you?

Question 12

Have you been influenced by the Figgis, Demant, Christendom strand of Anglican social thinking?

Question 13

So, let me be clear here. Are you arguing that the Temple, Preston, Atherton tradition can work together with the Figgis, Demant, Milbank / Radical Orthodoxy tradition as correctives to one another?

Question 14

So, to clarify, in 2010 were you, in your paper GS1804, where you advised the Church of England on the handling of the 'Big Society' project, trying to incorporate both of those traditions — trying to get the best of both?

Question 15

So, to clarify, is your view that GS1804 reflected an Anglican inclination to want to try to get different people from different traditions working together?

Question 16

But how can you seek to accommodate these stands of thinking in a way that is theologically coherent if they are so antithetical in so many ways?

Question 17

So, to be clear, is it the case that when you were seeking to advise the Church of England on the Big Society project, you were taking the Temple, Preston, Atherton legacy, though not uncritically, and consciously taking the Figgis, Demant, Christendom, Milbank, Blond, critique of that, and finding some positives there too, that could provide a theoretical entry point into that project?

Question 18

Do you consider the Church of England to have changed since the 1980s in a way that the Christendom perspective has become more prominent?

Question 19

So, did you see the Near Neighbours project as something coming out of Beveridge's thinking?

Question 20

Was there a five million pounds grant given?

Question 21

Did you have qualms about taking that money from government in the context of a Big Society project which you acknowledged in GS1804 was at a time when a Coalition Government had "set out to deliver dramatic cuts to public spending, not least in social welfare?"

Question 22

When did you start to think it was all presentation and no substance?

Question 23

In GS1804 you stated that if the Near Neighbours initiative proved to be successful, there may be: 'further opportunities for similar church/ government partnership under The Big Society agenda. Some of these may involve the church in direct service delivery'. What had you in mind for the Church of England vis-à-vis direct service delivery when you wrote this?

Question 24

So, let me be clear: when you wrote GS1804, did you have a plan of action for delivering on more direct service delivery or was it just an aspiration?

Question 25

And the document 'The Enemy Isolation' as well?

Question 26

So you consider the Red Tory/Blue Labour thing was a crossover and synergistic to what you were trying to do?

Question 27

In your article 'Civil Society, Welfare and the State', you refer critically to Phillip Blond's *ResPublica* think tank, which proposes that the Church of England should take over large tranches of what has hitherto been state welfare provision as 'an example of how communitarians risk retreating into nostalgic utopianism when direct experience of the institutions they discuss is deficient.' Can I ask you to develop your thinking on this specific point?

Question 28

You are aware, no doubt, that John Milbank gave that report an out-an-out endorsement?

Question 29

Coming back to the Big Society project, in retrospect, what, if any, lessons do you think that the Church of England can take from it?

Question 30

Do you think that the Church of England's overall positive response to the 'Big Society' project in 2010/11 and, specifically, your advice in GS1804, was a change in the Church of England's theological perspective on the state to the one it had adopted in 1948?

Question 31

Do you think there is a need to review the current dominant model?

Question 32

Are there any other points you want to make about what we have been discussing?

Bibliography

Works by John Milbank

Books

Beyond Secular Order (Chichester: Wiley-Blackwell, 2013)
The Future of Love: Essays in Political Theology (London: SCM Press, 2009)
Theology and Social Theory: Beyond Secular Reason (1990), 2nd edn (Oxford: Blackwell, 2006)
The Word Made Strange: Theology, Language, Culture (Oxford: Blackwell, 1997)

Scholarly Articles and Talks

'Against Human Rights', available at: http://theologyphilosophycentre .co.uk/papers/Milbank_AgainstHumanRights.pdf (accessed on 14 December 2021)
'Associationism, Pluralism and Post-liberalism: The Theo-political Legacy of David Nicholls and Current British politics', a lecture delivered in 2014 in Oxford to the David Nicholls' Memorial Trust, available as a podcast at: http://www.dnmt.org.uk/ (accessed on 15 August 2015)
'The Blue Labour Dream', in I. Geary and A. Pabst (eds), *Blue Labour: Forging a New Politics* (London: I.B. Tauris, 2015), pp. 27–49
'Blue Labour, One-Nation Labour and Postliberalism: A Christian Socialist Reading', available as a PDF download at: http://theologyphilosophycentre .co.uk/papers/Milbank_BlueLabourOneNationLabourAndPostliberalism .pdf (accessed on 21 December 2021)
'Enclaves, or Where Is the Church?', June 1992, Wiley Online Library
'Liberality versus Liberalism', available at: http://www.theologyphilosophy centre.co.uk/papers/Milbank_Liberality.pdf (accessed on 18 April 2015)
'The Peculiarity of the Secular', *Public Spirit*, available at: http://www .publicspirit.org.uk/religion-and-secularity-in-britain-today/ (accessed on 9 September 2017)
'Postmodern Critical Augustinianism: 42 Answers to Unasked Questions', *Modern Theology* 7, no. 3 (April 1991), Wiley Online Library

'The Real Third Way', in A. Pabst (ed.), *The Crisis of Global Capitalism: Pope Benedict XVI's Social Encyclical and the Future of Political Economy* (Eugene, OR: Wipf & Stock, 2011), pp. 27–70

'Socialism of the Gift, Socialism by Grace', 2007, Wiley Online Library

Journalistic Articles

'Anglican Church Spectacularly Blind to Protest Symbolism', ABC Religion & Ethics, 2 November 2011, available at: http://www.abc.net.au/religion /articles/2011/11/02/3354567.htm (accessed on 19 May 2015)

'The Big Society Depends on the Big Parish', ABC Religion & Ethics, 30 November 2010, available at: http://www.abc.net.au/religion /articles/2010/11/30/3080680.htm (accessed on 3 March 2015)

'Breaking the Faustian Pact: The End of Thatcherism and the Promise of Blue Labour', ABC Religion & Ethics, 30 April 2015, available at: http:// www.abc.net.au/religion/articles/2015/04/30/4226515.htm (accessed on 23 March 2016)

'Can the Market Be Moral? Peace and Prosperity Depends on a Regimented Socialism', ABC Religion & Ethics, 24 October 2014, available at: http:// www.abc.net.au/religion/articles/2014/10/24/4114040.htm (accessed on 23 October 2016)

'Christian Vision of Society Puts Economics and Politics in Their Place', ABC Religion & Ethics, 8 December 2011, available at: https://www.abc. net.au/religion/christian-vision-of-society-puts-economics-and-politics-in -their/10100960 (accessed on 14 February 2021)

'The Church Is the Site of the True Society', *Church Times*, 14 December 2011

'Dignity, not Rights: Against Liberal Autonomy', ABC Religion & Ethics, 8 January 2016, available at: http://www.abc.net.au/religion /articles/2016/01/08/4385494.htm (accessed on 20 October 2016)

'How Democracy Devolves into Tyranny', *ABC* Religion & Ethics, 18 November 2011, available at: https://www.abc.net.au/religion /how-democracy-devolves-into-tyranny/10101002 (accessed on 21 December 2021)

'How Liberalism Is Undoing Itself', *The World Post*, updated 6 December 2017, available at: http://www.huffingtonpost.com/john -milbank/liberalism-undoing-itself_b_7104638.html (accessed on 14 April 2016 and 18 February 2020)

'How Politics Lost Its Soul: Liberalism and Its Discontents', ABC Religion & Ethics, 10 February 2015, available at: http://www.abc.net.au/religion /articles/2015/02/10/4177458.htm (accessed on 20 October 2016)

'Labour Is Right to Be Cautious about Knocking Workfare Plans', *The Guardian*, 11 November 2010, available at: https://www.theguardian.com /commentisfree/belief/2010/nov/11/workfare-labour-cautious-christian -attitude-poor (accessed on 19 January 2017)

'The Left and the Politics of Atheism', ABC Religion & Ethics, 28
    September 2010, available at: https://www.abc.net.au/religion/the-left-and
    -the-politics-of-atheism/10102072 (accessed on 21 December 2021)
'The Politics of Paradox', *Telosscope*, 13 March 2009, available at: http://www
    .telospress.com/the-politics-of-paradox/ (accessed on 21 December 2021)
'The Poor Are Us: Poverty and Mutual Fairness', ABC Religion & Ethics,
    22 November 2010, available at: http://www.abc.net.au/religion
    /articles/2010/11/22/3073193.htm (accessed on 15 December 2016)
'The Problem of Populism and the Promise of a Christian Politics',
    ABC Religion & Ethics, 16 February 2017, available at: http://www
    .abc.net.au/religion/articles/2017/02/16/4621192.htm (accessed on 11
    September 2017)
'Thatcher's Perverse Victory and the Prospect of an Ethical Economy', ABC
    Religion & Ethics, 15 April 2013, available at: http://www.abc.net.au
    /religion/articles/2013/04/15/3737062.htm (accessed on 3 March 2016)
Untitled: reply by J. Milbank to an analysis of his work by C. Baker, J.
    Atherton and J. Reader, 'A Case of Ecclesial Over-Optimism? A Response
    to Milbank's Return to Christendom's Social Vision', *Political Theology
    Network*, 23 February 2012, p. 5, available at: http://www.politicaltheology
    .com/blog/a-case-of-ecclesial-over-optimism-a-response-to-milbanks
    -return-to-christendoms-social-vision/ (accessed on 12 August 2015)
'What a Christian View of Society Says about Poverty', The Contextual
    Theology Centre and The Children's Society, December 2011, available at:
    http://www.theology-centre.org.uk/wp-content/uploads/2013/04/windsor
    -consultation-milbank.pdf (accessed 21 December 2021)

Joint Publications
_____ and P. Blond, 'No Equality of Opportunity', *The Guardian*, 27
    January 2010
_____ and A. Pabst, 'The meta-crisis of liberalism: "The downward spiral"',
    The European, 13 April 2015. Available at: https://www.theeuropean.de
    /en/john-milbank/10019-the-meta-crisis-of-liberalism (accessed on 30
    December 2021)
_____ and A. Pabst, 'The Anglican Polity and the Politics of the Common
    Good', *Together for the Common Good*, 2014, available at: https://
    togetherforthecommongood.co.uk/leading-thinkers/the-anglican-polity
    -and-the-politics-of-the-common-good (accessed on 13 December 2021)
_____ and A. Pabst, *The Politics of Virtue: Post-liberalism and the Human
    Future* (London: Rowman & Littlefield International, 2016)
_____ and A. Pabst, 'Post-liberal Politics and the Alternative of Mutualising
    Social Security', in N. Spencer (ed.), *The Future of Welfare: A Theos
    Collection* (London: Theos, 2014), pp. 90–100, available at: https://kar.kent
    .ac.uk/38380/1/The%20future%20of%20welfare%20-%20a%20theos%20
    collection.pdf (accessed on 19 April 2017)

_____, C. Pickstock and G. Ward (eds), *Radical Orthodoxy* (London: Routledge, 1999)

Other Works

Abbas, M., and R. Lachman, *The Big Society: The Big Divide?* (Bradford: JUST, 2012)

Abu-Lughod, J., *Before European Hegemony: The World System A.D. 1250–1350* (New York: Oxford University Press, 1989)

A Group of Churchmen, *The Return of Christendom* (New York: The Macmillan Company, 1922)

Alcock, P. *Partnership and Mainstreaming: Voluntary Action under New Labour*, Third Sector Research Centre, 2010, Working Paper 32. University of Birmingham. Available as a PDF download at http://epapers.bham.ac.uk/793/ (accessed on 1 January 2022)

Alcock, P., 'Voluntary Action, New Labour and the "Third Sector"', in M. Hilton and J. McKay (eds), *The Ages of Voluntarism: How We Got to the Big Society* (Oxford: Oxford University Press, 2011)

Aldred, J., S. Hebden and K. Hebden, *Who Is My Neighbour? A Church Response to Social Disorder Linked to Gangs, Drugs, Guns and Knives* (London: Churches Together in England, 2008), available at: https://www.cte.org.uk/Groups/236211/Home/Resources/Pentecostal_and _Multicultural/Reports_Papers_Videos/Who_is_my/Who_is_my.aspx (accessed on 2 July 2019)

Alexander, R.J., *International Trotskyism, 1929–1985: A Documented Analysis of the Movement* (Durham, NC: Duke University Press, 1991)

Anderson, D., *Come Back Miss Nightingale: Trends in Professions Today* (London: Social Affairs Unit, 1998)

Anderson, D., J. Lait and D. Marsland, *Breaking the Spell of the Welfare State* (London: Social Affairs Unit, 1981)

Alim, M.S., 'How Advanced Was Europe in 1760 After All?', *Review of Radical Political Economy* 32, no. 4 (September 2000), pp. 621–25

Aquinas, T., *Aquinas Ethicus: or, the Moral Teaching of St Thomas: A Translation of the Principal Portions of the Second Part of the Summa Theologica*, with notes by Joseph Rickaby SJ (London: Burns & Oates, 1892), Vol. 2, available at: http://oll.libertyfund.org/pages/aquinas-on-usury (accessed on 4 November 2016)

Aristotle, *Prior Analytics Book 1* (c. 350 BCE), Clarendon Aristotle Series (Oxford: Oxford University Press, 2009)

Atherton, J., C. Baker and J. Reader, *Christianity and the New Social Order: A Manifesto for a Fairer Future* (London: SPCK, 2011)

Attlee, C.R., *The Labour Party in Perspective* (London: Left Book Club, 1937)

Aves, G.M., *The Voluntary Worker in the Social Services*, Report of a committee jointly set up by the National Council of Social Service and the

National Institute for Social Work Training, under the chairmanship of Geraldine M. Aves (London: Allen & Unwin, 1969)

Baker, C., 'A Case of Ecclesial Over-Optimism? A Response to Milbank's Return to Christendom's Social Vision', *Political Theology Network*, 23 February 2012 (article later attributed to C. Baker, J. Atherton and J. Reader), available at: http://www.politicaltheology.com/blog/a-case-of-ecclesial-over-optimism-a-response-to-milbanks-return-to-christendoms-social-vision/ (accessed on 20 August 2016), pp. 1–3

Baker, C. 'Lead Author' *Keeping the Faith: Partnership Between Faith Groups and Local Authorities, 2020.* Available for downloading at: https://www.faithandsociety.org/wp-content/uploads/APPG_CovidReport_Full_V4.pdf (accessed on 31 December 2021)

Baker, C.R., and E. Graham, *Theology for Changing Times: John Atherton and the Future of Public Theology* (London: SCM Press, 2018)

Becker, S., S. Pfaff and J. Rubin, 'Causes and Consequences of the Protestant Reformation', available at: https://pdfs.semanticscholar.org/d680/a29a28682b933d75e35d5aec902c843ab770.pdf (accessed on 18 January 2017)

Beech, M., and R. Page, 'Blue and Purple Labour Challenges to the Welfare State: How Should "Statist" Social Democrats Respond?', *Social Policy & Society* 14, no. 3 (2015), pp. 341–56

Beer, M., *A History of British Socialism* (Nottingham: Spokesman Books, 1984)

Belloc, H., *The Servile State* (1912) (London: Constable & Co., 1950)

Benedict XVI, *Caritas in Veritate: Encyclical Letter on Integral Human Development in Charity and Truth* (London: Catholic Truth Society, 2009)

Bentham, J., *Defence of Usury; Shewing the Impolity of the Present Legal Restraints on the Terms of Pecuniary Bargains in a Series of Letters to Adam Smith* (1787), available at: http://socserv2.mcmaster.ca./~econ/ugcm/3ll3/bentham/usury (accessed on 2 November 2016)

Bentley, M., 'History, Truth and Changing Perspectives', The Social Affairs Unit, 2 August 2006, available at: http://www.socialaffairsunit.org.uk/blog/archives/001046.php (accessed on 18 July 2018)

Berlau, A.J., *The German Social Democratic Party, 1914–1921* (New York: Columbia University Press, 1949)

Beveridge, W.H., *Papers by W.H. Beveridge to Inter-Departmental Committee on Social Insurance and Allied Services* (1942), cited in D. Fraser, *The Evolution of the British Welfare State* (London: Palgrave Macmillan, 2009), pp. 358–61

Beveridge, W.H., *The Pillars of Security* (London: George Allen & Unwin, 1942)

Beveridge, W.H., *Social Insurance and Allied Services* (London: HMSO, 1942)

Beveridge, W.H., *Voluntary Action: A Report on Methods of Social Advance* (London: George Allen & Unwin, 1948)

Beveridge, W.H., and J. Beveridge, *On and Off the Platform* (Wellington, New Zealand: Hicks, Smith & Right, 1949)

Billis, D., *Organising Public and Voluntary Agencies* (London: Routledge, 1993)

Billis, D., and M. Harris, *The Challenge of Change in Local Voluntary Agencies*, Working Paper 11 (London: Centre for Voluntary Organisations, London School of Economics, 1992)

Bingham, J., 'Church of England's Pre-election Blast Revives Memories of *Faith in the City*', *Daily Telegraph*, 3 October 2019

Blair, T., interview with the BBC, 8 April 2013, available at: http://www.bbc.co.uk/news/uk-politics-22073434 (accessed on 26 August 2016)

Blake, H., 'Dr Rowan Williams: Two and a Half Cheers for the Big Society', *Daily Telegraph*, 24 July 2010

Blaut, J. M., *The Colonizer's Model of the World* (New York: Guilford Press, 1993)

Blond, P., 'Allow Me to Suggest, George', *The Guardian*, 27 September 2008, available at: http://www.theguardian.com/commentisfree/2008/sep/27/conservatives.toryconference (accessed on 2 October 2010)

Blond, P., 'The Austerity Drive Must Not Derail the Winning "Big Society"', *The Guardian*, 3 October 2010, available at: http://www.theguardian.com/commentisfree/2010/oct/03/cuts-big-society-treasury-civic-state (accessed on 4 November 2017)

Blond, P., 'David Cameron Has Lost His Chance to Redefine the Tories', *The Guardian*, 3 October 2012

Blond, P., *Red Tory: How Left and Right Have Broken Britain and How We Can Fix It* (London: Faber & Faber, 2010)

Blond, P., and J. Noyes, *Holistic Mission: Social Action and the Church of England* (London: ResPublica, 2013)

Brenton, M., *The Voluntary Sector in British Social Services* (London: Longman, 1985)

Bretherton, L., 'Big Society and the Church', *The Guardian*, 7 October 2010

Bretherton, L., *Christ and the Common Life* (Grand Rapids, MI: William B. Eerdmans Pub. Co., 2019)

Bretherton, L., 'Vision, Virtue and Vocation: Notes on Blue Labour as a Practice of Politics', in I. Geary and A. Pabst (eds) *Blue Labour: Forging a New Politics* (London: I.B. Tauris, 2015), pp. 217–33

Briggs, A., 'The Welfare State in Historical Perspective', *Archives Européennes de Sociologie 2*, no. 2 (1961), pp. 221–59. Cited in R. Lowe, *The Welfare State in Britain Since 1945*, Third Edition (London: Palgrave Macmillan, 2005), p.17

Brown, A., and L. Woodhead, *That Was the Church That Was: How the Church of England Lost the English People* (London: Bloomsbury, 2016)

Brown, C.G., *The Death of Christian Britain: Understanding Secularisation 1800–2000* (London: Routledge, 2001)

Brown, G., *My Life: Our Times* (London: Bodley Head, 2017)

Brown, M., 'A State We Can Believe in? The Church of England, the Welfare State and the NHS', *Crucible: The Christian Journal of Social Ethics*, July-September 2012, pp. 21–27

Brown, M., *After the Market* (Bern, Switzerland: Verlag Peter Lang, 2004)

Brown, M., 'Anglican Social Theology: Today and Tomorrow', in S. Spencer (ed.), *Theology Reforming Society: Revisiting Anglican Social Theology* (London: SCM Press, 2017), pp. 125–43

Brown, M., 'Annex', *Near Neighbours: By Faithful Interaction Draft Proposals*, Church of England, 15 October 2010

Brown, M., *"The Big Society" and the Church of England*, General Synod Paper GS1804, Church of England, September 2010

Brown, M., 'Civil Society, Welfare and the State', *Modern Believing* 56, no. 1 (2015), pp. 11–21

Brown, M., *The Church and Economic Life: A Documentary Study, 1945 to the Present* (London: Epworth Press, 2006)

Brown, M., 'The Church of England and Welfare Today', in N. Spencer (ed.), *The Future of Welfare: A Theos Collection* (London: Theos, 2014), pp. 52–60

Brown, M., 'The Church of England and the Common Good', in N. Sagovsky and P. McGrail (eds), *Together for the Common Good: Towards a National Conversation* (London: SCM Press, 2015), pp. 120–36

Brown, M., 'John Atherton: Industry, the City and the Age of Incarnation', in C.R. Baker and E. Graham (eds), *Theology for Changing Times: John Atherton and the Future of Public Theology* (London: SCM Press, 2018), pp. 81–95

Brown, M., 'Red Tory and Blue Labour: More Theology Needed', *Political Theology* 13, no. 3 (2012), pp. 348–66

Brown, M., 'Society Needs Us to Be Anglican, not Sectarian, *Church Times*, 11 May 2018

Brown, M., *Thinking Afresh about Welfare: The Enemy Isolation*, Internal Policy Document, Church of England, 2016, available at: https://www.churchofengland.org/sites/default/files/2017-11/The%20Enemy%20Isolation.pdf (accessed on 16 December 2018)

Brown, M. (lead author), 'Who Is My Neighbour: A Letter from the House of Bishops to the People and Parishes of the Church of England for the General Election 2015 (London: Church of England, 2015)

Brown, M. (ed.), *Anglican Social Theology* (Croydon: Church House Publishing, 2014)

Brown, S., P. Nockles, and J. Pereiro (eds), *The Oxford Handbook of the Oxford Movement* (Oxford: Oxford University Press, 2017)

Bryant, C., *Possible Dreams* (London: Hodder & Stoughton, 1996)

Bull, P., 'The Kingdom of God and the Church Today', in A Group of Churchmen, *The Return of Christendom* (New York: The Macmillan Company, 1922), pp. 217–44

Burke, E. *Reflections on the Revolution in France*, 2nd edn (1790) (London: J. Dodsley, 1955)

Burns, J., 'The Great Strike', *New Review* 1, no. 5 (October 1889), pp. 40–82. Cited in L. McCluskey 'foreword', *The Great Dock Strike of 1889* (London: Unite the Union, 2015), p. 54. Available at: https://markwritecouk.files .wordpress.com/2018/07/the-great-dock-strike-of-1889-web-booklet11 -23272.pdf (accessed on 29 December 2021)

Butler, P., 'Food Bank Use Tops Million Mark over the Last Year', *The Guardian*, 22 April 2015

Butler, P., 'Local Charity Cuts Jeopardise David Cameron's "Big Society"', *The Guardian*, 23 July 2010

Butler, R.A., *The Art of the Possible* (London: Penguin, 1973)

Butler, R., and D. Wilson, *Managing Voluntary and Non-Profit Organisations: Strategy and Structures* (London: Routledge, 1990)

Butt, R., 'The Church of England Gets £5m for Community Cohesion Project', *The Guardian*, 20 February 2011

Cabinet Office, 'Community Organisers: Inspiring People to Build a Bigger, Stronger Society', Cabinet Office Analysis and Insight Team blog, 11 August 2015, available at: https://coanalysis.blog.gov.uk/2015/08/11 /community-organisers-inspiring-people-to-build-a-bigger-stronger -society/ (accessed on 17 November 2017)

Callaghan, J., 'Leader's Speech, Blackpool 1976', available at: http://www. britishpoliticalspeech.org/speech-archive.htm?speech=174 (accessed on 25 August 2016)

Cambridge University Hospitals, *History of Chaplaincy*, 2017, available at: https://www.cuh.nhs.uk/chaplaincy/history-chaplaincy (accessed on 25 August 2017)

Cameron, D., 'David Cameron's Speech in Full', BBC News, 6 October 2010, available at: http://www.bbc.co.uk/news/uk-politics-11485397 (accessed on 23 April 2018)

Cameron, D., 'Transcript of a Speech by the Prime Minister on the Big Society, 19 July 2010', available at: https://www.gov.uk/government /speeches/big-society-speech (accessed on 1 December 2016)

Campion, W.J.H., 'Christianity and Politics', in C. Gore (ed.), *Lux Mundi* (1889) (London: John Murray Press, 1890)

Chaplin, J., 'Evangelical Contributions to the Future of Anglican Social Theology', in M. Brown (ed.), *Anglican Social Theology* (Croydon: Church House Publishing, 2014), pp. 102–32

Chapman, M., *Anglican Theology* (London: T&T Clark, 2012)

Chapman, M., *Bishops, Saints and Politics* (London: T&T Clark, 2007)

Chapman, M., 'Pluralism, Welfare and the "Common Good": Three Varieties of Christian Socialism', *Political Theology* 1, no. 2 (2000), pp. 33–56

Chapman, M., 'Red Toryism, Common Good, and One Nation', in J. Kidwell and S. Doherty (eds), *Theology and Economics* (London: Palgrave Macmillan, 2015), pp. 65–82

Chapman, M., 'Red Toryism: Some Historical Reflections', *Political Theology* 13, no. 3 (2012), pp. 277–91

Chapman, M.D., S. Clarke and M. Percy (eds), *The Oxford Handbook of Anglican Studies* (Oxford: Oxford University Press, 2018)

Chase, M., *Chartism: A New History* (Manchester: Manchester University Press, 2007)

Churchill, W., 'Blood, Toil, Tears and Sweat', First speech to the House of Commons as Prime Minister, 13 May 1940, available at: http://www .winstonchurchill.org/resources/speeches/1940-the-finest-hour/blood-toil -tears-and-sweat (accessed on 25 August 2016)

Church of England, *Faith in the City: A Call for Action by Church and Nation: The Report of the Archbishop of Canterbury's Commission on Urban Priority Areas* (London: Church House Publishing, 1985)

Church of England, the Archbishops' Commission on Housing, Church and Community, *Coming Home: Tackling the Housing Crisis Together*, April 2019, available at: https://www.churchofengland.org/ABChousing (accessed on 10 June 2019)

Church of England, *Not Just for the Poor: Christian Perspectives on the Welfare State: Report of the Social Policy Committee of the Board of Social Responsibility* (London: Church House Publishing, 1986)

Church of England, *Report of Proceedings 2010: General Synod: November Group of Sessions*, Vol. 41, no. 3

Church of England, *Recent Survey/Mapping Exercises Undertaken across the English Regions to Measure the Contribution of Faith Groups to Social Action and Culture*, 2006, available at: http://www.ihbc.org.uk/recent _papers/docs/RegionalreportsTable.pdf (accessed on 25 October 2017)

Clark, J., 'Obedient Disobedience: Living the Anglican Catholic Tradition in Today's London', paper given at a conference on *London: The Exceptional Case? Honouring Kenneth Leech's London Ministry Today*, St Botolph's Aldgate, 23 February 2019

Clark, J., A. Cochrane and C. Smart, *Ideologies of Welfare: From Dreams to Disillusion* (London: Hutchinson, 1987)

Clarke, S., 'The Neoliberal Theory of Society', in A. Saad-Filho and D. Johnston (eds), *Neoliberalism: A Critical Reader* (London: Pluto Press, 2005)

Coates, D., and P. Lawler (eds), *New Labour in Power* (Manchester: Manchester University Press, 2000)

Cobbett, W., *Rural Rides* (1830) (London: Penguin Classics, 2001)

Colloms, B., *Charles Kingsley* (London: Constable, 1975)

Commission for Urban Life and Faith, *Faithful Cities: A Call for Celebration, Vison and Justice* (London: Church House Publishing, 2006)

Conservative Party, *A Better Tomorrow* (London: Conservative Central Office, 1970)

Corbett, S., 'The Big Society Five Years On', in L. Foster, A. Brunton, C. Deeming and T. Haux (eds) *In Defence of Welfare 2* (Bristol: Policy Press, 2015), pp. 165–67

Council of Churches for Britain and Ireland, *Unemployment and the Future of Work: An Enquiry for the Churches* (London: CCBI Publications, 1997)

Crossman, R., 'The Role of the Volunteer in the Modern Social Service: Sidney Ball Memorial Lecture, 1973', in A. H. Halsey (ed.), *Traditions in Social Policy* (Oxford: Blackwell, 1976), pp. 259–85

Crowson, N., M. Hilton and J. McKay, *NGOs in Contemporary Britain: Non-State Actors in Society and Politics since 1945* (Basingstoke: Palgrave Macmillan, 2009)

Cruddas, J., *The Dignity of Labour* (Cambridge: Polity Press, 2021)

Dalroy Jones, P., *The Christian Socialist Revival 1877–1914* (Princeton, NJ: Princeton University Press, 1968)

Darlington, T., *Management Learning and Voluntary Organisations* (London: NCVO, 1989)

David, A., and K. Edwards, *Twelve Charity Contracts: Case Studies of Funding Contracts between Charities and Local Authorities and Other Bodies* (London: Directory of Social Change, 1990)

Davie, G., *Religion in Britain since 1945: Believing Without Belonging* (London: John Wiley & Sons, 1994)

Davies, M., 'Southampton Church Will Change Its Spots to Attract a Student Congregation', *Church Times*, 18 May 2018, available at: https://www .churchtimes.co.uk/articles/2018/4-may/news/uk/southampton-church -will-change-its-spots-to-attract-a-student-congregation (accessed on 13 September 2019)

Davis, C., J. Milbank and S. Zizek (eds), *Theology and the Political* (Durham, NC: Duke University Press, 2005)

Davis, F., E. Paulhus and A. Bradstock, *Moral, But No Compass: Government, Church and the Future of Welfare* (Chelmsford: Matthew James Publishing, 2008)

Davis, R., *Tangled Up in Blue: Blue Labour and the Struggle for Labour's Soul* (London: Ruskin Publishing, 2011)

Davis Smith, J., *100 Years of NCVO and Voluntary Action: Idealists and Realists* (London: Palgrave Macmillan, 2019)

Davis Smith, J., C. Rochester and R. Hedley (eds), *An Introduction to the Voluntary Sector* (London: Routledge, 1995)

Deakin, N., and J. Davis Smith, 'Labour, Charity and Voluntary Action', in M. Hilton and J. McKay (eds), *The Ages of Voluntarism: How We Got to the Big Society* (Oxford: Oxford University Press, 2011), pp. 69–93

Deakin, N., and J. Kershaw, *Meeting the Challenge of Change: Voluntary Action into the 21st Century* (London: NCVO, 1996)

Dean, H., and P. Taylor-Gooby, *Dependency Culture: The Explosion of a Myth* (London: Harvester/Wheatsheaf, 1992)

Demant, V.A., *Religion and the Decline of Capitalism* (London: Faber & Faber, 1952)

Demant, V.A., *Theology of Society: More Essays in Christian Polity* (London: Faber & Faber, 1947)

Department of Health, *The NHS Plan: A Plan for Investment, a Plan for Reform* (Norwich: HMSO, July 2000)

Digby, A., *British Welfare Policy: Workhouse to Workfare* (London: Faber & Faber, 1989)

Dimont, M.I., *Jews, God and History* (New York: Simon and Schuster, 1962)

Doak, M., 'The Politics of Radical Orthodoxy: A Catholic Critique', *Theological Studies* 68, no. 2 (2007), pp. 368–93, available at: https://journals.sagepub.com/doi/abs/10.1177/004056390706800207 (accessed on 1 July 2019)

Domoko, J., 'Jobcentres "Tricking" People out of Benefits to Cut Costs, Says Whistleblower', *The Guardian*, 1 April 2011

Donnison, D., *A Radical Agenda: After the New Right and the Old Left* (London: Rivers Oram Press, 1991)

Dowler, E., *The Church and the Big Society* (Cambridge: Grove Books, 2013)

Edwards, J., (ed.), *Retrieving the Big Society* (Oxford: Wiley-Blackwell, 2012)

Ekklesia, *Common Wealth: Christians for Economic and Social Justice*, November 2010, available at: http://www.ekklesia.co.uk/CommonWealthStatement (accessed on 5 November 2017)

Elford, r.j., and I.S. Markham (eds), *The Middle Way: Theology, Politics and Economics in the Later Thought of R.H. Preston* (London: SCM Press, 2000)

Elliott, C., *Whatever Happened to the Big Society?*, Centre for Policy Development Occasional Paper 25, February 2013, available at: https://cpd.org.au/2013/02/whatever-happened-to-the-big-society/ (accessed on 20 December 2021)

Evans, E., *Thatcher and Thatcherism* (London: Routledge, 2018)

Faith Survey, 'Introduction: UK Christianity 2005–2015', *Church Statistics* (no author cited), available at: https://faithsurvey.co.uk/download/csintro.pdf (accessed on 23 April 2018)

Fanfani, A., *Catholicism, Protestantism and Capitalism* (London: Sheed & Ward, 1935), available at: http://www.strobertbellarmine.net/books/Fanfani--Catholicism_Protestantism_Capitalism.pdf (accessed on 22 January 2017)

Farnell, R., R. Furbey, S. Shams al-Haqq Hills, M. Macey and G. Smith, *'Faith' in Urban Regeneration? Engaging Faith Communities in Urban Regeneration* (Bristol: Policy Press, 2003)

Faucher-King, F., and P. Le Galès, *The New Labour Experiment: Change under Blair and Brown* (Stanford: Stanford University Press, 2010)

Fawcett, H., and R. Lowe (eds), *Welfare Policy in Britain: The Road from 1945* (London: Palgrave Macmillan, 1999)

Field, F., *Inequality in Britain: Freedom, Welfare and the State* (London: Collins, Fontana, 1981)

Field, F., *Making Welfare Work: Reconstructing Welfare for the Millennium* (London: Institute of Community Studies, 1995)

Figgis, J.N., *Churches in the Modern State* (London: Longmans, Green & Co., 1913)

Figgis, J.N., *From Gerson to Grotius* (Cambridge: Cambridge University Press, 1907)

Figgis, J.N., *The Political Aspects of St Augustine's 'City of God'* (1921) (London: Bibliotech Press, 2013)

Filby, E., 'Faith, Charity and Citizenship', in Hilton and McKay (eds), *The Ages of Voluntarism*

Filby, E., *God and Mrs Thatcher: The Battle for Britain's Soul* (London: Biteback Publishers, 2015)

Finlayson, G., *Citizen, State and Social Welfare in Britain 1830–1990* (Oxford: Clarendon Press, 1994)

Fletcher, J., *William Temple: Twentieth-Century Christian* (New York: Seabury, 1963)

Forde, J., 'Anglican Socialism and Welfare: John Milbank's 'Blue Socialist' Thinking and the Church of England's Approach to Welfare since 2008' (PhD thesis, University of Manchester, 2020)

Forde, J., 'Popular Front Strategy in France and Spain in the 1930s: Betrayal or Reaffirmation of the Socialist Cause?' (Unpublished MA dissertation, University of Sheffield, 1987)

Forde, J., 'The Third Way: Industrial Partnerships in the NHS' (Unpublished MA dissertation, University of Huddersfield, 2000)

Forrester, D.B., *Christianity and the Future of Welfare* (London: Epworth Press, 1985)

Foss, B., *War Paint: Art, War, State and Identify in Britain 1939–1945* (New Haven, CT: Yale University Press, 2007)

Francis, (Pope), *Fratelli Tutti: Encyclical Letter on Fraternity and Social Friendship*, issued 2020, available at: http://www.vatican.va/content /francesco/en/encyclicals/documents/papa-francesco_20201003_enciclica -fratelli-tutti.html (accessed on 27 October 2020)

Fraser, D., *The Evolution of the British Welfare State* (London: Palgrave Macmillan, 2009)

Freeman, M., *Edmund Burke and the Critique of Political Radicalism* (Oxford: Blackwell, 1980)

Friedman, M., *Capitalism and Freedom* (Chicago: University of Chicago Press, 1962)

Furbey, R., A. Dinham, R. Farnell, D. Finneron, G. Wilkinson, C. Howarth, D. Hussain and S. Palmer, *Faith as Social Capital: Connecting or Dividing?* (Bristol: Policy Press, 2006)

Garraghan, G.J., *A Guide to Historical Method* (New York: Declan X. McMullan, 1946)

Geary, I., and A. Pabst (eds), *Blue Labour: Forging a New Politics* (London: I.B. Tauris, 2015)

Giddens, A., *The Third Way: The Renewal of Social Democracy* (London: Polity Press, 1998)

Glasman, M., 'The Good Society, Catholic Social Thought and the Politics of the Common Good', in I. Geary and A. Pabst (eds), *Blue Labour: Forging a New Politics* (London: I.B. Tauris, 2015), pp. 20–36

Glasman, M., 'Labour as a Radical Tradition: Labour's Renewal Lies in its Traditions of Mutualism, Reciprocity and Common Good', Soundings, no. 46 (September 2010), pp. 31ff

Glasman, M., J. Rutherford, M. Stears and S. White (eds), *The Labour Tradition and the Politics of Paradox: The Oxford London Seminars 2010–11* (London: Lawrence and Wishart, Ebook, 2011)

Glennerster, H., *British Social Policy since 1945* (Oxford: Oxford University Press, 1995)

Goldman, L., 'Founding the Welfare State: The Collective Biography of William Beveridge, R.H. Tawney and William Temple', a lecture given at the Institute of Historical Research on 7 April 2016, available at: https:// www.history.ac.uk/podcasts/franco-british-history-external/founding -welfare-state-collective-biography-william (accessed on 19 June 2019)

Goodhart, D., 'Globalisation, Nation States and the Economics of Migration', in I. Geary and A. Pabst (eds), *Blue Labour: Forging and New Politics* (London: I.B. Tauris, 2015), pp. 121–40

Gore, C., (ed.), *Lux Mundi* (1889) (London: John Murray Press, 1890)

Graham, E., 'From Where Does the Red Tory Speak? Phillip Blond, Theology and Public Discourse', *Political Theology* 13, no. 3 (2012), pp. 292–307

Gramsci, A., *Selections from the Prison Notebooks* (London: Lawrence & Wishart, 1971)

Green, T.H., *Collected Works*, Vol. III (1888) (Cambridge: Cambridge Library Collection, 2011)

Greengrass, M., *Christendom Destroyed: Europe 1517–1648* (London: Penguin, 2015)

Grice, A., '£850 bn: Official Cost of the Bank Bailout', *Independent*, 4 December 2009, available at: http://www.independent.co.uk/news/uk /politics/163850bn-official-cost-of-the-bank-bailout-1833830.html (accessed on 4 November 2017)

Griffin, E., 'The Making of the Chartists: Popular Politics and Working-Class Autobiography in Early Victorian Britain', *The English Historical Review* 129, no. 538 (June 2014), pp. 578–605

Griffiths, B., *Morality and the Market Place* (London: Hodder & Stoughton, 1982)

Grimley, M., *Citizenship, Community and the Church of England* (Oxford: Oxford University Press, 2004)

Grimley, M., 'Civil Society and the Clerisy: Christian Elites and National Culture, c. 1930–1950' in J. Harris (ed.) *Civil Society in British History: Ideas, Identities, Institutions* (Oxford: Oxford University Press, 2005), pp. 231–47

Gutiérrez, G., *A Theology of Liberation* (Maryknoll, NY: Orbis Books, 1973)

Hadley, R., and S. Hatch, *Social Welfare and the Future of the State* (London: George Allen & Unwin, 1981)

Harman, C., *A People's History of the World* (London: Verso, 1999)

Harman, C., 'The Rise of Capitalism', *International Socialism 2*, no. 102 (Spring 2004), available at: https://www.marxists.org/archive/harman/2004/xx/risecap.htm (accessed on 23 January 2017)

Handy, C., *Improving Effectiveness in Voluntary Organisations: Report of the Charles Handy Working Party* (London: NCVO, 1981)

Harris, B., *The Origins of the British Welfare State* (London: Palgrave Macmillan, 2004)

Harris, J., (ed.), *Civil Society in British History: Ideas, Identities, Institutions* (Oxford: Oxford University Press, 2003)

Harris, J., 'Phillip Blond: The Man Who Wrote Cameron's Mood Music', *The Guardian*, 8 August 2009, available at: https://www.theguardian.com /theguardian/2009/aug/08/phillip-blond-conservatives-david-cameron (accessed on 3 December 2016)

Harris, J., 'Voluntarism, the State and the Public-Private Partnerships in Beveridge's Social Thought', in M. Oppenheimer and N. Deakin (eds), *Beveridge and Voluntary Action in Britain and the Wider British World* (Manchester: Manchester University Press, 2011), pp. 9–20

Harris, J., *William Beveridge: A Biography* (Oxford: Oxford University Press, 1988)

Harris, M., and C. Rochester (eds), *Voluntary Organisations and Social Policy in Britain: Perspectives on Change and Choice* (Basingstoke: Palgrave, 2001)

Harvey, D., *A Brief History of Neoliberalism* (Oxford: Oxford University Press, 2005)

Hattersley, R., *Choose Freedom: The Future of Democratic Socialism* (London: Michael Joseph, 1987)

Hattersley, R., and K. Hickson, 'In Praise of Social Democracy', *The Political Quarterly* 83, no. 1 (October-December 2011), pp. 5–12

Hattersley, R., and K. Hickson (eds), *The Socialist Way: Social Democracy in Contemporary Britain* (London: I.B. Tauris, 2013)

Hauerwas, S., 'How to Remember the Poor', *Together for the Common Good*, available at: https://togetherforthecommongood.co.uk/leading-thinkers /how-to-remember-the-poor (accessed on 20 December 2021)

Hauerwas, S., *The Peaceable Kingdom* (Paris: University of Notre Dame Press, 1984)

Hayde, P., E. Granter, J. Hassard and L. McCann, *Deconstructing the Welfare State: Managing Health Care in the Age of Reform* (London: Routledge, 2016)

Hayek, F.A., *New Studies* (London: Routledge & Kegan Paul, 1978)

Hayek, F.A., *The Road to Serfdom* (1944) (Chicago: University of Chicago Press, 2008)

Headlam, S., *The Guild of St Matthew: What It Is and Who Should Join It* (London: Guild of St Matthew, 1895)

Health Foundation, *Person-Centred Care Made Simple: What Every Person Should Know about Person-Centred Care* (London: The Health Foundation,

2014), available at: https://www.health.org.uk/publications/person-centred
-care-made-simple (accessed on 20 December 2021)

Healy, P., 'Extra £3.5m in Grants for Voluntary Services over the Next Four
Years', *The Times*, 9 December 1971

Heeney, B., *The Women's Movement in the Church of England, 1850–1930*
(Oxford: Clarendon Press, 1988)

Hegel, G.W.F., *Outlines of the Philosophy of Right* (1821) (Oxford: Oxford
University Press, 2008)

Helm, T., and J. Coman, 'Rowan Williams Pours Scorn on David Cameron's
"Big Society"', *The Guardian*, 24 June 2012

Hennessy, P., *Never Again: Britain 1945–1951* (London: Penguin, 2006)

Hibbert, C., *Disraeli: A Personal History* (New York: Harper Perennial, 2005)

Hill, A., 'Matt Hancock Asks MPs and Peers for Views on Adult Social Care
Reform', *The Guardian,* 6 March 2020

Hill, M., *The Welfare State in Britain: A Political History since 1945*
(Aldershot: Edward Elgar, 1993)

Hilton, M., 'Charities, Voluntary Organisations and Non-Governmental
Organisations in Britain since 1945', in A. Ishkanian and S. Szreter (eds),
The Big Society Debate: A New Agenda for Social Welfare (Cheltenham:
Edward Elgar, 2012)

Hilton, M., N. Crowson, J.-F. Mouhot and J. McKay, *Historical Guide to
NGOs in Britain: Charities, Civil Society and the Voluntary Sector since 1945*
(Basingstoke: Palgrave Macmillan, 2012)

Hilton, M., N. Crowson, J.-F. Mouhot and J. McKay, *The Politics of Expertise:
How NGOs Shaped Modern Britain* (Oxford: Oxford University Press, 2013)

Hilton, M., and J. McKay (eds), *The Ages of Voluntarism: How We Got to the
Big Society* (Oxford: Oxford University Press, 2011)

Hilton, R., *Class Conflict and the Crisis of Feudalism: Essays in Medieval
Social History* (1985) (London: Verso Books, 1991)

Hinsliff, G., 'Blair's Christianity', *The Guardian*, 8 April 2007

Hirst, P., (ed.), *The Pluralist Theory of the State* (London: Routledge, 1989)

Hobbes, T., *Leviathan* (1651) (London: Wordsworth, 1914)

Hobsbawm, E., *Labouring Men: Studies in the History of Labour* (London:
Weidenfeld & Nicolson, 1964)

Hobsbawm, E., *Worlds of Labour: Further Studies in the History of Labour*
(London: Weidenfeld & Nicolson, 2014)

Hovey, C., and E. Phillips (eds), *The Cambridge Companion to Christian
Political Theology* (Cambridge: Cambridge University Press, 2015)

Hughes, J., 'After Temple? The Recent Renewal of Anglican Social Thought',
in M. Brown (ed.), *Anglican Social Theology* (Croydon: Church House
Publishing, 2014), pp. 74–101

Husselbee, L., and P. Ballard (eds), *Free Churches and Society: The
Nonconformist Contribution to Social Welfare 1800–2010* (London:
Continuum International Publishing, 2012)

Illich, I., *Disabling Professions* (1997) (London: Marion Boyars, 2005)

Illich, I., *Limits to Medicine* (New York: Marion Boyars, 1976)

Insole, C., *The Politics of Human Frailty: A Theological Defence of Political Liberalism* (London: SCM Press, 2012)

Ishkanian, A., and S. Szreter (eds), *The Big Society Debate: A New Agenda for Social Welfare* (Cheltenham: Edward Elgar, 2012)

Jacobovits, I., *From Doom to Hope: A Jewish View of Faith in the City* (London: Office of the Chief Rabbi, 1986)

Jefferys, K., (ed.), *War and Reform: British Politics during the Second World War* Manchester: Manchester University Press, 1994

Jenkins, R., *Asquith* (New York: Harper Collins, 1988)

John Paul II, *Centesimus Annus: Encyclical Letter on the Hundredth Anniversary of Rerum Novarum*, available at: http://w2.vatican.va/content /john-paul-ii/en/encyclicals/documents/hf_jp-ii_enc_01051991_centesimus -annus.html (accessed on 29 October 2018)

Jones, P.D., *The Christian Socialist Revival, 1877–1914* (Princeton, NJ: Princeton University Press, 1968)

Jordan, B., *Why the Third Way Failed: Economics, Morality and the Origins of the 'Big Society'* (Bristol: Policy Press, 2010)

Joseph Rowntree Foundation, *The Cost of the Cuts: The Impact on Local Government and Poorer Communities* (York: Joseph Rowntree Foundation, 2015), available at: https://www.jrf.org.uk/sites/default/files/jrf/migrated /files/Summary-Final.pdf (accessed on 19 July 2018)

Kay, A., (ed.), *Dear NHS: 100 Stories to Say Thank You* (London: Trapeze, 2020)

Kent, J., *William Temple: Church, State and Society in Britain, 1880–1950* (Cambridge: Cambridge University Press, 1992)

Kidwell, J., and S. Doherty (eds), *Theology and Economics* (London: Palgrave Macmillan, 2015)

Kitson, A., A. Marshall, K. Bassett and K. Zeitz, 'What Are the Core Elements of Patient-Centred Care? A Narrative Review and Synthesis of the Literature from Health Policy, Medicine and Nursing', *JAN: Improving Practice and Policy Worldwide Through Research & Scholarship* 69, no. 1 (2013), pp. 4–15

Knott, G., *Investing More for the Common Good: National Church Social Action Survey Results 2014* (Shrewsbury: Jubilee Plus, 2014)

Kramer, R.M., 'Change and Continuity in British Voluntary Organisations 1976–1988', *Voluntas* 1, no. 2 (1990), pp. 33–59

Krinks, P., 'Social Enterprise in the Theologies of William Temple and John Milbank', *Journal of Beliefs & Values* 37, no. 3 (2016), pp. 282–95

Kuhnle, S., and P. Selle (eds), *Government and Voluntary Organisations: A Relational Perspective* (Aldershot: Avebury, 1992)

Labour Party, *Building Bridges: Labour and the Voluntary Sector* (London: Labour Party, 1992)

Labour Party, *Building the Future Together: Labour's Policies for Partnership between Government and the Voluntary Sector* (London: Labour Party, 1997)

The Lambeth Conference Resolutions Archive of 1948, available at: http://
www.anglicancommunion.org/media/127737/1948.pdf (accessed on 29
December 2017)

Lambie-Mumford, H., and D. Jarvis, 'The Role of Faith-Based Organisations
in the Big Society: Opportunities and Challenges', *Policy Studies* 33, no. 3
(2012), pp. 249–69, available at: http://www.tandfonline.com/doi/abs
/10.1080/01442872.2012.666395?journalCode=cpos20 (accessed on 17
November 2017)

Landry, C., *What a Way to Run a Railroad: An Analysis of Radical Failure*
(London: Comedia Publishing, 1985)

Laybourn, K., *The Rise of British Socialism* (Stroud: Sutton Publishing, 1997)

Leech, K., 'The Christian Left in Britain (1850–1950)', in R. Ambler and
D. Haslam (eds), *Agenda for Prophets: Towards a Political Theology*
(London: Bowerdean Press, 1990), pp. 61–72

Leech, K., 'Christianity and Social Services in Modern Britain: The
Disinherited Spirit', *Church Times*, 2 November 2006

Leech, K., 'Farewell to the Days of Birettas and Cassocks', *Church Times*, 2
November 2006, available at: https://www.churchtimes.co.uk/articles/2004
/23-april/features/farewell-to-the-days-of-birettas-and-cassocks (accessed
on 4 November 2016)

Leech, K., *Politics and Faith Today: Catholic Social Vision for the 1990s*
(London: Darton, Longman & Todd, 1994)

Leech, K., *The Radical Anglo-Catholic Social Vision*, a lecture given at the
Centre for Theology and Public Issues, University of Edinburgh, on 13
March 1989 (Edinburgh: CTPI, 1989), available at: https://books.google
.co.uk/books/about/The_Radical_Anglo_Catholic_Social_Vision.html?id
=NwR0Zk5WME8C (accessed on 23 April 2016)

Leech, K., 'Turbulent Priests', *Marxism Today* (February 1986), pp. 11–13

Leech, K., 'What Happened to the Anglo-Catholic Socialists?', 2011. This
article is held on a private web site (WordPress.com) for which access can
be obtained on request at the following link: https://robbbeck.wordpress
.com/2011/10/28/what-happened-to-the-anglo-catholic-socialists/

Leech, K., (ed.), *Conrad Noel and the Catholic Crusade: A Critical Evaluation*
(London: The Jubilee Group, 1993)

Leo XIII, *Rerum Novarum: Encyclical of Pope Leo XIII on Capital and Labor*,
issued 15 May 1891, available at: http://w2.vatican.va/content/leo-xiii/en
/encyclicals/documents/hf_l-xiii_enc_15051891_rerum-novarum.html
(accessed on 5 January 2017)

Lenin, V.I., *The State and Revolution* (1917) (Washington, DC: Regnery
Publishing, 2009)

Lenin, V.I., *What Is to Be Done?* (1902) (Oxford: Oxford University Press,
1963)

Lewis, J., 'The Voluntary Sector and the State in Twentieth-Century Britain',
in H. Fawcett and R. Lowe (eds), *Welfare Policy in Britain: The Road from
1945* (London: Palgrave Macmillan, 1999), pp. 52–67

Lindbeck, G.A., *The Nature of Doctrine: Religion and Theology in a Post-liberal Age* (Louisville, KY: Westminster John Knox Press, 1984)

Loughlin, G., 'Erotics: God's Sex', in J. Milbank, C. Pickstock and G. Ward (eds), *Radical Orthodoxy* (London: Routledge, 1999), pp. 143–62

Lowe, R., *The Welfare State in Britain since 1945*, 2nd edn (London: Macmillan Press, 1999)

MacIntyre, A., *After Virtue: A Study in Moral Theory* (Notre Dame, IN: University of Notre Dame, 1981)

Macmillan, H., speech at a Tory Party rally in Bedford, July 1957. Available at: http://news.bbc.co.uk/onthisday/hi/dates/stories/july/20/newsid_3728000/3728225.stm (accessed on 10 December 2021)

Magid, H., *English Political Pluralism: The Problem of Freedom and Organization* (New York, Columbia University Press, 1941)

Major, J., Speech to business leaders involved in charity work in October, 1993. Cited in J. D. Smith, C. Rochester and R. Hedley (eds), *An Introduction to the Voluntary Sector* (London: Routledge, 2005), p. 123

Manser, G., and R.H. Cass, *Voluntarism at the Crossroads* (New York: Family Service Association of America, 1976)

Marwick, A., *British Society since 1945* (London: Penguin Books, 1982)

Marwick, A., *The Nature of History* (London: Macmillan, 1970)

Marx, K., *Critique of the Gotha Programme* (1875) (London: Lawrence & Wishart, 1905)

Marx, K., *Critique of Hegel's 'Philosophy of Right'* (1843) (Cambridge: Cambridge University Press, 2009)

Marx, K., and F. Engels, *The Communist Manifesto* (1848) (London: Progress Publishers, 1966)

Marx, K., and F. Engels, *Economic and Philosophic Manuscripts of 1844* (London: Wilder Publications, 2011), available at: https://www.marxists.org/archive/marx/works/1844/manuscripts/labour.htm (accessed on 26 October 2016)

Marx, K., and F. Engels, *The German Ideology* (1846) (London: Lawrence & Wishart, 1997)

Masterman, N.C., *John Malcolm Ludlow: The Builder of Christian Socialism* (Cambridge: Cambridge University Press, 1963)

Mauss, M., *The Gift: Forms and Functions of Exchange in Archaic Societies* (Eastford, CT: Martino Fine Books, 2011)

May, T., 'Full Text: Theresa May's Conference Speech', *The Guardian*, 7 October 2002

Mayo, H.B., 'Marxist Theory and Scientific Methods', *The Canadian Journal of Economics and Political Science* 18, no. 4 (November 1952), pp. 487–99, available at: https://www.jstor.org/stable/138368?seq=1#page_scan_tab_contents (accessed on 3 November 2016)

McCann, D.P., 'A Second Look at Middle Axioms', *The Annual Society for Christian Ethics* 1 (1981), pp. 73–96

McGee, R.W., 'Thomas Aquinas: A Pioneer in the Field of Law and Economics', *Western State University Law Review* 18, no. 2 (1990), pp. 471–83

McKay, A.L., 'Wrong about Orwell Being on the Right', 28 August 2012, available at: https://www.e-ir.info/2012/08/28/wrong-about-orwell-being -on-the-right/ (accessed on 25 November 2019)

McKay, J., 'Voluntary Politics: The Sector's Political Function from Beveridge to Deakin', in M. Oppenheimer and N. Deakin (eds), *Beveridge and Voluntary Action in Britain and the Wider British World* (Manchester: Manchester University Press, 2011)

Medhurst, K.N., and G.H. Moyser, *Church and Politics in a Secular Age* (Oxford: Clarendon Press, 1988)

Merrick, M., 'The Labour Family', in I. Geary and A. Pabst (eds), *Blue Labour: Forging a New Politics* (London: I.B. Tauris, 2015), pp. 235–52

Michener, R.T., *Postliberal Theology: A Guide for the Perplexed* (London: T&T Clark, 2013)

Milliken, D., 'Factbox: UK on Course for Highest Borrowing since World War Two', Reuters, 25 November 2020, available at: https://www.reuters. com/article/us-health-coronavirus-britain-borrowing/factbox-uk-on -course-for-highest-borrowing-since-world-war-two-idUSKBN28500D (accessed on 12 January 2021)

Moffatt, V., (ed.), *Reclaiming the Common Good: How Christians Can Help Rebuild Our Broken World* (London: Darton, Longman & Todd, 2017)

Morgan, K., *Labour in Power 1945–1951* (Oxford: Oxford University Press, 1985)

Morgan, R., (ed.), *The Religion of the Incarnation: Anglican Essays in Commemoration of Lux Mundi* (Bristol: Bristol Classical Press, 1989)

Morris, J., *To Build Christ's Kingdom: An F.D. Maurice Reader* (Norwich: Canterbury Press, 2007)

Morton, A.R., 'The Future of Welfare', Occasional Paper No. 41 (Edinburgh: Centre for Theology and Public Issues, University of Edinburgh, 1997)

Murray, S., *Post-Christendom: Church and Mission in a Strange New World* (Milton Keynes: Paternoster, 2005)

Nathan, H., *Effectiveness and the Voluntary Sector* (London: NCVO, 1990)

Near Neighbours, *Near Neighbours Impact Report: April 2011-March 2017*, available at: https://static1.squarespace.com/static/5a68889a90bade 540b4da177/t/5b239001aa4a99a4bb1ac216/1529057287026/Near+Neighbours +Impact+Report.pdf (accessed on 20 December 2021)

New King James Version Reference Bible (Nashville, TN: Thomas Nelson Publishers, 2019)

Nicholls, D., 'Christianity and Politics', in R. Morgan (ed.), *The Religion of the Incarnation: Anglican Essays in Commemoration of Lux Mundi* (Bristol: Bristol Classical Press, 1989), pp. 172–88

Nicholls, D., *Church and State in Britain since 1820* (London: Routledge & Kegan Paul, 1967)

Nicholls, D., *Deity and Domination: Images of God and the State in the Nineteenth and Twentieth Centuries* (London: Routledge, 1989)

Nicholls, D., *God and Government* (London: Jubilee Group Pamphlet, 1991)

Nicholls, D., *The Pluralist State* (London: The Macmillan Press, 1975)

Nicholls, D., *Three Varieties of Pluralism* (London: The Macmillan Press, 1974)

Nicholls, D., 'William Temple and the Welfare State', *Crucible: The Christian Journal of Social Ethics*, October/ November 1984, pp. 161–68

Noel, C., *Socialism in Church History* (London: Frank Palmer, 1910)

Norman, J., and J. Ganesh, *Compassionate Conservatism: What It Is – Why We Need It* (London: Policy Exchange, 2006)

Norman, J., *Compassionate Economics: The Social Foundations of Economic Prosperity* (Buckingham: University of Buckingham Press, 2008)

Norman, J., and P. Oborne, *Churchill's Legacy: The Conservative Case for the Human Rights Act* (London: Liberty, 2009)

Norman, J., *The Big Society: The Anatomy of the New Politics* (Buckingham: University of Buckingham Press, 2010)

Norman, J., 'The Intellectual Origins of the "Big Society"', *Total Politics*, 18 February 2011, available at: https://www.totalpolitics .com/articles/interview/intellectual-origins-big-society (accessed on 4 November 2017)

Oakeshott, M., *Rationalism in Politics and Other Essays* (York: Methuen, 1981)

O'Donovan, O., *The Desire of the Nations: Rediscovering the Roots of Political Theology* (Cambridge: Cambridge University Press, 2008)

Oldham, J.H., *The Church and Its Function in Society* (London: G. Allen & Unwin, 1937)

Oppenheimer, M., and N. Deakin (eds), *Beveridge and Voluntary Action in Britain and the Wider British World* (Manchester: Manchester University Press, 2011)

Owen, J., 'Hidden Homeless: Benefit Sanctions Blamed as Rough Sleepers Increase by a Third in Five Years', *Independent*, 22 May 2015 Available at: https://www.independent.co.uk/news/uk/politics/hidden-homeless-benefit -sanctions-blamed-as-rough-sleepers-increase-by-a-third-in-five-years -10021643.html (accessed on 1 January 2021)

Pabst, A., (ed.), *The Crisis of Global Capitalism: Pope Benedict XVI's Social Encyclical and the Future of Political Economy* (Eugene, OR: Wipf & Stock, 2011)

Partington, R.J., 'UK Should Respond to Economic Crisis with 1945-style Reboot, Says CBI Chief', *The Guardian*, 3 February 2021

Philpot, R., (ed.), *The Purple Book: A Progressive Future for Labour* (London: Biteback Publishing, 2011)

Pierotti, S., 'Backup of the Protestant Ethic and the Spirit of Capitalism: Criticisms of Weber's Thesis', available at: http://dearhabermas.org /weberrelbk01.htm (accessed on 15 December 2021)

Pierson, C., *Beyond the Welfare State: The New Political Economy of Welfare* (Philadelphia: Pennsylvania State University Press, 2007)

Pius XI, *Quadragesimo Anno: Encyclical of Pope Pius XI on Reconstruction of the Social Order,* issued 15 May 1931, available at: https://w2.vatican .va/content/pius-xi/en/encyclicals/documents/hf_p-xi_enc_19310515 _quadragesimo-anno.html (accessed on 5 January 2017)

Polanyi, K., *The Great Transformation: The Political and Economic Origins of Our Time* (Boston: Beacon Press, 1944)

Pomeranz, K., *The Great Divergence: China, Europe, and the Making of the World Economy* (Princeton, NJ: Princeton University Press, 2001)

Poole, H.R., *The Liverpool Council of Social Service 1909–1959* (Liverpool: The Liverpool Council for Social Service, 1960)

Powell, F., *The Politics of Civil Society: Big Society and Small Government* (Bristol: Bristol University Press, 2007)

Preston, R., *Church and Society in the Late Twentieth Century: The Economic and Political Task* (London: SCM Press, 1983)

Preston, R., 'Middle Axioms in Christian Social Ethics', *Crucible: The Christian Journal of Social Ethics,* January/February 1971, pp. 9–15

Preston, R., *Religion and the Persistence of Capitalism* (London: SCM Press, 1979)

Price, D., *Office of Hope: A History of the Public Employment Service in Great Britain, 1910–97* (London: Policy Studies Institute, 2000)

Prime Minister's Office, 'Government Launches the Big Society Programme', Briefing from the Prime Minister's Office, 18 May 2010, available at: https://www.gov.uk/government/news/government-launches-big-society -programme--2 (accessed on 2 December 2016)

Prochaska, F., *Christianity and Social Service in Modern Britain: The Disinherited Spirit* (Oxford: Oxford University Press, 2006)

Prochaska, F., 'The Church of England and the Collapse of Christian Charity', Social Affairs Unit, 8 November 2004, available at: http:// www.socialaffairsunit.org.uk/blog/archives/000207.php (accessed on 16 December 2021)

Prochaska, F., 'Mrs Thatcher, the Voluntary Sector and Victorian Values', Social Affairs Unit, 16 February 2005, available at: http://www .socialaffairsunit.org.uk/blog/archives/000294.php (accessed on 22 December 2021)

Prochaska, F., 'New Labour and the Voluntary Sector', Social Affairs Unit, 15 March 2005, available at: http://www.socialaffairsunit.org.uk/blog /archives/000324.php (accessed on 11 June 2019)

Prochaska, F., 'The State of Charity: Charity Commission Lecture', September 2014, available at: https://assets.publishing.service.gov.uk /government/uploads/system/uploads/attachment_data/file/356191/Lecture _-_Dr_Frank_Prochaska.pdf (accessed on 15 December 2021)

Prochaska, F., 'Voluntary Action – Renaissance or Decline?', *History & Policy: Connecting Historians, Policy Makers and the Media* .http://

www.historyandpolicy.org/docs/voluntary_sector.pdf (accessed on 28 August 2017; the article is no longer available at that source. The present writer has a hard copy that can be made available on request.)

Prochaska, F., *Women and Philanthropy in Nineteenth-Century England* (Oxford: Clarendon Press, 1980)

Radice, L., *Beatrice and Sidney Webb* (London: Palgrave Macmillan, 1984)

Rainey, H.G., *Understanding and Managing Public Organisations* (San Francisco: John Wiley & Sons, 2003)

Raven, C., *Christian Socialism 1848–1854* (London: Frank Cass & Co., 1968)

Rawls, J., *A Theory of Justice* (1971) (Cambridge, MA: Harvard University Press, 2005)

Reckitt, M.B., *The Meaning of National Guilds* (New York: Macmillan, 1918)

Reckitt, M.B., (ed.), *Prospect for Christendom* (London: Faber & Faber, 1945)

Reisman, D., *State and Welfare: Tawney, Galbraith and Adam Smith* (London: Macmillan, 1982)

Report of the Committee on Local Authority and Allied Personal Social Services (the Seebohm Report), Cmnd 3703 (London: HMSO, 1968)

Rich, H., *Growing Good: The Future of the Church?* (London: Theos, 2020)

Rodger, T., P. Williamson and M. Grimley, *Church of England and British Politics since 1900*, (Woodbridge: Boydell Press, 2020)

Rooff, M., *Voluntary Societies and Social Policy* (London: Routledge & Kegan Paul, 1957)

Rousseau, J.-J., *The Social Contract* (1762) (London: Wordsworth, 1958)

Rowland, C., and J. Vincent (eds), *British Liberation Theology: For Church and Nation* (Sheffield: Urban Theology Union, 2013)

Sacks, J., 'The Jewish Community Could Not Exist for One Day without Its Volunteers', *Daily Telegraph*, 28 October 2012

Saad-Filho, A., and D. Johnston (eds), *Neoliberalism: A Critical Reader* (London: Pluto Press, 2005)

Sagovsky, N., and P. McGrail (eds), *Together for the Common Good: Towards a National Conversation* (London: SCM Press, 2015)

Sampson, A., *The Changing Anatomy of Britain* (London: Hodder & Stoughton, 1982)

Samuelson, K., *Religion and Economic Action* (Toronto: University of Toronto Press, 1993)

Saunders, R., 'Chartism from Above: British Elites and the Interpretation of Chartism', *Historical Research* 81, no. 213 (August 2008), pp. 463–84

Scotland, N., 'Methodism and the English Labour Movement 1800–1906', *Anvil* 14, no.1 (1997), available at: https://biblicalstudies.org.uk/pdf/anvil /14-1_036.pdf (accessed on 25 January 2017)

Scott, P., 'Red Toryism and the Case of the Lost Revolution', *Political Theology* 13, no. 3 (2012), pp. 308–29

Scuffham, F.,'foreword', *Action on Unemployment: 100 Projects with Unemployed People* (London: Church Action with the Unemployed, 1984).

Produced by the National Extension College Trust Ltd, and the ISBN number for this publication is 0860824705

Seldon, A., *Wither the Welfare State*, Occasional Paper 60 (London: Institute of Economic Affairs, 1981)

Sentamu, J., 'Hope Today for a Brighter Future', in J. Sentamu (ed.), *On Rock or Sand* (London: SPCK, 2015), pp. 1–26

Shakespeare, S., *Affirming Common Wealth: A Response to Milbank*, ABC Religion & Ethics, 10 December 2010, available at: http://www.abc.net.au /religion/articles/2010/12/10/3090394.htm (accessed on 27 August 2017)

Shakespeare, S., *Radical Orthodoxy: A Critical Introduction* (London: SPCK, 2007)

Sheppard, D., *Bias to the Poor* (London: Hodder & Stoughton, 1983)

Sheppard, D., 'Foreword', in Council of Churches for Britain and Ireland, *Unemployment and the Future of Work: An Enquiry for the Churches* (London: CCBI, 1997)

Siddique, H., 'ATOS Quits £500m Work Capability Assessment Contract Early', *The Guardian*, 27 March 2014, available at: https://www.theguardian .com/society/2014/mar/27/atos-quite-work-capability-assessment-contract -early (accessed on 19 January 2018)

Skorton, D., and A. Bear (eds), *The Integration of the Humanities and Arts with Sciences, Engineering, and Medicine in Higher Education: Branches from the Same Tree* (Washington, DC: National Academies Press, 2018)

Slocock, C. (ed.), *Whose Society? The Final Big Society Audit* (London: Civil Exchange in Partnership with DHA Communications, 2015), available at: https://www.civilexchange.org.uk/wp-content/uploads/2015/01/Whose -Society_The-Final-Big-Society-Audit_final.pdf (accessed on 16 March 2017)

Smith, A., *The Theory of Moral Sentiments* (1759) (London: Penguin Classics, 2010)

Smith, A., *An Inquiry into the Nature and Causes of the Wealth of Nations* (1776) (Oxford: Oxford University Press, 2008)

Smith, G., *More than a little Quiet Care: The Extent of the Churches' Contribution to Community Work in East London in the 1990s* (London: Aston Charities Community Involvement Unit, 1998)

Smith, G., 'Pluralism and Justice: A Theological Critique of Red Toryism', *Political Theology* 13, no. 3 (2012), pp. 330–47

Smith, J.D., 'Volunteers: Making a Difference', in M. Harris and C. Rochester (eds), *Voluntary Organisations and Social Policy in Britain* (Basingstoke: Palgrave, 2001)

Smith, S.R., and M. Lipsky, 'Nonprofit Organisations, Government and the Welfare State', *Political Science Quarterly* 104, no. 4 (1989), pp. 625–48

Spencer, N., *Doing Good: A Future for Christianity in the 21st Century* (London: Theos, 2016)

Spencer, N., *'Doing God?': A Future for Faith in the Public Square* (London: Theos, 2006)

Spencer, N. (ed.), *The Future of Welfare: A Theos Collection* (London: Theos, 2014)

Spencer, S., *William Temple: A Calling to Prophecy* (London: SPCK, 2001)

Spencer, S., 'William Temple and the "Temple Tradition"', in S. Spencer (ed.), *Theology Reforming Society: Revisiting Anglican Social Theology* (London: SCM Press, 2017), pp. 85–107

Spencer, S., 'William Temple and the Welfare State: A Study of Christian Social Prophecy', *Political Theology* 3, no. 1 (2001), pp. 92–101

Spencer, S. (ed.), *Theology Reforming Society: Revisiting Anglican Social Theology* (London: SCM Press, 2017)

Stark, R., *The Victory of Reason: How Christianity Led to Freedom, Capitalism and Western Success* (New York: Random House, 2006)

Stott, M. (ed.), *The Big Society Challenge* (Thetford: Keystone Development Trust Publications, 2011)

Stratton, A., 'Labour: Now It's Kind of Blue', *The Guardian*, 24 April 2009, available at: https://www.theguardian.com/politics/blog/2009/apr/24/blue-labour-conservative-socialism (accessed on 2 December 2016)

Streek, W., and P. Schmitter (eds), *Private Interest Government: Beyond Market and State* (London: Sage, 1985)

Suggate, A.M., 'The Temple Tradition', in M. Brown (ed.), *Anglican Social Theology* (Croydon: Church House Publishing, 2014), pp. 22–73

Suggate, A., 'William Temple', in P. Scott and W.T. Cavanaugh (eds), *The Blackwell Companion to Political Theology* (Oxford: Blackwell, 2004)

Tawney, R.H., *The Acquisitive Society* (1921) (London: Fontana, 1961)

Tawney, R.H., *The Attack and other Papers* (London: George Allen & Unwin, 1953)

Tawney, R.H., *Equality* (1931) (London: Unwin Books, 1964)

Tawney, R.H., 'Max Weber and the Spirit of Capitalism' (1930), in J.M. Winter (ed.), *History and Society: Essays by R.H. Tawney* (London: Routledge & Kegan Paul, 1978), p. 195

Tawney, R.H., *The Radical Tradition* (1964) (London: Penguin Books, 1966)

Tawney, R.H., *Religion and the Rise of Capitalism* (1926) (London: Penguin Books, 1938)

Tawney, R.H., *R.H. Tawney's Commonplace Book* (1912), ed. with an Introduction by J.M. Winter and D.M. Joslin (Cambridge: Cambridge University Press, 1972)

Tawney, R.H., *The Western Political Tradition* (London: SCM Press, 1949)

Taylor, C., *Radical Tories: The Conservative Tradition in Canada* (Toronto: Anansi Press, 2006)

Taylor, M., *New Times, New Challenges: Voluntary Organisations Facing 1990* (London: NCVO, 1990)

Temple, W., *Christianity and Social Order* (1942) (London: Shepheard-Walwyn, 1971)

Temple, W., *Christianity and the State* (London: Macmillan and Co., 1928)

Temple, W., 'The Church and the Labour Party: A Consideration of Their Ideals', *The Economic Review* 18, no. 2 (1908), pp. 190–202

Temple, W., *Citizen and Churchman* (London: Eyre & Spottiswoode, 1941)

Temple, W., *Essays in Christian Politics and Kindred Subjects* (1933) (London: Hardpress Publishing, 2014)

Thane, P., 'The "Big Society" and the "Big State": Creative Tension or Crowding Out?', The Ben Pimlott Memorial Lecture 2011, *Twentieth Century British History* 23, no. 3 (September 2012), pp. 408–29

Thane, P., 'There Has Always Been a "Big Society"', *History Workshop*, 30 April 2011, available at: http://www.historyworkshop.org.uk/there-has-always-been-a-big-society (accessed on 10 April 2017)

Thane, P., 'Voluntary Action – Renaissance or Decline?', History & Policy, 2006, *Connecting Historians, Policy Makers and the Media*. Available at: http://www.historyandpolicy.org/docs/voluntary_sector.pdf (accessed on 23 August 2017)

Thatcher, M., *The Downing Street Years* (London: Harper-Collins, 1993)

Thatcher, M., 'Facing the New Challenge', Speech delivered on 19 January 1981 to the Women's Royal Voluntary Service National Conference, available at: http://www.margaretthatcher.org/document/104551 (accessed on 18 April 2017)

Thompson, E.P., *The Making of the English Working Class* (1963) (London: Pelican, 1972)

Thornton, E., 'Keir Starmer: Best of British Values Are the Best of Christian Values', *Church Times*, 18 December 2020

Thorpe, A., *A History of the British Labour Party*, 3rd edn (London: Palgrave Macmillan, 2008)

Timmins, N., *The Five Giants: A Bibliography of the Welfare State* (London: Harper-Collins, 1995)

Togliatti, P., *On Gramsci and Other Writings* (London: Lawrence & Wishart, 1979)

Tomlin, G., and M. Brown, *Coming Home: Christian Perspectives on Housing* (London: Church House Publishing, 2020)

Townsend, P., *Poverty in the United Kingdom* (London: Allen Lane and Penguin Books, 1979)

Trotsky, L., *History of the Russian Revolution* (1930) (Chicago: Haymarket Books, 2008)

Trotsky, L., *The Permanent Revolution and Results and Prospects* (1929) (Seattle: Red Letter Press, 2010 edition)

Trotsky, L., *The Revolution Betrayed* (1936) (Mineola, NY: Dover Publications, 2004)

Tuck, R., *Hobbes: A Very Short Introduction* (Oxford: Oxford University Press, 2002)

Turner, M.J., 'Local Politics and the Nature of Chartism: The Case of Manchester', *Northern History* 45, no. 2 (2008), pp. 323–45

UK Government, Academies Act 2010, available at: https://www.legislation.gov.uk/ukpga/2010/32/contents (accessed on 17 November 2017)

UK Government, *Decentralisation and the Localism Bill: An Essential Guide*, 13 December 2010, available at: https://www.gov.uk/government/publications/decentralisation-and-the-localism-bill-an-essential-guide--2 (accessed on 17 September 2015)

UK Government, *Take Part: National Citizen Service*, available at: https://www.gov.uk/government/get-involved/take-part/national-citizen-service (accessed on 17 November 2017)

U.K. Government, Home Office Research Study 289. Home Office Citizenship Survey: People, Families and Communities (2003). Published by Home Office Research, Development and Statistics Directorate (2004). Available as a pdf download at https://dera.ioe.ac.uk//7943/ (accessed on 1 January 2022)

University of Nottingham, Impact Assessment (no author cited), 'Shaping the Ideology of Red Tory and Blue Labour', an 'Impact Assessment' document produced by the University of Nottingham, available as a PDF download at: http://impact.ref.ac.uk/casestudies2/refservice.svc/GetCaseStudyPDF/28886 (accessed on 13 March 2017)

Viner, J., *Religious Thought and Economic Society* (Durham, NC: Duke University Press, 1978)

Visser't Hooft, W.A., and J.H. Oldham, *The Church and its Function in Society* (London: G. Allen & Unwin, 1937)

Walker, C., and L. March, *The House of Good* (London: National Churches Trust, 2020), available at: https://www.houseofgood.nationalchurchestrust.org/wp-content/uploads/2020/10/House-of-Good-AW-digital-small.pdf (accessed on 20 December 2020)

Wanless, D., *Securing Our Future Health: Taking a Long-Term View* (London: HM Treasury, 2002)

Ward, G., *Cities of God* (New York: Routledge, 2000)

Weber, M., *The Protestant Ethic and the Spirit of Capitalism* (1905) (London: Create Space International Publishing Platform, 2013)

Webb, S., and B. Webb, *The Prevention of Destitution* (London: Longman, 1912)

Weeks, J., '1945 and 2015: They Really Don't Match', *Compass: Together for a Good Society*, 28 June 2013, available at: http://www.compassonline.org.uk/1945-and-2015-they-really-dont-match/ (accessed on 24 October 2017)

Welby, J., 'Building the Common Good', in J. Sentamu (ed.), *On Rock or Sand* (London: SPCK, 2015), pp 27–52

Welby, J., *Reimagining Britain: Foundations for Hope* (London: Bloomsbury Continuum, 2018)

Wells, S., R. Rook and D. Barclay, *For Good: The Church and the Future of Welfare* (Norwich: Canterbury Press, 2017)

Wempe, B., *T.H. Green's Theory of Positive Freedom* (London: Impact Academic, 2004)

Wilkinson, A., *Christian Socialism: Scott Holland to Tony Blair* (London: SCM Press, 1998)

Williams, R., 'Convictions, Loyalties and the Secular State', *Political Theology* 6, no. 2 (2005), pp. 153–64

Williams, R., and L. Elliott, *Crisis and Recovery: Ethics, Economics and Justice* (New York: Palgrave Macmillan, 2010)

Wilson, D., and B. Butler, 'Corporatism in the British Voluntary Sector', in W. Streek and P.C. Schmitter (eds), *Private Interest Government: Beyond Market and State* (London: Sage, 1985), pp. 72–86

Wolch, J.R., *The Shadow State: Government and the Voluntary Sector in Transition* (New York: Foundation Centre, 1990)

Wolfenden, J., *The Future of Voluntary Organisations: Report of the Wolfenden Committee 1978* (London: Croom Helm, 1978)

Woodfield, P. (ed.), *Efficiency Scrutiny on the Supervision of Charities*, Report to the Home Secretary and the Economic Secretary to the Treasury (London: HMSO, 1987)

Woolley, R., *The Ethical Foundations of Socialism: The Influence of W. Temple and R.H. Tawney on New Labour* (Lewiston, NY: Edwin Mellen, 2007)

Woolley, R., 'Tawney and Temple's Legacy to New Labour: Values for a Moral Society', *Political Theology* 8, no. 2 (2007), pp. 171–95

Woolf, M., 'Labour Considers "New Localism" as the Big-Banner Policy for a Third Term', *Independent*, 22 October 2013, available at: http://www.independent.co.uk/news/uk/politics/labour-considers-new-localism-as-the-big-banner-policy-for-a-third-term-108522.html (accessed on 3 October 2015)

Wright, O., 'Red, Purple or Blue: Which Kind of Labour Are You?', *Independent*, 26 September 2011, available at: http://www.independent.co.uk/news/education/education-news/red-purple-or-blue-which-kind-of-labour-are-you-2361433.html (accessed on 26 January 2017)

Wuthnow, R., and C. Nass, 'Government Activity and Civil Privatism: Evidence from Voluntary Church Membership', *Journal for the Scientific Study of Religion* 27, no. 2 (1988), pp. 157–74

Wykes, M., 'Devaluing the Scholastics: Calvin's Ethics of Usury', *Calvin Theological Journal* 38, no. 1 (2003), pp. 27–51, available at: http://web.mit.edu/aorlando/www/SaintJohnCHII/CalvinUsury.pdf (accessed on 1 December 2016)

Yeo, S., *Religions and Voluntary Organisations in Crisis* (London: Croom Helm, 1976)

Index

Page numbers with a suffix 'n' refer to footnotes. For example, 87n42 means note number 42 on page 87. The suffix 'app' indicates an appendix.

Christian Socialism:

The Promise of an Almost Forgotten Tradition

By Philip Turner

Christian Socialism arose in England in the mid-nineteenth century as a response to the philosophy of 'political economy' – now commonly called neoliberalism. Seeking not institutional change or nationalisation, but a reform of the moral underpinnings of society, it refuted the assumption that people are essentially selfish, competitive individuals seeking nothing but personal happiness. Although they did not deny the presence of selfishness, its proponents believed that the social nature of humankind lies deeper than such egotism and conflict, and pursued a society built on this belief.

Less prominent now than at the time of its inception, Christian Socialism nevertheless continues into the twenty-first century, its goal nothing less than a new society built upon the virtues of equality, fellowship, cooperation, service and justice. Philip Turner's careful exposition traces the history of this strand of Anglican political thought and restores confidence in its message for the future.

'a *timely book that reclaims the insights of the Christian Socialist movement in the Church of England, tracing its roots and analyzing its present-day influence. Turner values this tradition's emphasis upon ideals, but tempers it with his own emphasis on the church's practice of the virtues.*' – **John Bauerschmidt**, Bishop of the Episcopal Diocese of Tennessee

Philip Turner holds a PhD in Christian Ethics from Princeton University and is the retired Associate Dean of the Yale Divinity School. He is the author of Christian Ethics and the Church.

Published 26 May 2022

Paperback ISBN: 978 0 227 17791 4
PDF ISBN: 978 0 227 17808 9

BV - #0003 - 120522 - C0 - 234/156/18 - CC - 9780227177808 - Gloss Lamination